Art Buchwald has performed a commendable public service. You, the citizen, no longer have to ask yourself:

* Is there life after Love Canal?
* If Reaganomics is supposed to trickle down to the people, who trickles down on Reaganomics?
* Does David Stockman put catsup on his tofu?
* If your children pray in school, will they learn to read and write in church?
* Why does the government want to sell Yellowstone National Park and buy Times Beach, Missouri?
* Is a limited nuclear war better than no war at all?

WHILE REAGAN SLEPT

Art Buchwald

Illustrated by
Steve Mendelson

FAWCETT CREST • NEW YORK

A Fawcett Crest Book
Published by Ballantine Books

Library of Congress Catalog Card Number: 83-10900

ISBN 0-449-12762-1

This edition published by arrangement with G.P. Putnam's Sons

Manufactured in the United States of America

First Ballantine Books Edition: September 1984

Contents

About the Artist   xiii
At Last   xv

Part One:
BONZO IN THE WHITE HOUSE   1

Bonzo in the White House   3
Wake Up, Mr. Reagan   5
Help Wanted   8
Damage Control at the White House   10
Best Book of the Year   13
Watt's on First   15
Patton in the Garden   17
Doctor in the House   19
Get the Secular Humanists   22
"I Love New York"   24
Back to Bribery   26
What to Do with Knees   29
Wedding Present   31
Missing Persons Bureau   33
Rent a Plane   36
You Look Great   38
The Float   40
Sex and Violence   43
You'll Love This Bomb   45

Part Two: IF A TREE FALLS 47

If a Tree Falls   49
Jelly Bean Economics   50
Good News from Russia   53
Sandbagged   55
The New Airlines   57
No Law Is Good Law   60
Your Biggest Fear   62
The Nixon Library   64
Defrosting the Economy   66
Whither the Safety Net?   68
Pity the KGB   70
Diablo Country   72
Everyone Is in Retail   74
The Political Spectrum   77
Designer Chocolates   79
State Visit   81
We Socked It to Them   84

Part Three: VOODOO ECONOMICS 87

Voodoo Economics   89
Watch Out, Kadafi   91
Ah So!   93
The Corporate Safety Net   95
Anybody Home?   97
A Question of Civil Rights   100

Some Call It Art   102
What Consultants Do?   104
Fear of Tipping   107
Newspaper Sources   109
The Man's Story   111
No Business Like CIA Business   114
We Got Shortchanged   116
Buy American   119
Tanks a Billion   121
The Black Republican   123
Foreclosing on Poland   126

Part Four: OUR TOWN
(With Apologies to Thornton Wilder)   129

Our Town (With Apologies to Thornton Wilder)   131
Eight Out of Ten Doctors   133
Ask Not   135
And Now, Here's Juanie   137
Chatting with Eastern   139
Half a War Is Better than None   141
Smoking and Research   143
Tora! Tora! Tora!   145
Enchilada Wins a Victory   148
Trouble in the Schools   150
Riffing   152
Let It All Hang Out   154
Youthful Job Trading   157
A Question of Shrinks   159

Part Five:
WHY JOHNNY CAN'T EAT   163

Why Johnny Can't Eat   165
Dinner at the White House   167
The Airline Price War   169
My Latest Nightmare   171
School Prayers   174
A Dry Run   176
Poor-Mouthing Defense   178
Acrimony Payments   181
The Gates' Syndrome   183
The High Cost of Messages   185
Catch-22   188
Paris Under Mitterrand   190
New French Souvenirs   192
"I Love a Parade"   194
Who Needs College?   197
The Computer Widow   199

Part Six: MAKE ME AN OFFER   203

Make Me an Offer   205
Invasion of Privacy   207
Psychological Baggage   209
It's All in the Waist   211
Business Is Good   213
Letters from Jim Watt   216
A Barrel of Laughs   218
Copping a Plea   220

The Human Comedy 222
Smart Bombs and Dumb Kids 224
Moscow Hot Line 226
Unnecessary Roughness 229
Takeover Lane 231
A Great Sport 233
Filling the Tubes 236
Splat! 238
The Hazards of EPA 240
The DeLoreans Are Selling 243
Our Election Endorsements 245

Part Seven:
100 NEEDIEST FAMILIES

249

100 Neediest Families 251
The Woman Behind the Woman 253
Gas Lighting the Consumer 255
The High Price of Politics 258
Love Boat USA 260
Dooley Lives 262
On Her Majesty's Service 265
Andropov's Honeymoon 267
Telling the Truth 269
Cannibalism in Hi-Tech 271
Defensive Medicine 274
Certifying Human Rights 276
The Battleships Are Back 278
The Worst TV Commercial 280

Part Eight: GOODBYE, MA 283

Goodbye, Ma   285
Social Security Sweepstakes   287
A Lot of Bull   290
Northrop Has a Better Idea   292
Hello Out There   294
A Good News Story   297
"Oh Boy"   299
Recessions Hurt Everyone   302
Nice Guys Finish Last   304
The Sweet Smell of EPA   306
Shouting at the President   309
A Dirty Movie   311
An American Hero   313
The U.S. Garage Sale   315
Retraining Horatio Alger   318
Why Jason Can't Read   320
"Is Paris Burning?"   322
No Conflict of Interest   324
Play Ball   327
IRS Squealers   329

List of Illustrations

STEVE MENDELSON, ARTIST xii

BONZO IN THE WHITE HOUSE 2

IF A TREE FALLS 48

VOODOO ECONOMICS 88

OUR TOWN (WITH APOLOGIES TO THORNTON WILDER) 130

WHY JOHNNY CAN'T EAT 164

MAKE ME AN OFFER 204

100 NEEDIEST FAMILIES 250

GOODBYE, MA 284

STEVE MENDELSON, ARTIST

About the Artist

Steve Mendelson, the artist whose pen-and-ink sketches adorn this book, works for *The Washington Post*, where he can usually be found illustrating world leaders, as well as many who have failed to lead, for political and international *Post* stories. When he is not at *The Washington Post*, he is either in bed, or in Norway. Mendelson is twenty-five years old, but is already considered one of the most talented people in his business.

He comes from a long line of sculptors, painters, and graphic artists.

His first involvement in politics came at the age of ten, when he wrote a letter to President Johnson in RED CRAYON, demanding the President stop the bloodshed in Vietnam. When Johnson failed to do it, Steve decided he would use crayons (and pen and ink) as a way of speaking out against the stupidities of people in power.

He has won several awards, and his twenty-foot-long pen-and-ink mural based on Jean Sibelius' Seventh Symphony is on permanent display in the Sibelius Academy in Helsinki.

Not only does Steve have a wicked pen, but he also has a wicked sense of humor. Somewhere in each drawing in this book is a hidden Reagan. If you find all eight of them you will be entitled to no less than seventy-five dollars for the rest of your life after you reach sixty-five years of age. The money will be sent to you in the form of a United States Social Security check, and neither Mr. Mendelson, nor the author, nor the publisher is responsible if for some reason it doesn't arrive.

Besides his enormous talent, one of the reasons Mr. Mendelson said he wanted to illustrate this book is that he is a big fan of Ronald Reagan's, and wanted to make sure the President was treated with respect.

At Last

This may be the last book you will ever have to read about Ronald Reagan.

You might as well admit it. You've tried to understand Reaganomics, the MX missile system, the Environmental Protection Agency, James Watt, OPEC, unemployment, Social Security, Nancy Reagan's china, the School Lunch Program, the prime rate, political action committees, California, Caspar Weinberger, the Soviet Union and the Middle East—and all you've managed to do is have nightmares, or stay awake all night long.

Now for the first time a writer has managed to put everything you have wanted to know about the President and the country in ONE volume.

You no longer have to ask yourself:

- Is there life after Love Canal?
- Is the world safer today than it was under Amy Carter?
- If Reaganomics is supposed to trickle down to the people, who trickles down on Reaganomics?
- Does David Stockman put catsup on his tofu?
- If your children pray in school, will they be able to learn to read and write?
- Why don't the banks give you the same respect when you can't meet a car loan payment that they give to Poland?
- Why does the government want to sell Yellowstone National Park and buy Times Beach, Missouri?
- Is a limited nuclear war better than no war at all?

These are only a few of the many questions that this book answers to MAKE YOU A BETTER AND MORE INFORMED PERSON, finally able to deal with problems that were too much for you to handle before.

We guarantee to cure you of your PARANOIA about Washington. The author helps you to understand that if you believe the government is trying to control your life, and make you do things you don't want to do, you are not HALLUCINATING, but are as normal as the next American.

If you get DEPRESSED because you feel your elected officials are serving special-interest groups rather than the people who put them in office, you are not sick, but are just reacting to what they are doing.

This book will show you how to deal with mental problems without the aid of expensive psychiatrists. By the time you reach the last page, you will no longer have FEARS about turning on the evening news, or reading the front pages of the newspapers.

Everything is explained in language you can UNDERSTAND.

Here are a few testimonials from people who have studied this book.

- Jeannie Aiyer of Spring Valley: "Before I read *While Reagan Slept* I had no idea what the administration was doing. Now it's all crystal-clear to me, and I no longer wake up in the middle of the night screaming."
- Martin Riley of Boston: "I've been unemployed since 1981 and I couldn't understand why my wife cried so much. Then I read your book, and now her crying doesn't bother me anymore. I figure it's her problem."
- Hilda Marton of Los Angeles: "I used to blame

Ronald Reagan for everything that happened to California, including mudslides, forest fires, and coastline disasters. Thanks to you I now realize it wasn't his fault. He inherited these problems from forty years of mismanagement in the government by the Democrats."

- Adolphus Hinkle of Philadelphia: "I used to be a small-time stickup man and I believed my profession was recession-proof. Then I found nobody had anything in their cash registers but food stamps. Luckily, another inmate recommended your book, and I discovered if you spent the same amount of time and energy overcharging the government for military equipment, the Justice Department couldn't lay a glove on you. So I'm now building airplanes for the Pentagon, and I'm a millionaire and a pillar of my community."

- Ira Harris of Chicago: "I read your chapters about Reagan's foreign policies and LOST thirteen pounds in one week. It was a miracle."

These are just a few of the testimonials from satisfied readers. Now it's your turn to change your life and become a happier, richer, and more contented person. No matter how you felt about Ronald Reagan in the past, once you read this book YOU'LL NEVER BE THE SAME PERSON YOU WERE BEFORE.

Part One

BONZO IN THE WHITE HOUSE

BONZO IN THE WHITE HOUSE

Bonzo in the White House

It has been one of the best-kept secrets of the administration. When the Reagans first moved into the White House, they brought "Bonzo," the President's favorite chimpanzee, with them. Bonzo keeps to himself playing in the attic or down in the basement, and swinging on trees on the south side of the White House lawn at night when no one is around.

When the Reagans are alone in their upstairs living quarters, Bonzo might sit in the President's lap while they reminisce about their days on the old Warner Brothers' lot.

Bonzo has never caused the President any embarrassment until recently.

What happened was that the Reagans had decided not to take Bonzo to California for the holidays because he had a cold.

Bonzo was very angry about this and as soon as everyone in the White House had gone, he managed to get out of the attic and began exploring the West Wing, a place he had never been before. The West Wing is where the Oval Office is situated, and the place where all the President's top administration officials work.

The chimp walked into an empty office and saw a computer standing in the corner. Bonzo hit a couple of keys and the words MORE BUDGET CUTS came up on the screen. This delighted him, and he started to hit some more keys. The word UNEMPLOYED came up on the screen and Bonzo clapped his hands, and tapped the keys again. The words

TAX UNEMPLOYMENT BENEFITS appeared and then Bonzo hit a communications key and the message was dumped into a computer that prints out White House press releases.

The printer immediately went to work: THE WHITE HOUSE ANNOUNCED TODAY THAT IT WAS CONSIDERING TAXING UNEMPLOYMENT BENEFITS AS A WAY OF GETTING PEOPLE TO LOOK FOR JOBS.

An AP man picked up the press release and sent it out on the wires, and that night on all the news shows it was announced as the lead story of the day.

When the news got to the West Coast White House headquarters in Santa Barbara, everyone was confused as to what had happened. There had been some talk about taxing unemployment benefits, yet it was just one of the many options the Office of Management and Budget was going to show the President. But since the word had been officially released, the staff assumed that someone had given the green light to send it out.

Larry Speakes, the White House deputy press secretary, didn't want to appear ignorant, so he confirmed to reporters that the unemployment tax was being given serious consideration.

Ed Meese, one of the President's top aides, had a tough decision to make. He could either defend the tax that afternoon or wake up the President. He opted for defending the tax rather than interrupt the President's nap.

In the meantime, Bonzo was back at the White House having a great time. He got the hang of working the computer and pretty soon he was feeding it stuff like BUDGET CUT IDEAS FOR CHRISTMAS, TAX ALL MEDICAL BENEFITS AS INCOME, RECOMMEND USER TAX ON WHEELCHAIRS, PUT SURCHARGE ON SALVATION ARMY, DO AWAY WITH TAX SHELTER FOR UNMARRIED MOTHERS, and ADD TEN PER-CENT EXCESS PROFITS TAX FOR BLOOD BANKS.

After a while, Bonzo got bored and started jumping around. He saw a Telex machine which said HOTLINE TO THE KREMLIN and started hitting the keys. The screen lit up with HAPPY THANKSGIVING TO AMERICAN CAPITALISTS. THIS IS NOT A TEST. Bonzo responded, ANDROPOV IS THE BIGGEST TURKEY IN THE SOVIET UNION. THIS IS NOT A TEST.

Fortunately, at that moment a Secret Service man walked into the West Wing office and grabbed Bonzo away from the hotline and gave him a banana. The agent then called the Western White House and told them he had caught Bonzo working the hotline.

Someone asked the agent to check the budget computer. When he reported what was on it, the pieces all started to fall into place concerning the unemployment tax announcement on Thanksgiving Day. The next morning, the President had to assure everyone there would be no such tax and also had to send an apology to Andropov.

But when a member of his staff suggested they move Bonzo out of the White House and send him to the Old Actors' Home in Hollywood, President Reagan wouldn't hear of it. "He's the best friend I ever had," the President said. "And just because he was in show business doesn't mean he can't come up with some good ideas."

Wake Up, Mr. Reagan

"Mr. Reagan, Mr. Reagan. Wake up, your honeymoon is over."

"So soon?"

"You've had a longer one than most Presidents, sir. If you weren't such a lovable guy we would have asked you to leave the honeymoon suite three months ago."

"Gosh, I was having such a good time. I wish it could have gone on forever."

"Don't we all? But no honeymoon can last forever—or it wouldn't be called a honeymoon. Now you have to go and find out what it's really like to be married to the American people. Don't forget when you took your presidential vows it was for better or for worse."

"How does a President know when his honeymoon is over?"

"When the population starts to question all those beautiful things you whispered in their ears. They've heard them before, but when they're in love, they want to believe them. Then one day they say, 'He promised us a rose garden, and all we got was cheddar cheese.'"

"It's the media that have done it. They've made me into a Scrooge. I am a compassionate, kind, generous person and the softest touch they've had in a long time. But all they talk about are budget deficits, and unemployment and high interest rates. Why do they do that?"

"Because the press is in show business, Mr. President. They're always playing up the bad news in South Succotash and they never talk about the good news. Now will you please get out of bed so the maid can clean up the room?"

"You know who really ruined my honeymoon?"

"No, sir."

"Congress. They're out to get me because they hate to see anyone happy."

"I couldn't agree with you more. Congress always promises a President a honeymoon, and then when he turns out the lights, they start dropping shoes on his head. Here, Mr. Reagan, is your bathrobe. Would you like to take a shower before you go?"

"Business hasn't been any help either. They're all so skeptical and downbeat, they don't believe anything I told them. If anyone ruined my honeymoon it was the gloom and doom boys on Wall Street. I gave them everything they wanted, and they still turned against me when I needed them."

"Businessmen are terribly fickle. They'll applaud you in the East Room and as soon as you leave for the Oval Office, they'll sell you short. I'll start packing your clothes while you're shaving."

"I'll tell you who really ruined my honeymoon. It was all those government bureaucrats who kept screaming about what I was doing to the old and the poor. I was willing to take care of the old and poor, but I wasn't going to let people who could work get a free ride any more. Did I ever tell you about that lady in Chicago who was getting ten welfare checks at the same time?"

"Many times, Mr. Reagan."

"How about the student who took his college loan, and put it into a twenty percent money fund?"

"That was one of your best ones."

"Or the guy who took his food stamps and bought vodka with them?"

"You told that one to everybody."

"They say I never get my facts right."

"They'll say anything, Mr. Reagan, when the honeymoon is over."

"Maybe my problem is everyone thinks I'm just a nice guy. As long as they ruined my honeymoon, I can now be myself, and show them I'm as tough and mean as they are."

"It's worth a try, Mr. Reagan. Well, I guess it's time to leave the suite. We've enjoyed having you, sir. Here, I'll carry those bags for you."

"I'm going to miss this place. I had some wonderful times here. Can I say goodbye to the help?"

"I don't think that would be wise, sir. The TV reporters will just start interviewing the people I had to lay off."

Help Wanted

A few weeks ago President Reagan, in response to a reporter's questions on unemployment, replied that he had picked up the Sunday *Washington Post* and read twenty-four pages of "Help Wanted" ads. He said, "What we need to do is make more people qualified to go and apply for these jobs."

I happened to remember this when Frederico, a chauffeur, who had been laid off by the government, came to see me to complain he couldn't find a job.

"Why don't you look in the 'Help Wanted' section of *The Washington Post*?" I asked angrily.

"I can't afford to buy the *Post*."

"Here," I said, throwing the "Help Wanted" pages at him. "Now you have no excuse."

Frederico started studying the pages. "This sounds good," he said. "Some company wants a cellular immunologist."

"Well, there you are," I told him. "Why don't you apply for it?"

"What's a cellular immunologist?"

"I don't have the slightest idea. But I'm sure you can fake it until you learn the ropes."

He circled it, and kept reading. "Do you know what a psychiatric nurse is supposed to do?"

"I would assume he or she must take care of mentally sick people, counsel them, provide them with drugs, and look after their physical needs."

"I did that when I was a chauffeur in the government,"

8

Frederico said brightly. "Most of the people I drove were crazy or they wouldn't be entitled to a chauffeured car."

I encouraged him. "All it takes to be a psychiatric nurse is common sense. You'd be perfect for the job."

Frederico circled that one.

"Here's one that sounds interesting. 'Wanted: Nuclear Energy Safety Inspector for Breeder Reactor Facility.' I wonder what would be required for that."

"It's a snap. All you have to do is walk around the plant and if you see a water pipe leaking or a red light blinking, report it to the janitor."

"Is it safe?"

"Of course it's safe. They give you a white badge to wear, and if it turns a motley green, that means the reactor is giving off more radioactivity than the human body can absorb."

"What do I do then?"

"You clear everyone out of the building until the public relations people announce it's safe to go back in again."

"Well, it's a job," Frederico said, circling it. "Listen to this one. 'If you are unhappy in your present Data Systems position, we are looking for you. The position we have open requires a computer programmer who can evaluate stress factors on aerospace high-tension materials, and devise new methods of factoring mathematical blueprint formulae with heat intensities of eight thousand degrees Fahrenheit. Starting salary forty thousand dollars a year and medical benefits.' That's more money than I can make as a psychiatric nurse."

"And the work is probably more fulfilling too," I said. "I wouldn't be surprised if you were put to work on the B-one bomber."

"The ad says people will be interviewed tomorrow at the Holiday Inn in Bethesda."

"You can stop off there after your interview with the breeder reactor plant," I said.

Frederico said, "Hey, look, Saudi Arabia is advertising

for a neurosurgeon, and they provide housing and ser-
vants with the job. What do you think?"

"Better talk it over with your wife. You'll be busy
operating all day long, and she might get bored there with
nothing to do. Do you see anything else that appeals to
you?"

"Can I take the pages home with me and study them
at my leisure with a dictionary?"

"Be my guest."

"Thanks a million. I didn't know there were so many
jobs going begging these days."

"Neither did I. Thank God, President Reagan reads
The Washington Post."

Damage Control at
the White House

Just when the White House staff thought it was safe
to send the President out to meet the people, Ronald
Reagan blew his entire "My Heart Goes Out to the Poor
'State of the Union'" speech by telling hi-tech business
executives in Boston that he might be in favor of abol-
ishing the corporate income tax. He said, "I realize there
may be a great stirring and I will probably kick myself
for having said this. But when are we going to have the
courage to point out in our tax structure [sic], the corporate tax is very hard to justify its existence."

White House staffers who stayed behind to see how
the President's speech was playing on Capitol Hill were
dumbfounded when someone rushed in and said, "He

blew it in Boston. Get the damage control team right away."

Sirens rang in the White House and six men dressed in asbestos Brooks Brothers suits with fire extinguishers rushed into the political war room. They gathered around the AP news ticker and read the statement.

"Oh, my God," one of them said. "This is worse than announcing on Thanksgiving Day we were thinking of taxing unemployment benefits."

The chief damage control officer said, "Let's not panic, men. We have to think clearly. Dave, start flooding the media with confusion."

"Should I say he didn't say it, or he didn't mean it?"

"We can't say he didn't say it, because they'll show him making the statement on TV tonight. And we can't say he didn't mean it, because we'll make him look as if he doesn't know what he's talking about."

"So how can we snuff it out?"

"We'll say he was speaking for himself and not as President of the United States."

"That won't fly."

"We'll say it's an idea the President would like to implement at some future time when the country is on the mend."

The phones were ringing in the war room. An aide picked one up and said, "We know all about it. We're trying to get the fire under control. . . ." He turned to the others. "It's the Treasury Department. They're asking what happened."

"Tell them nothing happened. The President was just having a little fun in Boston with corporate executives about taxes."

The aide repeated the message and then turned to the damage control team. "They say they've just issued a press release that we're planning to tax medical bills and make old people pay more of their hospital costs. The President's remarks are going to blow them out of the water."

"We can't worry about their problems now. We'll call them back when we figure out how we're going to handle it."

An aide on another phone yelled, "It's Larry Speakes in Boston. He says he's under siege by the press traveling with the President."

The head damage control officer grabbed the phone.

"How bad is it, Larry?...Real bad?...The press boys are licking their chops and doing back flips over the statement?...What about the President visiting the job training program in Roxbury or a blue-collar bar in Boston?...I was afraid of that. Look, hold on as long as you can, Larry, until we can come up with something here that can turn the tide....Stonewall them. That's what you're paid for."

Another aide was on the phone. "It's Howard Baker on the Hill. He says the Democrats are dancing in the aisles."

The chief grabbed the phone. "Cool down, Howard...No, I haven't spoken to the President yet, but I swear to you this is the first time anyone ever heard of this idea. Howard, we know this is making your life tougher, but we'll get it straightened out...No, Howard, he doesn't have his feet in concrete on this one. At least we don't think he has."

The chief damage control officer hung up. "No more calls."

An aide who was on the phone said, "It's the President in Boston. He wants to know how he's doing."

The chief took the receiver. "Yes, sir. You're doing just great. The calls on your 'State of the Union' have been phenomenal, and the telegrams are pouring in....Where do we want you to go next? We think you had better stay in the White House until your budget is passed. A trip to Boston can be pretty taxing for you. By the way, Mr. President, speaking of taxing..."

Best Book of the Year

The most important book published in Washington this year is titled *The Budget of the United States Government, Fiscal Year 1984*.

I haven't had time to read it myself, though I've browsed through it to see if my name was mentioned. But I asked a friend who reviews fiction and nonfiction for *The Washington Post* what he thought of it.

"It's the best book I've read this year," he said. "Frankly, I think it's going to be another *Winds of War*."

"That good, huh?"

"I couldn't put it down. I kept turning the pages to see what government program would be cut next. It's more frightening than *Rosemary's Baby*."

"You mean it's a thriller?"

"More of a whodunit. Or, specifically, who's doing it to whom. It's about money and power, the struggle for survival, death and taxes, and man's fate in a world he never made."

"Any sex?"

"The military chapters are very sexy, particularly the love scenes between the President of the United States and the new weapons that the Pentagon has seduced him into buying."

"You mean the President of the United States is in bed with the military-industrial complex?"

"All through the book. Some of the scenes between them are so hot that Tip O'Neill has threatened to ban the book in Boston."

"Does the President's wife know he's in love with the new weapons?"

"Everybody knows. But the President says he has to do it in the name of national security."

"Is that the main plot?"

"No, it's just one of the subplots. The main plot is about a rich uncle, who has lost so much of his money that he is down and out and in debt up to his ears."

"How did he fall on such bad times?"

"He was caught up in a recession and couldn't pay his bills. Finally, he got so sick that the President's doctors had to operate to save his life. They cut everything down to the bone, and froze everything they couldn't cut."

"Does he live?"

"In the book he does. The President's doctors maintain they just removed the fat, and although the patient will have to suffer pain, it's the only way he can get well. The White House doctors admit the medicine they've prescribed is a bitter pill to swallow, but the uncle is now on the mend."

"That makes sense to me."

"The only problem is that Democratic doctors who've read the book claim the President's surgeons have cut out the uncle's vital organs to save his life. In its present form they find the plot not very believable, and they're calling for changes in the next edition before they buy it."

"Everybody's a critic. What book would you compare this work to?"

"The first one that comes to mind is *The Grapes of Wrath*, though of course it's not as well written. The poor, the sick and the aged are the ones who get hurt the most."

"It sounds depressing. I'm not sure I want to read it."

"You have to because that's all people will be talking about this spring."

"Well, tell me this. Does it have an upbeat ending?"

"All budget books written by a President have an upbeat ending. This one predicts that in 1986 the uncle will be fully recovered and regain his fortune again. And everyone will live happily ever after."

"Will it make a good movie?"

"It's been optioned by all three TV networks. They don't know yet if they'll make it into a soap opera, a docudrama or a situation comedy."

"If the book is as good as you say it is, I hope they don't ruin it when it comes to the screen."

"The networks usually do."

Watt's on First

"Who's on first?"

"No, Watt's on first."

"Who is What?"

"Watt is the secretary of the interior. He wants to sell all the mineral rights on federal lands."

"What for?"

"I don't know."

"I thought 'I Don't Know' was on second."

"Watt's on second, too. He's touching all the bases."

"How can What be on first and second?"

"Because he is playing both ends against the middle."

"What for?"

"Because Watt doesn't believe you should support large tracts of wilderness which don't produce one nickel for the government."

"If What is on first and second, Who is on third?"

"Watt is on third."

"Why is he on third?"

"Because he thinks there is oil and gas under it. He's just leased it to you-know-who."

"I don't know Who."

"It doesn't matter who as long as they pay royalties to Watt."

"If What is on first, second and third Who is at shortstop?"

"No one is at shortstop because it's being strip-mined for coal."

"Can What do that?"

"I don't know."

"If What is playing all the bases, then Who is on the mound?"

"Who is not on the mound. Watt won't let anybody on the mound because he's the only one who can pitch to the mining interests."

"Let me get this straight. What is on first. What is on second, and What is on third, and What is also pitching to the coal companies. Then Who is catching?"

"Wrong again. Watt is catching."

"What is he catching?"

"Hell from the environmentalists, the Sierra Club, the National Audubon Society, and the National Wildlife Federation."

"What for?"

"Because he won't play ball with them."

"Who is in the outfield?"

"No, Watt is in the outfield. He's trying to sell it to private developers for resort condominiums."

"How can you have a game if you sell the outfield?"

"Who knows?"

"Isn't there an umpire to call What out when he's off base?"

"Watt says he's the umpire and he calls them as he sees them."

"Why doesn't someone kick dirt in his face?"

"Because the President keeps cheering him on from the side."

"What President?"

"Watt's President."

"I thought Reagan was President."

"He is. Reagan is Watt's President."

"You mean What doesn't have to follow the book as long as Reagan eggs him on?"

"Watt makes up his own rules as he goes along."

"He sounds like a foul ball."

"He's a hit with the people who hate conservationists."

"What's going to happen to all of us if he wins?"

"Exactly."

Patton in the Garden

"The vegetable garden is ready for your inspection, sir."

"Thank you, Sergeant. Now hear this. As commander of this spring garden I want every plant to line up in rows, four abreast. Let's move it, on the double. You asparagus down there: I want your shoulders back, and your spears straight up. If you tomato plants don't stop sagging, I'm going to pull you up by your roots. Do you hear me? I SAID, DO YOU HEAR ME? That's better.

"This is the sorriest excuse for vegetable life I've ever seen. But let me tell you something: By the time I get finished, every last one of you is going to be fit to eat, or I'll know the reason why.

"You think all it takes is a little mulch and fertilizer to be a vegetable? Well, you're wrong, wrong, wrong. You've had an easy time of it sacking out and slouching in your beds. Now you're going to start producing or I'll know the reason why.

"From this day on you're going to shape up or ship out. Is that understood? And that goes for the rhubarb, too.

"Sergeant, why do these corn stalks look so sick?"

"I don't know, sir. I've tried to get them to straighten up, but they keep flopping over."

"Maybe they could use a little discipline. Perhaps if we tie them to a stick for a week, they'll know how to stand at attention."

"But that's cruel and unusual punishment."

"It's nothing compared to what they'll face when they go up against the corn borer. I'm trying to save these plants' lives, and we can't do that by coddling them. Tie 'em up, and that's an order."

"Yes, sir."

"Why do these new wax beans look so sallow?"

"I don't know, sir. I think they've been high on nitrogen."

"They're all zonked out. From now on, no one gets any nitrogen until you check with me. Let me tell you wax beans something, and hear me loud and clear. I didn't even want you in my garden. I accepted you against my better judgment. But since you're here, you are going to play by my rules or else wind up in the compost heap. I want your pods polished every morning, so I can see my face in them. I want you tough on the outside and tender on the inside. If you can't hack it, I can always replace you with squash. Do you read me? I SAID, DO YOU READ ME? You scraggy plants give all wax beans a bad name.

"What do we have over here, Sergeant?"

"Carrots, sir. Off the record, they haven't caused us any trouble so far."

"Well, at least we have something in this garden we can count on. Give them an extra shovelful of topsoil as a reward. Where are the eggplants?"

"Dead, sir."

"Dead! How the hell did they die?"

"The early frost got them, sir. It's all in my report."

"Oh, well, it's no great loss. I don't know too many people who like eggplants. We can always fill out the ranks with cucumbers. How are the potatoes doing?"

"They're a great young crop, sir. But then we never have had trouble with the potato. It's a tough little vegetable and it doesn't mind wallowing in the dirt."

"What's wrong with this head of lettuce?"

"It was wounded by an army worm in the trenches and doesn't want to grow any more."

"It's not sick. It's malingering. I can't stand a yellow head of lettuce. Our vegetables are out there giving their all for America, and this little coward just sits in its bed faking illness. Well, I won't have it. DO YOU HEAR ME? I WON'T HAVE IT! Take that, you miserable excuse for a salad."

"Sir, you slapped it in the face."

"That's exactly what it needed. If we coddle these rotten shirkers, we won't have anything to eat this summer at all."

Doctor in the House

When I saw Glover the other day, he looked sick.

"Why don't you go to your doctor?" I asked him.

"I did. He wants me to see a specialist."

"So, why don't you go to see the specialist?"

"He's delivering a paper in Sydney, Australia, on his specialty. He won't be back until July."

"All right, then go to another specialist."

"I called another one and his secretary said he can't see me until September. I told her I might be dead by then. So she said she'd move me up to August."

"This is May—that seems like a long time to wait. Did you go back to your regular doctor?"

"Yeah. He called around and he finally found a guy who would see me right away."

"That's great," I said. "Why don't you go to see him?"

"Because I'm not sure how good he is."

"Why? Did you check him out?"

"No. But if he's such a hot doctor, how come he isn't delivering a paper in Vienna, instead of seeing patients?"

"Maybe he is in between lectures," I suggested.

"All right. But if he knows his stuff, why doesn't he have a two-month waiting list like everybody else?"

"That's a good question. He can't be a great medical man if he's willing to see you right away. Maybe he's just starting out in practice."

"I thought the same thing. So that means if I go see him, I'm going to have to get a second opinion."

"Wasn't your family doctor suspicious when the specialist said you could come over so soon?"

"It did make him nervous. He said he had never known a specialist who would see a patient right away. But he also said I didn't have any choice. It was either go to him or NOT see the best man in the field because he was in Australia."

"Maybe the guy who will see you had a cancellation?" I said, trying to cheer him up. "I once knew of a case where a top orthopedic man saw a friend of mine just four weeks after he called."

"What did the orthopedist tell him?"

"That there was nothing wrong with him. Whatever the problem was had cleared up."

"So you think if I wait for the specialist to come back from Sydney, I'll get better, too?"

"I'm not a doctor. But I've heard of many cases where

a patient has had to wait so long to see the top man in the field, that he's cured himself."

"But don't you look like a fool if you wait all that time and when you finally see the specialist, he can't find anything wrong?"

"Specialists don't care. They're so busy, it saves them spending a lot of time with you."

"I still wonder if I should cancel the appointment with the specialist who will see me, and try to get one with the one who can't."

"Well, the one who can't is probably the better man, and you'd be more confident with him. At the same time, if you kept your appointment with the doctor who will see you, you could be pleasantly surprised. Maybe he's good at what he does, but doesn't live to deliver papers at medical meetings. You know, there are some doctors who are afraid to fly."

"Why can't the top specialists in their fields just practice medicine?" Glover asked. "Why do they have to keep going to Nairobi and Cairo and Stockholm all the time to read papers?"

"Because if they just took care of patients, no one would know they were the top men in their field. Look, I think you're hurting yourself wrestling with the problem. My suggestion is to go to the specialist who told you to come over right away. But before you let him examine you, ask him how many conventions he's been to this year. If he replies, 'None,' walk out of his office without taking your clothes off."

Get the Secular Humanists

The new threat to this country, if you believe the Moral Majority and the television preachers, is not coming from Communists or fellow travelers, but "secular humanists."

The "secular humanists" are the ones who are brainwashing our children with books about evolution, sex, race relations, ERA, and naughty words.

This means we have to get the books out of the schools and libraries. The book censors are starting to organize, the moral crusade has begun and the hunt for secular humanists is on.

I am always intimidated by book-burners, so I want to get on the bandwagon as soon as possible.

My problem is, unlike the Red-baiting witch hunts of the McCarthy days, I find it impossible to know who a secular humanist is.

It was easy to tell a Commie or fellow traveler in the '50s because he always carried a *Daily Worker* under his arm, and didn't bother to shine his shoes. He never had a nice thing to say about Senator Joe McCarthy or Roy Cohn, and he kept taking the Fifth Amendment when he was called in front of the House Un-American Activities Committee. Also, you could check up on him by finding out if he once belonged to one of the hundreds of subversive organizations listed by the government as being for the violent overthrow of the democratic system.

But a secular humanist is a different breed of cat. From

what I can gather, he is much harder to identify unless he openly admits he thinks Darwin's theory of creation makes sense.

Secular humanists are not joiners. They don't have cells where they plot anti-American and anti-God propaganda. Most of them work alone, doing historical research, writing textbooks and novels, and explaining how babies are born. They pollute children's minds with how the world is, rather than how the antihumanists would like it to be.

What makes them so dangerous is that secular humanists look just like you and me. Some of them could be your best friends without you knowing they are humanists. They could come into your house, play with your children, eat your food and even watch football with you on television, and you'd never know that they have read *Catcher in the Rye, Brave New World,* and *Huckleberry Finn.*

Of course there are some who flaunt their humanism, and will brag they're for abortion, and against prayers in public schools. You can throw them out of the house.

But for every secular humanist who will tell you where he or she stands on a fundamentalist issue, there are ten who keep their thoughts to themselves and are working to destroy the American family.

No one is safe until Congress sets up an Anti-Secular Humanism Committee to get at the rot. Witnesses have to be called, and they have to name names of other secular humanists they know.

Librarians and teachers must be made to answer for the books they have on their shelves. Publishers have to be held accountable for what they print. Writers must be punished for what they write.

The secular humanists should be put on notice that they can no longer hide behind the First Amendment.

If we're going to go back to the old moral values that

made this country great, we're going to have to do it with search-and-destroy methods. First, we must burn the books—and, if that isn't enough, then we must burn the people.

"I Love New York"

NEW YORK— New Yorkers are always complaining that "foreigners" (those who don't live there) are giving the city a bad name. Actually, we "foreigners" would have no idea what was going on unless New Yorkers told us.

I had occasion to visit New York on a Sunday recently, and spent the afternoon in Queens at a gathering of friends. Then I announced that I had to go into the city.

"How are you planning to go?" someone asked.

"I thought I'd take the subway," I replied.

"You can't take the subway!" the person said.

"Why? It's Sunday. The subway shouldn't be too crowded."

"That's just the point," another friend told me. "It's much more dangerous to take it when it isn't crowded. You could be sitting in a car all by yourself, and that's when they'll get you."

"If they don't get you, the subway will," another person said.

"How could the subway get me?" I wanted to know.

"It's always breaking down. You could be stuck under the East River all night long."

"Maybe I'd better take a taxi."

"Be careful. Don't tell the cab driver you're from out

of town, or he'll take you to Manhattan via Staten Island. They wait all day for people like you."

Another friend said, "If he does take you by way of Staten Island, don't argue with him. There was a story in the newspaper the other day about a man who complained the taxi was taking the long way from Kennedy Airport, and the driver beat him up with a tire iron."

"How long are you staying in Manhattan?" someone inquired.

"Just a couple of days."

"I'd take off that watch if I were you. They're getting awfully good at ripping off watches. If your wife is going to be with you, tell her not to wear any gold chains. They'll rip them off, too."

"Where are you staying?"

"Down in Gramercy Park," I said.

"You weren't planning on going out at night, were you?"

"I was hoping to. I understand there's a lot to see in New York City at night."

Someone said, "It depends on where you go. Always walk on a lighted street near the curb, and if they ask for your money, give it to them without arguing."

"Better still, don't walk anywhere. Take a taxi, and tell the driver to wait until you get into the hotel lobby," a friend added.

"It is all right to go to the theater?" I asked.

"It's all right to go. But coming back is when you could get into trouble. Whatever you do, stay off Eighth Avenue. That's where all the crazies hang out."

"Before you go, put all your valuables in the hotel safe, and be sure when you get back to your hotel to double-lock your door. I know a guy who was sleeping in one of the best hotels in the city and found someone going through his trousers looking for his wallet."

"I think I better take notes," I said. "I hear the restaurants are pretty good in New York."

"It depends if they know you or not. If you go to one

of the better ones, make sure you slip the headwaiter a twenty-dollar bill, or you'll be standing at the bar until eleven o'clock at night."

"When you're leaving for the airport during the rush hour, give yourself two hours. If one car breaks down on the East Side Drive, you're a dead duck."

"Gosh," I said. "This sounds like a tough city."

"Why do you say that?" someone asked defensively.

"No reason," I replied, realizing I was on dangerous ground.

"That's the trouble with you out-of-towners. You're always knocking New York because you don't live here. It's the greatest place in the world."

"I wouldn't live anywhere else," another friend added. "I love New York."

"I better get going," I said.

"Why? It's only four o'clock."

"Well, if I'm going to get beaten up with a tire iron, I better allow some time to go to the hospital."

"If you go to the emergency room on Sunday," a friend said, "make sure there's an English-speaking doctor on duty."

Back to Bribery

The White House has proposed a serious relaxation in the 1977 Foreign Corrupt Practices Act, which was intended to prevent American companies from bribing foreign officials.

The administration maintains that the United States is

losing too much business to competitors because we can't grease the palms of some of our best customers.

If Congress goes along with it, American executives are going to have to do a complete switch, as most of them had given strict orders not to offer bribes for contracts abroad. The truth of the matter is, United States company sales reps are out of practice.

A friend of mine from a multinational confessed this to me the other day. "I was pretty good at bribing politicians abroad in my time," he told me, "but I think I've lost my touch."

"It will come back," I assured him. "It's like a foreign language. All you need is a little practice."

"That's why I came over tonight," he said. "I was hoping you would help me to brush up."

"Sure," I told him. "Why don't you play yourself and I'll play the brother-in-law of the president of a country where you're trying to get a big order."

"That would be great. Let's pretend that we're having dinner at the brother-in-law's palace."

"You're on."

"Your Excellency, thank you for your wonderful hospitality. I have never had such a sumptuous banquet in my life."

"It is my pleasure, Mr. Doppel. Tell me, what brings you to Enchilada?"

"My company is interested in arranging a contract for the sale of puppy formula. We believe this could make a great health contribution to Enchilada, as it would save your dogs from having to breast-feed their young."

"Everyone has been offering us puppy formula. What are your terms?"

"A five-year, low-interest, financed contract in which you would guarantee to buy ten million dollars of formula at world market prices."

"That's very interesting. My brother-in-law would like that. But what about his wife's foundation for the widows and orphans of Enchilada?"

"We would be happy to make a contribution."

"Good. The money is to be deposited in Switzerland."

"Why Switzerland?"

"That's where the foundation has its headquarters."

"No problem. Then it's a deal?"

"Not yet. I am sure your country is interested in the welfare of our people. I'm the president of Enchilada United Way, and we are in the middle of our fund drive."

"Of course. Our company always gives to the United Way."

"Here is the numbered bank account of the Enchilada United Way in Liechtenstein. Just have your bank wire my cousin's bank in Miami. He is treasurer of the fund."

"Our bank will attend to it. Can we sign a letter of agreement now?"

"I'm not in a position to sign such a letter. That has to be done by my uncle, who is minister of commerce. I will write a note to him, but I warn you he's a tough man to deal with. He only accepts diamonds."

"We'll find diamonds. Anyone else on the list I should know about?"

"If you could find it in your heart to spare a few dollars for Army Chief General Valdez's Veterans Hospital, he would be eternally grateful."

"Of course. Where is the hospital?"

"It hasn't been built yet. But he'll be happy to show you the plans."

"If my company has anything to say about it, he shall have his hospital."

"You were great," I told Doppel. "You're going to make a great comeback in the international bribery business."

"Whew," he said, relieved, "for a while I thought I had lost my fastball."

What to Do with Knees

Anyone who has been flying tourist class these days has noticed that the airlines are placing their rows closer and closer to each other, making it more difficult to get your entire body into a seat.

I was on a shuttle to New York City the other morning, and the stewardess announced that all carry-on luggage had to be placed under your seats.

The man next to me called her over and said, "What do I do with my knees?"

The stewardess said, "I beg your pardon?"

"My briefcase is under the seat in front of me, but I don't have any place for my knees."

"Neither do I," I told her.

"Could I put my knees in the overhead rack?" he wanted to know.

"No," she said. "That would be against regulations. It would present a safety hazard in case we hit turbulence."

"Why don't you put them on your chest?" I suggested to my seatmate.

"I was hoping to read my newspaper," he replied. "It's almost impossible to turn a page if you have your knees on your chest."

The stewardess said, "FAA regulations forbid you to put your knees on your chest while the safety belt sign is on."

"Why doesn't the FAA have a rule that an airline has to provide room for a passenger's knees?"

"Because the airlines have been deregulated to increase competition. They can now put the rows as close together as they want. The government is no longer concerned with leg room."

My seatmate said, "I'm in the cattle business and the government still has strict regulations about how many cattle may be shipped in a car. You'd think we would have the same rights as animals."

"I'm only a stewardess. If you have any complaints, why don't you make them to management?"

"Could I check my knees in the baggage compartment?" he asked.

"I'm sorry, we're just about to take off and we can't check anything."

The stewardess went away. I turned to the man and said, "I have a suggestion, if you don't mind. Why don't you put your knees on my lap and I'll put my knees on your lap. In that way we'll both be more comfortable."

"You're not gay, are you?" he wanted to know.

"Heck no, and I assume you're not either."

"Well, let's give it a try," he said.

"Try not to take the crease out of my pants," I begged him. "I have to speak at a lunch today."

"I'll be careful."

We put our legs across each other's laps.

The pilot announced that we were third in line for takeoff.

The stewardess came down the aisle to check if our safety belts were fastened.

"That's not permitted," she said sternly.

"Where does it say so in the regulations?" my seatmate demanded.

"Look what you've started," she said. "Everyone is doing it."

It actually wasn't a bad trip, and when we got to La Guardia, we shared a taxi into New York. Fortunately it was a Checker cab and we could both stretch our legs as far as we wanted. The ride put shuttle airlines to shame.

Wedding Present

The June weddings are upon us, and once again everyone is trying to figure out what kind of present to buy newlyweds. Many friends call up parents and ask, "What do Phillippe and Jacqueline need?"

The Whelans have decided to deal with their son's wedding in a very practical way.

I was over at their house while the calls were coming in.

Phil, the father, said to the first caller, "They would like a window. Yes, that's right, a window. No, it doesn't have to have shutters. Any window will do."

He told the next caller, "The kids would love a chimney attached to a fireplace."

The third caller was told, "They're dying for a linoleum floor. I don't have the measurements, but I'll let you know in a few days."

Phil marked everything down in a book.

I asked him what he was doing.

"Well, people want to buy the kids something they need. What they need is a house. So every time someone calls, Sherry or I ask the person for a piece of it. We've got twelve windows promised, a ceiling for the living room, two walls for the bedroom, and light fixtures for the bathroom. If the Holbrookes come through with a front door, and the Evanses with a kitchen door, we can start telling people they want a roof."

"A roof is an awfully expensive wedding present," I said.

"We don't expect one person to give them a roof. But if we can talk ten of our friends into going in on it, we can get Phillippe's aunt to give them the shingles."

"That's a great idea. What happens if a wedding present arrives without consultation with you?"

"We take it back to the store and exchange it for a bag of cement."

The phone rang again. Phil said, "Yeah, it was a lovely wedding, wasn't it? What do they want? I heard Jacqueline say she'd love a kitchen sink. What pattern? It really doesn't matter as long as it goes with her cabinets. No, she doesn't have cabinets yet, but we're still hoping. That's very nice of you."

Phil made a notation in the book. "We're moving right along."

"Once you've got all the stuff together, who is going to build the house?"

"Phillippe's best man and ushers said they would work on it. My present to the kids is to pay someone to supervise the construction. It will be a rather tricky job since most of the presents won't match."

"Anyone come through with lumber yet?"

"People have offered, but we're holding out for redwood. I think Jacqueline's uncle might come across because she's his favorite niece. The Dumbartons sent us a stack of plywood, and Sherry was outraged because we gave their son a Cuisinart when he got married."

The phone rang again. "Teresa," said Phil, "how nice of you to call. No, the kids have linens and towels. Someone beat you to a coffeemaker. They also have an electric can opener. Let me think, what do they really want? I've got it! A gas furnace. They told me that if anyone asks just to say the thing that would make them the happiest would be a nice furnace to keep their love warm. Thanks for calling, Teresa, and best to Joe."

"I didn't think she'd go for it," Phil said, writing it in his book. "Particularly because when their kids got married, we only gave them bookends. By the way, what brings you over?"

"Ann asked me to drop by and find out what Phillippe and Jacqueline needed, but I see they have everything, so we'll just get them a nice pair of candlesticks."

"They don't want candlesticks," Phil said. "They want a lot."

"A lot of what?"

"A lot to build their house on. It doesn't have to be a large one. Phillippe hates to mow the grass."

"Can I think about it?"

"Sure. Talk it over with Ann. Women know more than men do about what kind of lots newlyweds want."

Missing Persons Bureau

"Bureau of Missing Persons, Sergeant Callahan speaking."

"I wish to report the disappearance of a kitchen appliance repairman."

"Come again, lady."

"My kitchen appliance man is missing. He was here one day working on my dishwasher, and said he was going back to the shop for a part, and I haven't seen him since."

"When was that?"

"Ten days ago. The dishwasher is in my kitchen in a hundred parts and I'm worried sick."

"Did you call the shop to see if he was there?"

"He's never there when I call. His answering service says they haven't heard from him in over a week."

"Don't start crying, lady. Did you have a quarrel with him?"

"It wasn't really a quarrel. I thought the hose had broken, but he said the washer needed a new motor. He said he had been having a lot of trouble with this particular type of machine, and I'd be better off buying a new one. I said I'd rather he fix it, and he just muttered to himself as he took it apart."

"Do you have a name we can work on?"

"I never got his name. I found his company in the Yellow Pages, under 'Twenty-four-hour Service—Satisfaction Guaranteed.'"

"That doesn't help us much. Did he take his tool kit with him?"

"Yes, he did. Why do you ask?"

"It sounds as though he really meant business. When a repairman packs up his tool kit, it usually indicates he's running away."

"But I was so good to him. I gave him an ice-cold beer, and a turkey sandwich. I treated him as if he were part of the family."

"Don't blame yourself, lady. A lot of repairmen take off before they finish the job. He's probably somewhere in town working on another dishwasher."

"But suppose he was in an accident and was hurt? I'd never forgive myself. My husband and I can't sleep at nights wondering if he's all right."

"We'd check the hospitals for you, lady. But it isn't easy without a name."

"Wait a minute. I think he did have a name. He made a telephone call when he was in the kitchen and identified himself to the other person as Jerry."

"At least that's something to go on. Could you give us a description of him?"

"He was about five-feet-eight, rather heavyset, and had grease all over his face and hands."

"We can't put out an all-points bulletin on that. You have to understand something. We get reports on maybe fifty runaway repairmen a day. They don't like to finish a job. They love to take things apart, but they don't like to put them back again. They don't even care if they get paid or not. We don't have the manpower to track them down, and even if we did we don't have the legal authority to send them back to your house to finish the work.

"All we can do, if we find your man, is try to persuade him to call you, and then it's up to you to talk him into coming home."

"So what you are saying is that I may never see him again?"

"I think you have to face reality. We haven't had too much luck in locating missing repairmen. Once they decide to leave an unfinished job, they're rarely heard from again. The only thing you and your husband can do is hope that perhaps someday he'll come back and put your dishwasher together of his own free will. If you were as kind to him as you say you were, he might turn up on your doorstep any day."

"If you hear anything, will you let me know?"

"We'll put his name on the ticker. But don't get your hopes up. He could be in California by now working on a garbage disposal unit, under another name. If a repairman doesn't want to be found, there isn't a Missing Persons Bureau in the country that can locate him."

Rent a Plane

The Defense Department keeps insisting that the United States is short of all types of military weapons, from tanks to airplanes. We probably are. But every time you pick up the newspaper, there is an announcement that we're selling off our stuff to some other country, or giving it away. No wonder we can't stockpile anything for ourselves.

The latest news bulletin, which came right after the Israeli raid on the nuclear facilities in Baghdad, was that the President had agreed to sell F-16s to Pakistan. Now anyone in the United States Air Force will tell you that they need every F-16 they can get. The question is, how do we keep supplying arms to all our friends and still have any left to equip our own armed forces?

There is a solution. Instead of selling our equipment to every ally who asks for it, we could rent the hardware on a daily or weekly basis. Working with Hertz, Avis, and other leasing companies, we could set up booths at air, naval, and army bases where all our military hardware would be kept.

Pretty women officers in attractive uniforms would be behind the counters.

This is how it would work: A foreign general and his staff would come up to the counter and say, "We'd like to rent five F-sixteens for a preemptive strike on our archenemy, Balanteria."

"That's no problem. I assume you want them fully equipped with rockets, bombs, and gas."

36

"I certainly do."

"Well, that's included in the price of the rental. But if you have to rearm and refuel, you will have to pay for it yourself. The first five hundred miles are on us, but you would be charged a thousand dollars a mile after that."

"That's reasonable. Can we charge it to our credit card?"

"Of course. Now when were you planning on making your strike?"

"Why?"

"Well, if you made it on a Saturday or Sunday, we could give you our special tourist weekend rate of five thousand dollars per plane, though you would have to return them on Monday morning."

"The weekend is as good a time as any. It might even be a better surprise. Do we have to return the planes to the same airfield?"

"No, you can drop them off at any American Air Force base after your raid. Now would you like liability insurance in case you are brought in front of the United Nations Security Council after the raid?"

"Sure, why not?"

"Here you are, sir. Take the Hertz bus right outside, and you can pick up your planes from our hangar."

"Oh, by the way, we also wanted to rent an AWAC airplane in case Balanteria decides to attack our oil installations in retaliation."

"All our AWACs have been rented to Saudi Arabia. Maybe Avis could help you."

The general would be directed to the next counter. The woman officer would punch his request into a computer. "We have a new AWAC coming in this afternoon. It's a sports model with only ten thousand miles on it. It will be fifty thousand dollars a day, but that's with unlimited mileage."

"That will be just fine."

"While you're here, sir, would you be interested in joining our VIP Nuclear Club?"

"What's the advantage of that?"

"You don't have to run through airports to get your planes. You can telephone in your order to the toll-free number and they will be ready when you get to the counter."

"That's a good idea."

"You also get a twenty-percent discount on our F-four fighter aircraft, and when you produce your card you will have priority on the latest air-to-air missiles just off the production line."

"Give me your application. You Americans certainly do have a wonderful customer relations program."

"Thank you, sir. When you're second-best in defense, you have to try harder."

You Look Great

Something happens to people when they visit friends or relatives in the hospital. I was forced to spend a few days in one not long ago for minor surgery, and had an opportunity to observe the peculiar behavior of the people who came to comfort me.

As a patient, I discovered you are at a complete disadvantage. Dressed in hospital garb, and stuck in a bed, you're no longer on equal terms with your pals. Without their realizing it, the entire relationship has changed.

From being a friend on equal footing with the Parkers, I suddenly found myself being treated like a senile uncle when they appeared at the hospital room door.

"You look great," Yvonne Parker said. "Doesn't he look great, Bill?"

"You certainly do," Bill agreed. "I've never seen you looking better."

"I feel great. I'm sore, but I feel just great."

"You have good color in your face," Yvonne said.

"Thanks," I replied. "Won't you sit down?"

"We can't stay too long," Bill said nervously, as he sat down. Then he got up. "Would you like a drink of water?"

"I don't think so, right now. But if I do I can pour one from this pitcher next to my bed."

"Isn't that great, Yvonne? He can pour his own water."

"I think it's just wonderful. Can I help you with your pillow?"

"No, thank you. I'm very comfortable."

"You look comfortable. I wouldn't even know you had been sick," Yvonne said.

"What does the doctor say?"

"He says I'm doing just fine. He doesn't think I'll have to stay the week."

"If he says so, he should know," Bill said.

"He wouldn't let you go home unless you were better," Yvonne said.

"That's what I thought," I said. "The reason he wants me to stay here is if I go home, I'll overdo it. At the same time, he doesn't want me to stay in bed all day because I'll get stiff. He wants me to walk around."

Yvonne said, "We'll leave if you want to walk around."

"No. I don't want to walk around now. I'll walk around later."

"I can't believe how good you look," Bill commented. "Doesn't he look good, Yvonne?"

"I've never seen him look better."

"Well, what's going on in the outside world?" I asked.

"Don't think about the outside world. Your job is to get well," Bill said. "Isn't that right, Yvonne?"

"That's right. There's no sense thinking about other things until you're on the mend."

"Well," Bill said, "we don't want to tire you out."

"You're not tiring me out. I feel great."

"You don't think you're tired," Yvonne said, "because you feel so good. But you have to rest. Do you want me to put your bed down?"

"No, if I want to put my bed down, I can do it with this button right here."

"We don't want to interfere with your dinner," Bill said.

"It's only three o'clock. They don't serve dinner around here until five."

Yvonne said, "Then you probably want to wash up for it. Bill, we'd better be moving along."

Bill got up. "You look just great."

Yvonne agreed. "I wouldn't believe it if I hadn't seen it with my own eyes."

Bill said, "You're going to be okay, guy. Isn't he going to be all right, Yvonne?"

"Of course he's going to be all right. He'll be his old self in no time."

"You hear that, fellow? Yvonne says you're going to be your old self in no time. And when she says something like that, you'd better listen to her. She knows what she's talking about."

The Float

Everyone can understand it when a little guy owes you money and is late in paying it back. But it's hard for most people to comprehend when a big corporation plays games with you.

Because of high interest rates, more and more of the

larger companies are dragging their feet when it comes to paying their bills. These are the same outfits who threaten an individual with the death penalty if he doesn't pay his bill on time.

The reason for this can be attributed to what is known in the banking business as "the float."

"The float" is the amount of cash that a company has on hand at any given time to invest in short-term bonds, notes, or certificates of deposit paying fourteen or fifteen or eighteen percent interest.

The longer the corporations hold on to your money, the more money they make on it for themselves. When interest rates were low, companies didn't pay much attention to "the float." Now it's keeping many of them alive. With double-digit interest, "the float" can make money for its owners on nights, weekends, and holidays. Special divisions have been set up to ensure that every bit of cash in a company is earning interest at all times, whether it's money that belongs to the company, or money that is owed to you.

This is how it works: You have provided a small service for Corporation Busbee, and your bill comes to five thousand dollars—a mere pittance to this great conglomerate. One month goes by and you don't hear a word. Then the second month goes by, and you decide to call up the man who ordered the work.

Because you're hoping for more business from CB you're very polite on the phone.

(Large companies which deal in "the float" count on the little fellow not becoming belligerent when it comes to asking for the money owed to him.)

The man who ordered the five thousand dollars' worth of services is expecting the call. "I put in a voucher for that bill the day it was received," he says in his most surprised voice. "I'll call Wheat Bluff, Kansas, and see what happened to it."

"Why would you call Wheat Bluff, Kansas, when you're located in Philadelphia, Pennsylvania?"

"That's where our computers are. We pay all our bills from Wheat Bluff."

"Isn't that a bit out of the way for you?"

"Not really. They have two commuter flights going in there every week. I'll get on this right away."

The next time you call, the man is on sick leave, and the time after that he's on vacation. Two months later you get him back on the phone.

"Any news about my five thousand dollars?"

"Didn't you get your money yet?" the man says. "This is shocking. The people in Wheat Bluff promised me they would put your check in the mail the next day. I'll get right back to you."

The next week the man at CB calls. "Well, you'll be glad to hear I found out what the hold-up was. Your invoice never reached Boulder, Colorado."

"Where does Boulder fit into this?"

"The computer in Wheat Bluff won't issue a check unless the computer in Boulder confirms that the figure is correct. I've sent a duplicate of the invoice off today. I wouldn't be surprised if you get your money in a week."

Whether you finally get your money in a week or a month after this call depends on whether the treasurer of Corporation Busbee wants to let you out of the company's float.

You may be wondering where your five thousand dollars was while you were trying to keep your head above water. If it will make you feel any better, it wasn't just sitting in Wheat Bluff, Kansas. It was floating in United States Treasury bills, German marks, Japanese yen, tax-free hockey bonds, or an offshore Eurodollar fund and Oil of Olay futures in Toronto, Canada.

Who says the big companies don't give you a ride for your money?

Sex and Violence

"You know what confuses me?" said Pfizer, as we were watching the girls in their bikinis do their stuff on the beach.

"What's that?" I asked him.

"Why do they always link sex and violence together? Every time the Moral Majority or any other minority discuss the evils of the day, they make it sound as if you can't have one without the other. This is particularly true of people who want to censor what we see or read. Now I have no trouble with violence—I don't like it and I think there's way too much of it for the good of the country. And there may be a lot more unnecessary sex than there has to be, when it comes to entertaining the masses. But I don't see why they have to be attacked in the same breath."

"Well, what would you link with sex?"

"Banana bread."

"Why banana bread?" I asked.

"I happen to like banana bread, and I also happen to like sex. I don't consider banana bread any more violent than sex, providing the other person has no objection."

"You miss the point. The people who are in the censoring business would get nowhere if they said they were against sex and banana bread. They're unlinkable."

"So are sex and violence," Pfizer said. "Now if they want to attack rape and violence, then I might join their club. I might even go along with their reservations about very young teenagers involved with sex. What I think is wrong is that by generalizing and putting sex and violence together, they're making people believe that if you're indulging in one you're committing the other."

"Would you object to sex and frozen yogurt?" I asked him.

"Why? Does frozen yogurt turn you on?"

"It does," I admitted. "Every time I see a pretty girl on the beach I think to myself, 'I wish I had a frozen yogurt.'"

"Well, at least frozen yogurt isn't a violent act, unless you push it in someone's face."

"If I had a frozen yogurt I would never resort to violence," I assured him.

"How about linking sex with flying a kite," Pfizer said.

"I don't believe the Moral Majority would do it," I told him. "They see sex as a violent act."

"Maybe that's their problem," Pfizer said. "Anyone with an unhappy sex life is prone towards violence."

"Well, if everything you say is true, what can just two of us do about it besides look at girls in their bikinis?"

"Not much," he said. "Let's find a refreshment stand that sells banana bread and frozen yogurt."

"What good would that do?"

"It would be making a nonviolent statement about sex, which everyone on this beach seems to have on their minds."

You'll Love This Bomb

Despite constant assurances of people very high in the government, there are still some skeptics in this country and Western Europe who are not sold on the argument that we need to build a neutron bomb. The fact of the matter is that the United States not only *needs* it—but it is inconceivable that we could ever have lived without it.

The neutron bomb is the greatest thing to come along since sliced bread. When set off it produces high levels of radiation, cooking people, but leaving structures and buildings standing. Unlike present atomic weapons where blast and heat do most of the damage, the neutron bomb actually penetrates its target, frying anyone inside.

The same people who are always standing in the way of progress are asking, "Why do we need a neutron bomb?"

The question doesn't deserve a response, but I'll give one anyway. We need one if we hope to fight an integrated war on foreign soil.

The United States military's new strategy is to prepare itself for conventional nuclear and chemical war battles. Because the Soviets outnumber the NATO forces, the neutron bomb will give us the parity we need to deter the Russians from attacking the West.

You would think the Europeans would be overjoyed that we were going ahead with an enhanced bomb which might kill them but preserve all their beautiful palaces and churches.

The reaction has been just the opposite. Instead of

saying, "Thank you, Uncle Sam," they have told us to stuff our neutron bombs in the ground.

I say if that's the way they feel about it, we should keep our bombs in Utah and see what kind of conventional nuclear war they can fight without them. If they want to use the second-rate, low-yield atomic weapons they now have at their disposal, good luck to them.

But when they start crying for the high-yield mini-nukes that can really do a man's job, we'll remind them of the fuss they made when we offered to place the neutron weapon on their soil.

The point that opponents keep missing is that we are not building a bomb to start a war, but to stop one. If the Soviets know we have a neutron bomb ready, they're not going to attack the West, unless, of course, they have a neutron bomb of their own.

By this time, we should have our laser death beam weapon in production, which will deter the Soviets from starting anything with their enhanced weapons.

In the arms war, the trick is always to stay one step ahead of the other guy.

I don't want anyone to get the idea that the neutron bomb is our ultimate weapon, and that we can relax after we get enough stockpiled. The bomb, for all its publicity, is just a nice little option a field commander has at his disposal when the going gets tough. It's not the end-all for killing large segments of the population, but if we can save pieces of valuable real estate from being destroyed, it will pay for itself in no time at all.

Part Two

IF A TREE FALLS

IF A TREE FALLS

If a Tree Falls

Secretary of Interior Watt's press person was briefing him for a news conference.

"So what do you think they'll ask me?" Watt wanted to know.

"Here is one question you may get. 'If a tree falls in the forest and nobody hears it, did it really make a sound?'"

"One of our trees, or one of theirs?" the secretary wanted to know.

"Let's assume it was a tree on government property."

"What's a tree doing on government property?"

"For the sake of argument, let's say it was located in a national park."

"Why are we allowing trees to grow in our national parks? How are we ever going to find oil and coal if we have foliage all over the area?"

"I don't think that that's the question," the press person said.

"I beg to differ with you," Secretary Watt replied. "My job as secretary of interior is to see we don't have too many trees cluttering up our forests. It discourages private investors from exploiting our natural resources. I don't have anything against trees personally, but I don't like to see them romanticized and used by the environmentalists as a lobbying weapon against private industry."

"Mr. Secretary, I couldn't agree with you more; but besides the environmentalists, there are a lot of people out there who like trees."

"They like them because they don't have to pay to keep them up. It comes out of my budget, not theirs. Now if we could lease the park lands to oil companies and mining consortiums, the royalties would pay for the trees and the burden wouldn't fall on the taxpayer."

"That's true. But some people are afraid that once you start leasing public land to the private sector they'll cut down every tree in sight."

"I never heard of anything so ridiculous. I just came back from Appalachia, and I saw trees there."

"That's so. But we still haven't answered the question as to whether the fallen tree made a sound or not."

"Why don't we turn the question to our advantage?" the secretary said. "We could point out that if the land was leased to a proper company, then there would be somebody there to hear if the tree fell or not—and he wouldn't even be on our payroll."

"That's not a bad idea. The environmentalists couldn't attack us for that. After all it wasn't the Interior Department's fault that the tree fell."

"At the same time, I think I should make it clear that if someone pushed it over I'm not going to make a big deal of it."

"Of course not. A secretary of interior never should."

Jelly Bean Economics

My young nephew John came over to the house the other night and said his teacher had given him the assignment of doing a paper on Reaganomics.

I decided to explain it in terms he would understand:

"I have here," I said, "a jar of jelly beans."

"May I have one?" he asked.

"No, you may not. You see, these jelly beans belong to the government and for years people have been eating more jelly beans than they put back in the jar. We have a deficit in jelly beans. Now what President Reagan hopes to do by 1984 is to have as many jelly beans in the jar as we consume."

"How is he going to do that?"

"By cutting down on the number of people who can have jelly beans. The fewer people who get jelly beans, the less chance there will be of the jar getting empty."

"That makes sense," John said.

"Now I'm going to give you ten jelly beans."

"What for?"

"It's a tax cut to which you are entitled under the Kemp-Roth Jelly Bean Bill."

"I thought you just said President Reagan was going to see that less people got jelly beans."

"He's just taking jelly beans away from people who don't deserve them but if you're working and putting jelly beans into the jar, you don't have to give back as many as you did before."

"Then how does Mr. Reagan ever hope to fill the jar?" John asked.

"In several ways," I explained patiently. "He's hoping that you will take the jelly beans he gave you and put them in a jelly bean savings account. Then the banks can loan them out to companies, who will make more jelly beans, and provide jobs for people."

"What good will that do?"

"The more people who have jobs, the more jelly beans they will be able to put into the jar, and pretty soon the government will have a surplus of jelly beans."

"How much will the banks charge to loan the jelly beans?"

"At the moment, for every hundred jelly beans they give, the borrower has to pay back one hundred twenty-one jelly beans plus an extra jelly bean for the paper-work."

"That's a lot of jelly beans," John said.

"It seems like a lot, but President Reagan believes that as soon as more and more people get their jelly bean tax cut, the banks will charge less to loan them out. The problem at the moment is that the government still has to borrow a large amount of jelly beans to take care of its obligations, so it is paying a higher rate for jelly beans than the banks can offer."

"That doesn't seem right," John said.

"The President doesn't like it either so he's ordered another severe cutback in his jelly bean budget. For example, schoolchildren will no longer be served jelly beans with their lunch."

"Suppose people eat their jelly bean tax cut instead of investing it?" John said.

"Then the jar will be empty by 1984 and nobody will have a bean to his name."

"And that's all there is to Reaganomics?" John said.

"That's it in a nutshell," I said. "If it works, we're going to be in jelly beans up to our hips—and if it doesn't, we're all going to be selling apples."

John left to write his paper. A few days later I saw him and inquired what kind of grade he got on his paper.

He said he didn't know.

"Why not?" I asked.

"My teacher was fired because the school ran out of jelly beans."

Good News from Russia

The only good news story I could find in the paper recently was that the Russians are suffering from two-digit inflation also.

The state informed the people that it was making dramatic price rises, doubling the price of gasoline, informally rationing food, increasing the price of tobacco and vodka by seventeen to twenty-five percent, and raising the cost on many consumer goods so it would be impossible for the average Soviet citizen to buy them.

You can imagine what the Soviets are saying within the confines of their homes.

"Misha, did you hear what Comrade Glushkov, Chairman of the State Pricing Commission, said in his speech on television tonight?"

"I fell asleep after the first three hours. What did he say?"

"They're raising the prices on everything because of inflation. It's outrageous. I think I'll write a letter to the Party leaders and give them a piece of my mind."

"Are you crazy, Misha?"

"I didn't say I'd 'mail' the letter. I said I'd just write it."

"But somebody could find it and then you would be in serious trouble."

"Maybe you're right. I think I'll bring it up at our next union meeting."

"We don't have unions, Misha."

"Well, we can't just sit here and let the state double the price of gasoline without saying anything."

"Why not?"

"Because this is a free country and Lenin said every worker must speak his mind."

"Misha, how many times have I told you Lenin is dead?"

"No matter. His teachings live on. How can the average person in the Soviet Union live if they keep raising the price on everything?"

"By not saying anything, Misha, that's how."

"I'll tell you why we have inflation. It's because of all the money they're spending on weapons. The military gets anything it wants. No one questions any request the military makes. The Politburo thinks it can solve every defense problem by throwing money at it. I think we should organize a protest meeting in front of the Kremlin and demand a large cut in military spending."

"Why don't you do that, Misha? You've never seen Lubianka prison."

"Make fun of me, woman, but I'll tell you something. The leaders of the Communist party are a bunch of idiots. They haven't been able to deliver on one thing they've promised us. I say in the next election, we throw the rascals out."

"Misha, that's your second bottle of vodka. At the new prices, you've just drunk two weeks' salary."

"That's it. We'll send a message to Moscow. If they can't manage the economy, we'll find somebody who can."

"Misha, have you been listening to 'Voice of America' without telling me?"

"You know what's wrong with this country? We have a bunch of bureaucrats sitting on their tails, telling everybody what's good for them. Well, they don't know beans about what's good for us. Government spending is what's causing inflation and all these socialist experiments where people are rewarded for nothing."

"Misha, is there another woman in your life I should know about?"

"No. Why do you ask?"

"Because you sound as if you want to leave me and go somewhere to work in a labor camp."

"All right. So what you're really saying is that we should do nothing about double-digit inflation and miserable salaries, and a bunch of stupid planners who could lead us into the greatest depression in Russian history."

"Not necessarily. We could move to Siberia."

Sandbagged

President Reagan's attacks on television coverage have made the news executives take a hard look at what they are showing on the nightly news.

Durham, at the ACN network, told me, "You know, the President isn't all wrong. What people see on the nightly news can affect them one way or the other. We make a lot of tough decisions when it comes to what we show."

"Give me an example."

"Well, remember a couple of weeks ago when Mr. Reagan stopped off in Fort Wayne, and for ten minutes helped the people pass sandbags to one another to stop the flood?"

"Do I ever. It was a great piece of film, and showed the President really cared about the people."

"I'm glad you saw it that way. But when the tape came in, we had a lot of questions about it. The first one was, if we showed it, would the viewing audience think the entire Midwest was under water?"

"You cleared that up by saying only Fort Wayne was being threatened."

"The second question was, would the American people think that all President Reagan did all day was pass sandbags from one person to another?"

"He was dressed in a black suit and wore a shirt and tie. I got the impression he just stopped off because it was a great picture opportunity for him, and his press people couldn't pass it up."

"That occurred to us, too. If this was true, was it a news story or just a publicity stunt to get the President on the evening news?"

"It could have been both," I said. "Frankly, the fact that the President of the United States took time out from defending his budget to pass sandbags to the people of Fort Wayne made me feel very good."

"Some of us thought that, but there were others in the newsroom who argued that viewers would be frightened about what we showed them in Fort Wayne, and they'd say if it could happen to the Hoosiers, it could happen to them. That could prolong the recession."

"I hadn't thought about that. People do tend to stop buying cars when they see them floating down the streets."

"Yet, if we didn't show the President passing sandbags, the White House would start screaming that we were keeping Mr. Reagan off the air when he was doing something for the people, and only showing him when he was attacking the media."

"Why couldn't you have done both? First you could have shown the President talking about South Succotash, and then you could have used the film of him saving Fort Wayne from going under water. It would have portrayed Mr. Reagan as first in war, first in peace and first in the hearts of his countrymen."

Durham said, "That's what we finally decided to do. But then we followed it with a story about an unemployed steel-worker in Gary, Indiana, and the White House raised the roof. They wanted to know what the President passing sandbags out in Fort Wayne had to do with unemployment in Gary."

"They had a point. Mr. Reagan was trying to stop an act of God, and you were trying to dramatize a manmade calamity for which the Democrats are responsible."

"Maybe we made a mistake in news judgment. We should have devoted the whole program to President Reagan passing along the sandbags."

"That's all water under the bridge, Durham," I told him. "When you're under a deadline it's hard to judge what will play in Peoria. Maybe you'll have another chance to make it up to the President."

"How?"

"As soon as Mount St. Helens blows again, the White House might give the President a broom and have him help the people sweep up the lava dust in Montana."

The New Airlines

As more and more major airlines eliminate cities and towns from their schedules, the slack is being taken up by tiny, struggling commuter lines.

What makes this exciting is that the new airlines are flying everything from World War II DC-3s to little planes that carry no more than six passengers at one time. The planes have none of the frills of a Boeing or a Lockheed jetliner, but there is a sense of adventure about flying one that makes you think you're in a time warp, and part of the early days of flight, before they had stewardesses and inflight movies.

We have such an airline on Martha's Vineyard, which

provides service between the Vineyard, Boston, and New York. Every trip on and off the island is an experience that none of the major airlines can give us.

My friend Peter Stone took me to the airport for a flight to Boston. Since we both had flown the route before, we discussed it as if he were Spencer Tracy and I were Clark Gable.

"I'll take the flight, and you marry Jane," he said.

"No," I told him. "I'll take the flight and you marry Jane. She really loves you."

"How do you know?" he asked.

"Because she begged me not to let you take the flight."

"Why didn't she say something to me?"

"Because she was afraid you'd do something stupid like knock me out, and then take the flight so we could get married."

"Okay, you take the flight and I'll marry Jane. If the marriage doesn't work out, I'll take the next flight and you marry her if I don't make it."

When we got to the airport, I checked in my luggage. The man behind the counter was wearing a sharp blue uniform with four stripes on it.

"You counter people have snappy uniforms," I said.

"What do you mean 'counter people'?" he said. "I'm the pilot." He put my baggage on the scales, and then he asked me how much I weighed.

I lied and said 190. He wrote down 200.

"People always lie by ten pounds," he said. Then he gave me a boarding card. "Heavy people will sit up front— lighter ones in the back of the plane."

As flight time approached I stood outside with Stone. Suddenly Jane drove up. "I've changed my mind," she said, throwing her arms around me. "I want Peter to take the flight and I want to marry you."

We went back inside but the pilot said it was too late. He had to load the luggage on the plane. He picked up his microphone and said, "Cumulus Airlines' Flight one-seven-eight-six is now boarding for Boston with intermediate stops in Hyannisport, Provincetown, and Woods Hole."

"But," I protested, "there are eight of us already, and with two pilots that makes ten. Why do we have to stop?"

"Who said anything about two pilots?" he replied. "We have room for one more passenger in the copilot's seat, and we may get lucky and pick up one at an intermediate stop."

"Look," I said to Peter, "you take my place and I'll marry Jane."

"Are you crazy?" Peter said. "If you make it to Boston you can marry anybody you want."

The passengers walked towards the tiny plane and before climbing the two steps, the pilot took our boarding passes. Then he crawled in behind us, closed the door and crawled down to his seat.

"Welcome to Cumulus Airlines," he said. "On behalf of the entire crew we hope that you have an enjoyable flight. Government regulations require me to tell you that in the unlikely event of any trouble your seat is your flotation jacket, so please don't forget it when going out the emergency exit door, which is the same door you came in by."

The pilot got out of the plane, turned both propellers by hand, returned to the plane, and then we were barreling down the runway.

I looked out the tiny window of the plane and saw Peter and Jane waving. This didn't shake me. What shook me was that the pilot had taken his hands off the throttle and was waving back.

No Law Is Good Law

Beagle, who works in the United States Department of Justice, called me and asked, "Do you want to play tennis this morning?"

"It's only ten o'clock," I protested. "Don't you have any work to do?"

"Nope. We're not supposed to do any work, or we get in trouble."

"But surely someone is violating someone's civil rights in the country."

"We've been instructed to stay away from that sort of thing. We don't want Jesse Helms to get mad."

"What has Jesse Helms got to do with the Justice Department?"

"He doesn't have anything to do with Justice directly, but every time we try to carry out any of the civil rights laws, he starts screaming his head off to the White House, and then the word is passed down to lay off."

"But don't you have some antitrust cases to work on?"

"What's antitrust?"

"You know—one company swallowing up another so there will be less competition."

"Haven't heard of one since Reagan got elected. You know bigness isn't necessarily badness. The way we look at it here, no large company would ever do anything to stifle another company, and even if it did, it would take too much work to prove it."

"Well, if you're not suing anyone for civil rights violations, and if you're not taking on any antitrust cases, what are you doing about environmental protection violations?"

"Oh, we're very much into environmental protection laws. If we find anyone violating them, we write a stiff letter telling them that if they don't desist we'll be very upset. It's actually a form letter but they don't know it."

"And if they ignore the letter?"

"That's it. The Justice Department is not in the business of harassing people."

"But surely, Beagle, in spite of not wanting to get involved in too much litigation, there is something you people can find to do. What about white-collar crime?"

"We prefer to settle those cases out of court. If a guy makes a mistake and promises not to do it again, then there is no sense in making his life miserable."

"What about organized crime?"

"That's something else. We don't like organized crime any more than anybody else. But we have to make sure we're operating within the law when we go after those people. We can't violate their civil rights."

"I can see why you want to play tennis in the morning," I said. "But I should think you would feel badly that you can't carry out the laws of the land."

"I do, every once in a while. If I really feel bad, I go after someone who is cheating on welfare. Jesse Helms doesn't mind that."

"I recall when you were so busy prosecuting cases at Justice, you didn't have time to play tennis on Saturday."

"I remember those days too. But this administration has a different philosophy. We're not out for a pound of flesh every time someone breaks a liberal law that shouldn't have been on the books in the first place."

"Well, I can't play tennis with you."

"Okay, maybe I'll write a brief on school prayers as a friend of the court."

"For school prayers or against them?"

"For them. What kind of Justice Department lawyer do you think I am?"

Your Biggest Fear

The magazine *Psychology Today* has just done a survey on "America's Hopes and Fears." It is a follow-up on the ones they conducted in 1964 and 1974.

Things have changed, as far as our fears go. In 1964 the thing we were most afraid of was war. In 1981 our main fear is a "lower standard of living." War comes in a weak third.

When the survey was taken in 1964, Americans' second most prominent fear was "ill health in the family." In 1981, possibly because of the influence of the "me" generation, the respondents said their second greatest fear was "ill health for self."

No one wants to admit this, but even those of us who live in Washington have personal fears. We mask them with bravado and by smiling a lot. But underneath we're just as frightened as the person in Missoula, Montana, who has found a Mediterranean fruit fly in his grapefruit juice.

Armed with *Psychology Today*, I went to a large party the other night and took a survey about what people in Washington are really afraid of.

Here are some of the more memorable responses.

A lawyer told me, "I'm afraid I'll be seated next to Supreme Court Justice Sandra O'Connor at a dinner party and I'll say, 'What does your husband do?'"

"My biggest fear," a friend told me, "is that I'm going to be invited to the White House and break one of Nancy Reagan's thousand-dollar plates."

An administration aide said, "Off the record? I'm afraid Interior Secretary James Watt is going to give permission to strip-mine the Rose Garden at the White House."

A congressman said, "My biggest personal fear is that someone is going to offer me fifty thousand dollars for my election campaign and I'm going to turn it down because I think it's an FBI Abscam setup. Then I'm going to find out it was a legitimate donation."

A lady told me, "I have this nightmare that I'll be sitting at a funeral next to Vice-President George Bush and will say to him, 'What do you do?'"

A State Department official said, "I have a deathly fear that I'm going to get a call some night from Al Haig, who will ask me to produce evidence to prove that the only way to save El Salvador is give them a fleet of AWACs."

"My fear," a Democratic senator told me, "is that we're going to win back a majority in the Senate and then we're not going to know what the hell to do."

"I'm afraid," said a friend from the Department of Labor, "that with the new budget cuts, every unemployment office in the country is going to go condominium."

A broker said, "I have this fear that if the Dow Jones average goes down to five hundred, President Reagan is going to condemn all the buildings on Wall Street and put the MX missile system in their place."

A reporter from *The Washington Post* said, "My biggest fear is that I'll do a series on the right-to-life movement, and then they'll want to kill me."

Someone asked me what my biggest fear was, and the first thing that came to mind was that I was stuck in an elevator for four hours with Phyllis Schlafly, and only one of us could get out.

The Nixon Library

This may come as a surprise to many people, but I believe Duke University did the right thing when it decided to build a Richard Nixon Library on its campus.

The only stipulation I would make is that all the Nixon papers and ALL the tapes be deposited here. Since he is probably the most interesting President we've ever had, I would hate to think that future historians would be deprived of many of the more private aspects of the man, when he served our country so well.

We all know about the Nixon who ended the Vietnam war, opened up relations with the People's Republic of China, brought detente between the United States and the Soviet Union, and battled for the First Amendment rights of all American citizens.

But I have a feeling that behind the public image, there was another Nixon that no one knows. Behind that winning smile and demeanor of confidence that all of us loved could have been a man with doubts and fears.

As I conceive the library, it should be divided into two sections. The Presidential Nixon part of the building would contain all of his state papers, his speeches, his discussions with world leaders, the gifts and honors that were bestowed on him by a grateful citizenry, and photos such as the one of him talking to antiwar protestors about football on the steps of the Lincoln Memorial.

This section would capture the spirit of a President who had to deal with the great problems of his country and the world. It would be an inspiration for generations of Americans to come, and a tribute to the thirty-seventh President of the United States.

The second section of the library would be connected by a Watergate and chiseled over its entrance in marble would be the words "I Am Not a Crook."

I believe that this section should be designed by the Walt Disney people. When visitors entered they would be greeted with an exact replica of the Oval Office. A wax figure of President Nixon would be seated behind the President's desk wired for sound.

In chairs, and standing around the office, would be wax figures of Haldeman, Colson, Ehrlichman, Dean, and John Mitchell, constructed so they, too, would be able to speak.

There would be an amphitheater, where people could sit comfortably and listen to all the tapes as the inner circle discussed the private matters that took up as much of President Nixon's time as the public ones.

When the tapes indicated only one or two members of the President's staff were in the office, stagehands could remove the others.

To give visitors an opportunity to buy popcorn and soft drinks, there would be an eighteen-and-a-half-minute intermission during the show.

For the first time, a Presidential Library would provide American citizens with the human side of a man who held the highest office in the land. His spirit and those of the people around him would come alive for tourists, who could actually hear their voices discussing the tribulations and heartaches of an administration beleaguered by enemies from every walk of life.

Duke University has an opportunity to do the real Richard Nixon justice, and I hope they don't blow it by just showing him being pelted with tomatoes in Venezuela.

Defrosting the Economy

The thing I like the best about Ronald Reagan is that he is probably one of the greatest salesmen in the country. He owes this talent to his training when he was spokesman for General Electric products. Ronnie sells Reaganomics with the same sincerity he sold appliances, and every time I watch him on television I can't help thinking he wants me to buy a new refrigerator.

If he were still working for GE this is probably how his pitch would go:

"My fellow citizens,

"I am speaking to you tonight to set the record straight concerning the pricing of our new refrigerators. There has been a lot of confusion about it in the media and you, the American people, deserve to know what is going on.

"I'm sure you've heard that we are proposing the largest price increase in history, and I've reversed my previous policy on refrigerator rebates to get the economy moving again. Well, don't you believe it.

"We are not raising our prices on refrigerators—we are 'reforming' them. It is the greatest icebox reform package in history, and one that will benefit everyone in this country.

"When I became spokesman for GE, inflation and interest rates made it impossible for the average American to buy a refrigerator.

"The reason for this was I inherited forty years of reckless spending and fraud by previous managements who didn't care what it cost to build one. Since I took this job we cut out the fat and brought our costs under control. Last year we announced a twenty-five-percent rebate for the next three years. This price cut was our way of stimulating the sale of refrigerators, creating new employment, and making the economy strong.

"We are not going back on these rebates. But in order to get our GE house in order, we are now making certain reforms which, contrary to reports, will not hurt the old, the sick, and the poor. For example, we are closing the loopholes to make the cost of a refrigerator much fairer to the working man and woman. There are many people who have not been paying for ice cube trays at the present time. Dealers have been throwing them in free so favored customers will buy our product. From now on everyone will pay for an ice cube tray no matter what tax bracket he is in.

"We have added a surcharge to our vegetable compartments which will only cost the average family two dollars and fifty cents a month. Our meat storage drawers will now be priced separately.

"There will be a slight price rise in freezer drawer shelves for people over sixty-five years of age, and we are asking five dollars more for those who want a place to store eggs. If you like handles on your refrigerator we will add them for a mere twenty dollars, which you will easily make up in energy costs in a month.

"When I became spokesman for General Electric, I promised you the best refrigerator that money can buy. With your help I can achieve this goal. Write to your dealers today and tell them that you support my efforts to move their products out of their showrooms.

"The refrigerator recession is bottoming out, thanks to the firm actions my administration has taken. But without the new reform I am proposing, we will never see the light at the end of the defroster behind closed doors."

Whither the Safety Net?

The budget cutters were working late into the night in the OMB office. As they sat around the table, weary from lack of sleep, one of them said:

"That's it, Dave, we can't find one more thing to cut."

"I can't tell that to the boss. There must be something else we've overlooked."

"I have an idea, Dave, though I hate to suggest it."

"Go ahead. It won't leave this room."

"What about the safety net?"

"I'm not following you."

"If we took away the safety net we could save ten billion more dollars."

"We don't have to tell anyone we've removed the safety net. It will be our dirty little secret."

"But if there is no safety net and someone walking on the tightrope falls, they will hit the pavement with a thud."

"It's done in circuses all the time. I've never seen anyone fall off."

"Yeah, but in a circus the people walking the tightrope are all in condition. The ones we're providing the safety net for are old and sick and have no shoes."

"Look, Dave, when the President talked about a safety net for the elderly, the really poor, and the really sick, he was talking about one of reasonable size.

"If we go into the recession before our supply-side economics bear fruit, we're going to need a bigger safety net than Detroit. And even if the poor people fall into it, there is no guarantee that they're still not going to be badly hurt. Our original figures indicated our safety net could take care of all the people who are on a tightrope now. But we didn't take into account the ones who are going to be walking on it after all our budget cuts go into effect."

"He's right, Dave. Also, you have to remember, in our last cuts, we made the tightrope a lot thinner and weaker to save money. It's not going to be able to hold all the new people we're putting on it."

"I promised the boss the safety net would be the last thing we'd cut. Don't forget, we're not only talking about people walking on a tightrope—we're also talking about those who are going to start jumping out of windows."

"You're all heart, Dave. But if the President goes on television and explains to the American people that this country can't afford a safety net until it gets its economic house in order, they'll go along with him.

"Where does it say in the Constitution, Dave, that the President of the United States has to provide a safety net for people who can't hack it on their own in this country?"

"I'm still not sure I can sell it to the boss."

"Put it in personal terms; he was poor and no one ever put a safety net under him."

"I need more ammunition than that."

"Okay, here's a memo I drew up showing every budget cut we've made. The only choice the President now has is either to cancel the safety net, or hold off on building the B-one bomber."

"Holy smokes, why didn't you show me that in the first place?"

Pity the KGB

Pity the poor KGB spy who has just been recalled to Moscow from the United States to explain his recent reports on President Reagan's military decisions.

"Federov, up until the last few months your work in the United States has been impeccable. But lately we can't make head or tail out of anything that you have sent us."

"Is confusing, comrades, I confess. But is not my fault. I only report the truth."

"Let's start with this report. What is 'Window of Vulnerability'?"

"Is window President looks out from White House and sees missile gap with Soviet Union. He said on television he wants to close window."

"That leads us to this second microfilmed report. You said he would close the window by building an underground MX missile system in state of Nevada, and move live missiles around so we wouldn't know where they were."

"Is not my fault I sent that message. I saw it on NBC and confirmed it in *The New York Times*."

"Then you sent a third coded cable that President is going ahead with building the B-one bomber, which will be obsolete by the time it flies. The cost is one hundred eighty billion dollars."

"I have the tape where he announced it on television."

"All right, Federov, assuming the President said it,

where is he going to get the one hundred eighty billion dollars and still balance the budget by 1984?"

"Is simple, comrades. Is called supply-side economics. You cut federal spending, give everyone twenty-five-per-cent tax cut, and the less taxes people pay, the more money you get back from the working people. Look, is all here on Laffer curve."

"Is not funny, Federov. And nobody in Soviet Union believes it."

"Comrades, I am aware that on paper it makes no sense, but our mole in the Treasury says Reagan people are serious about it."

"Shall we continue? You left message in Rock Creek Park for Boris which said, 'Half of United States Army and Navy are *stoned*.' What is *stoned*?"

"Drugged. They go on trip by smoking cigarettes and taking pills."

"You want us to believe United States military chiefs would let stoned people near nuclear weapons and billion-dollar military ships and planes?"

"Is all in Congressional Report, comrades. I left out those who were drunk because I knew you wouldn't believe me."

"And now, final message which you sent in diplomatic pouch Monday. You say United States is now preparing for limited nuclear war, on assumption if they keep it small, we will do same thing.

"What kind of idiots do you think we are, Federov? You made this all up, or else you're being fed by CIA disinformation agents.

"Federov, you need a rest. It's time you came in from the cold. Perhaps six months in a nice sanitarium will do you a lot of good."

"No, please, comrades. I'm not insane. I just reported the facts."

"Go quietly, Federov. Here is a present from all of us in the KGB's North American section."

"What is it?"

"A pad and crayon. Just think. You will now have time to draw all the Laffer curves you want to."

Diablo Country

I pride myself on having a very open mind on things, such as nuclear energy as long as they don't build a plant near my home.

So when I saw the Diablo Canyon demonstration in California a while ago I watched it with the calm impartiality which I reserve for all things that don't affect me personally.

On one side were scruffy, unshaven, unshod protestors. On the other were well-dressed state troopers, and clean, good-looking spokesmen for the power company. The dispute, as I understand it, was the scruffy unbathed people claimed that the people in the white hats didn't know what they were doing. They had built a billion-dollar nuclear plant near the San Andreas fault, which everyone says is going to cause an earthquake in California sooner or later.

My wife, who doesn't know the first thing about nuclear energy, asked me one evening as we watched the scruffies being hauled off in sheriffs' vans, "Why would they build a nuclear plant next to an earthquake center?"

"Because it obviously makes sense. The people who construct those plants know what they're doing. If you had been listening to the nice, clean-cut men in white shirts, ties, and dark suits, you would know that the power company has done exhaustive tests, and the nuclear plant can withstand any earthquake shock known to man. Besides, we have a Nuclear Regulatory Commission that has the last word on whether a plant is safe or not. They would never have given their okay to open one if there was the slightest question that building a nuke plant next to an earthquake fault could hurt the environment."

"Then why are the people in the scruffy clothes willing to be arrested for trying to close down the plant?" she asked.

"Because they have an unrealistic fear of nuclear power. They don't understand it and, therefore, they're against it. Many of them are students who enjoy getting involved in civil disobedience. But they're willing to go to jail for their beliefs."

"Whose side are you on?"

"I'm afraid I have to be on the side of those wearing the ties and coats. After all, they've been dealing with nuclear power all their lives and they should know if it's safe or not."

"A few years ago, you would have been on the side of the unwashed."

"I guess age does that to you. At some point in time you have to say that just because a person needs a shave doesn't make him right—and just because a person has short hair and dresses properly doesn't make him wrong."

"That's a stupid reason for taking one side over the other."

"There's more to it than that. The people who build nuclear plants are scientists, trained in our finest technical institutions. They work with computers and consult with famous experts who have an answer for every problem. The engineers and designers take extraordinary steps to see that not one bolt is put in wrongly. If they say a nuclear plant can survive an earthquake, I have to accept their word for it.

"This is not to say I am unsympathetic with the poor

souls who are willing to go to jail because they lack faith in our great scientific establishment. But in this case, I believe they're making a mountain out of a molehill. I would bet my All Savers Bank Account that they are wrong."

Well, you can imagine my surprise when a week later, the evening news announced that the Diablo Canyon nuclear reactor could not go into service because someone had gotten the drawings all mixed up, and the wrong pipes had been installed in the wrong sections of the plant. It meant that every pipe had to be personally inspected and replaced if it was discovered that it didn't belong there.

A man from the power company in a nice white shirt, tie, and blue suit explained it wasn't a very serious mistake and could have happened to anybody.

Another well-dressed man from the Nuclear Regulatory Commission said he was appalled at the sloppy engineering and was ordering an immediate investigation.

They didn't put on any scruffy people for comment. I wish they had, because I wanted to find out where to send them my All Savers Bank Account.

Everyone Is in Retail

I went to see my broker, Durgin, Burgin, & Black the other day. I had to wade through TV sets, refrigerators, automobile parts, tool chests, and children's clothes.

"What's going on?" I asked Durgin.

"Sears Roebuck is buying Dean Witter and going into the brokerage business. So we've decided to go into consumer retailing. No one wants to stay in his own racket any more," he said angrily.

"Do you have the floor space?" I asked him.

"We're taking over two more floors for our toy department and women's accessories. We are trying to get all the brokers in town to do the same thing. If Sears wants to play dirty pool, they've taken on the wrong people."

"I wish you luck. Listen, I was thinking about buying one hundred shares of Xerox. What do you think?"

"How about four radial automobile tires? They're guaranteed for ten years."

"Durgin, I know you're mad at Sears, but I really didn't come in here to buy tires."

"Forgive me. I've just lost my cool. Did you say Xerox?"

"I was thinking of Xerox or maybe RCA. That stock, according to Forbes, is underpriced."

"I like RCA. Let me show you one of their twenty-five-inch television sets. We're having a Founder's Day special on them this week. Sears can't match them for price."

"I don't want a television set. I want to buy stocks."

"Right you are. Let me get RCA up on the screen. Hey, look at that. You can get an electric chain saw and a pair of gloves for $89.95. It's going to be a cold winter, and you're really going to need a saw if you've got a fireplace."

"Durgin, I'm worried about Wall Street. Joseph Granville is a menace. He writes one letter and my entire stock portfolio goes out the window. How do I hedge against another Granville panic?"

"You can hide in the freezer. Let me show you this latest GE model."

"I can't buy stock and also buy freezers," I said.

"We'll let you have the freezer on our lay-away plan. Once your stocks go up, we'll transfer the dividends to your freezer account. We're the only ones offering this. Sears Roebuck isn't set up to do the paperwork."

"You're really out to get them, aren't you?"

"Why shouldn't we be? They want to muscle in on everything. First, it was insurance, then real estate, and now they want to sell stocks in their stores. I used to push Sears Roebuck stocks, but now when I get an order, I recommend tax-free bonds instead. If Sears Roebuck gets lucky, everyone will go into the brokerage business. You'll be able to go into Woolworth's and get all the IBM stock you want."

"But there are still going to be some of us who will just want to deal with a stockbroker who will devote all his time to financial business."

"You say that now. But I can just see you going into Sears for a mattress, and picking up a futures contract in pork bellies, which they'll probably have a sale on to get you in the store."

"Can we get back to my portfolio? What are you people recommending in money funds?"

"We have a wide selection. But if I were you, I'd take advantage of our Thanksgiving Day sale on video games. They're a lot more fun and unlike money funds your whole family can enjoy them."

"I'll be back, Durgin."

"You don't have to come in. Here's our new Christmas Retailer's Catalogue. You can order anything you want over the phone. And our deliveries are faster than Sears'."

The Political Spectrum

One of the most fascinating things to watch in world politics is how once-militant governments suddenly become "moderate" ones and vice-versa. Professor Heinrich Applebaum of the "Institute for Political Spectrums" keeps track of who are the militants and moderates on the global scene.

When someone from the media wants to know how to refer to a personality, or a country, or an organization, he first checks with Applebaum, who charges a two-dollar fee for each consultation.

Curious as to how Applebaum arrived at his conclusions, I visited his office. On one entire wall he had a detailed map of the world. It was covered with white pins, red pins, blue pins, and black pins. On another wall, he had a large blackboard, listing various rebel organizations.

"The white pins stand for 'moderates,' the red pins for 'militants,' the blue pins for 'freedom fighters,' and the black pins for 'fanatical militants,'" Applebaum explained. "Now any country that's anti-Soviet, no matter what its ideology, is considered to have a 'moderate' regime.

"And a country that has thrown in its lot with the Soviets is considered 'militant' and gets a red pin. The blue pins are reserved for movements trying to overthrow a pro-Soviet regime, and black pins are for groups trying to overthrow a pro-American government."

"That seems simple enough," I said.

"It's not as easy as you might think. Take Kadafi of Libya. A few years ago, because of his oil fields, he was considered a 'moderate.' He was exporting revolution at the time, but he wasn't bothering the United States. So I gave him a white pin. Then he started putting out death contracts on Libyan students in the United States and I had to change his classification to a fanatic."

"It took a long time for you to recognize what he really was," I said.

"If it was easy," Applebaum replied defensively, "we wouldn't be in all the trouble we're in right now. Let me show you something. Up here in northern Iran is where the Kurds live. At one time, since they were fighting for their independence, the United States considered them 'freedom fighters,' and was giving them aid. Then the Shah complained to our State Department, and we changed their status to 'communist-led rebels' and cut off all help.

"After the Shah was deposed, and Khomeini and his religious fanatics took over the country, we reinstated the Kurds as 'freedom fighters' and gave them back their blue pin."

"I see you have Arafat of the PLO down as a 'moderate.'"

"He is a 'moderate' compared to the radicals in the Palestine Liberation Organization. Although he wants to drive the Israelis into the sea, we think we can deal with him. So on the political spectrum, we changed his classification to 'moderate' so we could differentiate between him and the fanatic militants in the PLO, who are trying to kill him."

"Is that a blue pin I see in Cambodia?"

"That's correct. Although Pol Pot killed millions of people, and drove them out of the cities, he is now being opposed by troops who are being supplied by the Soviets. I had no choice but to make him a 'freedom fighter' after his country was attacked by the Vietnamese."

"You don't have any pin in Iraq," I pointed out.

"Iraq presents a problem. They're fighting Iran, and

being supplied by France, Italy, and the Soviet Union. They're also selling their oil to the West. We really don't have a pin to fit this kind of situation, so we've decided to ignore them."

"I can understand the problem with Iraq. But why have you classified Syria as 'moderate,' since they get all their military equipment from the Soviet Union?"

"The only way we can resolve the problems in the Middle East is to deal with Syria, because they occupy Lebanon."

"That makes sense," I said.

Someone came in and handed Applebaum a message.

He went over to the blackboard and erased the word "totalitarian" against South Africa, and replaced it with "moderate."

"What gives?" I asked.

"It's a personal favor to United Nations Ambassador Jeane Kirkpatrick."

Designer Chocolates

As you may have noticed, the dress designers are putting their names on every product from pillowcases to automobiles. So I shouldn't have been surprised to see that Bill Blass, one of America's leading couturiers, was now designing chocolates.

The copy in the ad read, "Bill Blass, renowned for his brilliant interpretations of American fashion, has teamed with the true aristocrat of chocolate, Godiva, to create a unique confectionary collection."

How does a fashion designer create a collection of chocolates? Maybe like this:

"Where is the master?"

"Hush, he's in his atelier working on new bonbons for Mother's Day."

"Renee, come in here right away."

"Yes, Master."

"I believe I've got it. Look at these sketches. What do you think?"

"It's divine, Master."

"I've filled the bust of the chocolate with raisins, brought in the waist with vanilla cream, and put butter crunch on both hips."

"*Quelle* inspiration! Christian Dior in his greatest days would have never thought of it."

"Now look at this sketch. I call this 'Evening in Vienna.'"

"It's so gorgeous it makes your mouth water."

"Do you know what makes it different from any chocolate you've seen?"

"Tell me, Master."

"I've put the nuts on the outside like sequins, so that you can see them before you bite into the bonbon. Most designers hide their nuts inside the chocolate and you don't know they're there. But if you put the nuts, like so, it not only adds luster to the outside, but it says 'I'm yours.'"

"I can't wait to see it in a box."

"Now this is my daytime chocolate that you can eat at a lunch or a fancy tea."

"It's so simple and yet so chic."

"I've put a tiny dash of Grand Marnier in it so it will make you feel naughty."

"Oh, Master, only you could think of putting a liqueur in a plain chocolate bonbon."

"Now over here in the upper left-hand corner of the box I've designed a caramel. But it's not an ordinary caramel. One layer is brown, one layer is pink and one layer is peppermint."

"The candy critics will go wild when they see it. Even Yves St. Laurent never put brown, pink, and peppermint in the same caramel."

"Wait, there's more. Look at this one."

"A seashell chocolate?"

"That's what it looks like. But when you strip off the chocolate, there is a tiny white saltwater taffy ball inside. Elizabeth Taylor will go nuts over this one.

"Now for my second layer, I have a big surprise. In the very center of the box I'm placing a coffee-cream-filled star with a red cherry on the bias."

"*Mon dieu*. No wonder they call you the greatest bon-bon designer in the world."

"I've saved the best for last."

"A perfect chocolate sparrow's egg?"

"And what do you think is inside?"

"Tell me, Master. I can't stand the suspense."

"A jelly bean."

"I think I'm going to faint."

State Visit

King Naban of New Gurdy stepped out of the helicopter on the White House lawn and shook hands with the President of the United States. Four cannons fired off a twenty-one-gun salute.

"Thank you, Mr. President, for that wonderful salute. What kind of cannons are they?"

The President looked to his military aide. "A hundred and five millimeters, sir," the aide whispered.

"Would you like one?" the President asked the king.

"I'd rather have two hundred ground-to-ground missile launchers—if that's all the same to you," the king said.

"I'll talk to Cap Weinberger about it. Will you join me while we play your national anthem?"

"Just a minute. I want to write down the name of the United States Marine helicopter I just flew in on. We could use some of those."

"We don't have too many in stock now, Your Highness."

"We'll take what you've got, and you can send us the rest later."

"Couldn't we wait until the welcoming ceremonies are completed?"

"Of course. Forgive me."

"Nancy and I are honored you would take time out of your busy schedule to visit us."

"It's my pleasure. I was only saying to the queen last week how much I was looking forward to coming to Washington and meeting the man who singlehandedly won the AWACs battle for Saudi Arabia."

"It was really nothing, Your Highness. The Saudis are our friends, and if anyone deserved AWACs, they did."

"How much do they cost?"

"They're not for sale, Your Highness. We just made an exception in the case of the Saudis, because they've kept the price of oil down in OPEC."

"Then how come they raised it two dollars a barrel, and cut back production the day after you persuaded the Senate to give them the AWACs?"

"I'm sorry. I have to come to attention. They're playing the 'Star-Spangled Banner.'"

"That's no excuse. We're your friends too. But if we don't get AWACs, my people will think we're being treated as a third-rate power."

"The AWAC is overrated, Your Highness."

"Then why did you make such a big deal out of it in Congress?"

"It was a question of pride with the Saudis. Had we refused to sell them, they would have lost face in the Arab world."

"And you don't believe it's a question of face with my government if you refuse to sell them to me?"

"Your Highness, if we sell AWACs to every country, the Saudis will decide they're not worth much, and then we'll have to give them something else that nobody in the Middle East has."

"You always liked the king of Saudi Arabia more than you liked me."

"That isn't true, Your Highness. Didn't we give you fifty F-four fighter planes on your last visit?"

"Every banana republic in South America has F-four fighter planes."

"Why don't we talk about it at the state dinner we're giving for you tonight?"

"I'd rather eat in my room if you're not going to give me AWACs."

"But Nancy has invited one hundred and ten people and she had to borrow china from the Hilton Hotel. Look, I wasn't supposed to mention it until tomorrow when we meet with Al Haig, but how would you like a Stealth bomber for your air force?"

"Can it do more than AWACs?"

"It makes an AWAC look like a Mediterranean fruit fly."

"If it's so good how come you didn't give it to the Saudis?"

"Because they didn't ask for it."

We Socked It to Them

I was sitting in a bar in O'Hare Airport killing time, and struck up a conversation with the man on the next stool.

"Your plane been canceled, too?"

"Yep," he said. "I was going to Dallas. Now they've routed me through Rochester, New York. Where you going?"

"Washington, by way of Montgomery, Alabama. I guess this air controllers' business is catching up with all of us."

"It seems to be. But I think Reagan did the right thing, not letting them come back to work."

"You can say that again," I said. "He sure showed them who was boss."

"Those guys should have never gone out on strike. They cut off their noses to spite their faces."

"I like a President who hangs tough. What time does your plane leave for Rochester?"

"Midnight. My flight to Dallas takes off at six in the morning."

"You're lucky, you have only four hours to wait. I have seven."

"It's a small price to pay for showing the air controllers they couldn't violate the law."

"You can say that again. I don't care if I ever get home as long as the air controllers have been taught a lesson."

"Bartender, I'll have another one, and don't forget the lemon twist this time."

"Sorry," the bartender said. "I'm new at this job. I'm

really a pilot. I was laid off because of the air controllers'
strike. Now just when I'm getting the hang of bartending,
I'm going to be laid off here."

"How come?" my friend asked.

"Not enough people in the airport. The flights have
been cut down by seventy-five percent. All the conces-
sionaires are going broke."

"Well, someone has to suffer to show that the Department of Transportation isn't going to take any flak
from those guys on the picket line," I said. "Your wife
work?"

"She's a stewardess," the bartender-pilot said. "She
was laid off, too." He then went over to a man sleeping
in a chair and woke him roughly. "Look, Mac, how many
times have I told you you can't sleep in here. Now get
out before I kick your butt."

"Who was that?"

"He's an air controller supervisor. Every time he gets
a break, he comes down here and tries to catch a few
winks before he goes up to the tower again."

"That's a nervy thing for a guy to do," I said. "You
would think a guy could work in a tower for twelve hours
without getting sleepy."

"You know what?" a man a few stools down the bar
said. "I think Reagan should be a big enough man and go
on television and say the air controllers made a mistake
but he forgives them, and if they want to come back to
work they can."

"Are you a Commie or something?" I said angrily.
"What kind of signal do you think that would give to the
Russians if he showed he was soft on air controllers?"

"If they pardoned Nixon, they can pardon the air controllers," he said.

"There's always one bleeding heart in a bar," I said.
"I'm glad there's no one in the Reagan administration who
is thinking in terms of amnesty."

"You can say that again," my friend on the next stool

said. "I hear we'll have enough air controllers by 1985 to resume normal flight operations again."

"I can wait," I said.

"I'll drink to that," my friend on the next stool said. "You let one air controller return, and they'll all want to come back to work. Before you know it, we'd have radar screens all over the country manned by criminals."

Part Three

VOODOO ECONOMICS

VOODOO ECONOMICS

Voodoo Economics

During the election campaign, President Reagan's Republican opponent, George Bush, described Mr. Reagan's economic plans as "Voodoo Economics." I thought this was all political hyperbole, until I walked behind the White House on Halloween night, and found a witch doctor stirring up a broth in a large black kettle.

"What's cooking?" I asked him.

"A little recession," he said mournfully. "I think I made a mistake in my recipe."

"Let me taste it," I said. He handed me a wooden spoon. "Ughghgh," I spat it out. "It's much worse than I thought. What did you put in it?"

"I know it's bitter, but I thought that's what was needed. I took all the fat off the bone and then I cut up the bone. Then I added a dose of interest rates and the pot boiled over. I have to start all over again."

"What are you doing now?"

"I'm throwing out the baby with the bath water."

"What for?"

"If I don't, the recession will thicken and we'll be in a worse stew than we are now. I have to start from scratch."

"You Voodoo Economics witch doctors can really cook up a storm."

"Don't talk. Let's see. I have to throw in a little of this and a little of that."

"What did you put in the pot?"

"Sugar supports, peanuts, butter, and an Air Force

base President Reagan promised a Boll Weevil congressman in Florida."

"The stew is starting to boil over again," I said.

"Well, it's not my fault," the witch doctor said angrily. "They told me if I cut out all the waste and chopped up large cuts of taxes, there would be more pie for everyone."

"I thought you were making stew."

"It started out to be a glorious economic pie. Now I don't know what the hell it is."

"Maybe it needs more tax seasoning than you thought," I suggested.

"We don't call them taxes. We call them revenue enhancers. They're additives that I'm going to have to put in whether I want to or not."

"What are you dumping in now?"

"I'm peppering it with blame. When the people finally realize what a mess we've cooked up, we're going to show them where the blame is."

"What kind of blame are you putting in?"

"Congressional Blame Number One. You sprinkle it on everything, and people don't know what they're eating."

"That's some recipe for an economic stew."

"It might not be stew after it's finished. It could turn out to be gruel."

"I don't understand it. The way Reagan and his people described this dish, it was going to be tasty and delicious and there would be enough to go around for everyone."

"A Voodoo Economist can do just so much," the witch doctor said. "They promised me all the ingredients and couldn't deliver. I'll be grateful if this mess doesn't turn into a heavy recession hash."

He tasted it. "I think it needs some more working poor."

"You're not going to put more working poor into the pot?" I pleaded.

"Well, you don't expect me to throw in tobacco crops, do you?"

Watch Out, Kadafi

As a reader of spy thrillers, I have been following the CIA-Libyan Connection with a great deal of interest. It appears there are these two ex-agents named Frank Terpil and Edward Wilson who have a contract with Colonel Kadafi to train terrorists, organize assassinations, hire American pilots and ex-Green Beret types, and procure all sorts of lethal weapons which will help Kadafi knock off his enemies.

Now you may wonder why two Americans, who served their country, would go over to the other side to help a madman who runs one of the most heinous governments in the world.

Well, if you read thrillers the way I do, then you'll probably buy the answer. Wilson and Terpil really still work for the CIA. But in order not to blow their cover, they keep devising ways to knock off American diplomats.

"The Company" has known for a long time what the two men are up to, particularly when it comes to buying material in the United States to further the cause of world terrorism.

The two turncoats also have been permitted to recruit mercenaries in the United States while the United States has looked the other way, to convince Colonel Kadafi that they are on his side.

Unbeknownst to the CIA, Terpil and Wilson were photographed by the KGB in a compromising situation in a Tripoli hotel room, and the Soviets turned them around so they would work for them. The Russians don't trust Kadafi any more than the Americans, and threatened to release photographs of the two men to the *National Enquirer* unless they became double agents, which both men agreed to do.

What the KGB doesn't know is that the real Terpil and Wilson were spirited off to Israel, and replaced with two Israeli intelligence agents *pretending* to be Terpil and Wilson, but actually reporting on Kadafi's activities to Tel Aviv through a Swiss company that "Mossad" had set up.

The French found out about this and that's how they managed to get the Libyans to pull out of Chad. Terpil and Wilson advised Kadafi to give up Chad, because they said they couldn't supply him with any more planes from the United States.

British intelligence, which is not sure what game the CIA is playing, has planted a beautiful Italian countess on Terpil who will do anything to avenge the murder of her father by Kadafi.

Egyptian agents have offered Wilson one million dollars in an American tax-free All Savers account, if he will push Kadafi out of an airplane at thirty-five thousand feet.

In order to prove his loyalty to Kadafi, Wilson reported the offer to the colonel, which has made Kadafi believe more in Wilson and Terpil than he ever did.

The biggest problem Terpil and Wilson have at the moment is to keep Libya from building an atomic bomb in Pakistan.

The CIA has supplied the two men with blueprints of the Three Mile Island nuclear plant, and if the Pakistanis follow the plans, the bomb will blow up in their faces.

Now I know there are a few people out there who believe that this scenario is farfetched, but it's the only one that makes any sense.

Otherwise, you have to ask yourself why would the United States Central Intelligence Agency, which has terminated many of its enemies for far less, permit two of its ex-agents to organize a worldwide terrorist network, and supply them with weapons and American pilots and ex-Green Berets.

I'm sticking to my theory until a better one comes along. If I were in Kadafi's place, I would bury Frank Terpil and Edward Wilson in hot sand up to their necks, and let red ants have a go at them until they tell the real reason why they're so anxious to help Libya become the terrorist capital of the world.

Ah So!

A Japanese newspaperman came into my office the other day, bowed low, and said, "Forgive me for this awkward intrusion, but I am doing a story for a newspaper in Tokyo about Richard Allen and the Nancy Reagan interview."

"Ah so," I said, "I would be most honored to answer any of your questions."

"What do you personally think of this situation?"

"I would prefer not to comment on it," I replied, "until the Justice Department finishes its investigation."

He smiled and gave me a white envelope containing one hundred dollars in cash.

"Ah so," I said, smiling back. "But I cannot accept a bribe for granting an interview."

"It is not a bribe," he said indignantly. "It is a tradition in my country to give a small gift of appreciation when someone grants an interview."

"Why didn't you say that in the first place?" I said. I

called in my secretary and asked her to put the envelope in the safe.

"Do you feel," he continued, "that someone in high position in office should accept a gift from a newspaperman for arranging an interview with the First Lady of the land?"

"Mr. Allen expected nothing, but he has great respect for your traditions and would do anything not to insult you. When Mr. Reagan took office, the first thing he said to his foreign policy advisers was, 'Under no conditions do I want anyone in my administration to offend the Japanese.'"

The newspaperman smiled and handed me another white envelope. He looked at his notes. "What do you think Mr. Allen intended to do with the thousand dollars?"

"He says he intended to give it to charity."

"Why didn't he?"

"Because he forgot about it. You must understand, Mr. Allen is the President's national security adviser and he forgets very easily. One day he says a certain country is a threat to the United States and then he forgets all about it."

"Am I taking up too much of your time?" he asked.

"Heck no," I said. "Not as long as you keep passing over white envelopes."

"Mrs. Reagan knew nothing about the arrangement?"

"Mrs. Reagan doesn't even remember being interviewed by the Japanese magazine."

"That means she must be very unhappy with Mr. Allen."

"Well, she's not working on a needlepoint pillow for him for Christmas this year."

The Japanese newspaperman was writing furiously.

"I don't mean to offend you," I said, "but you forgot to give me another white envelope."

"Ah so," he said. "A thousand pardons."

"It's okay. But we Americans aren't used to answering questions for nothing."

"One final question. Is it your opinion that Secretary of State Al Haig is happy or unhappy about the way things are going for Mr. Allen?"

"He looked very disturbed the last time I saw him on television and I couldn't tell whether it was because of Mr. Allen or Nicaragua."

The Tokyo newspaperman handed me my last envelope.

As soon as he left, I called Tom Brokaw and said, "The next time you want me to do the *Today* show, it's going to cost you ten big ones."

"But that's checkbook journalism," he cried.

"Ah so."

The Corporate Safety Net

People keep insisting that I'm making it up, but under a tax law lobbied through the summer of 1981, companies that lost money in that year can sell their losses to firms that made money, so the latter will not have to pay any corporation taxes.

Whereas, in the past, company losses were something no one liked to talk about, they now have become a valuable commodity and are being traded on the open market.

This is how it works:

"Hello, John, Hal Lemster of International Pushbutton calling. I just read your financial report. I see you people lost seven hundred and fifty million this year. Congratulations."

"Thanks, Hal. I guess we were just lucky."

"Well, International Pushbutton had the best year ever. We made one billion-two before taxes."

"Sorry to hear that, Hal."

"Everyone has an off year. I'm calling to buy your tax losses, John. If we can deduct your losses against our profits, and own the tax credits against new equipment, the government will owe us money."

"How much are you offering, Hal?"

"We'll give you one hundred million in cash, retool your plant, and lease the equipment back to you at a very favorable rate. Our accountants figure that with speeded-up depreciation, we'll pay less taxes this year than the kid who works in the mail room."

"Gosh, Hal, I'd like to help you out, but my account-ants figure our tax losses are worth at least two hundred million."

"You must be crazy. Just because you had a bad year, and we had a good year, there's no sense holding us up."

"This is strictly business, Hal. Our losses are our only assets. United Bull has offered us a hundred fifty million and I just had a call from Dimblebee Oil, which is willing to give us a hundred seventy million in preferred notes. We're sitting in the catbird seat."

"John, I'll be very honest with you. If I don't find a company with large tax losses, I'll be in serious trouble with my stockholders. I'll never be able to explain to them why we had to pay taxes to the government on our profits. They could sue me for mismanagement."

"I don't want to hear about your troubles, Hal. Who told you to make a lot of money in the first place?"

"Someday you'll have a good year, John, and then you're going to need help from a losing company."

"Look, Hal, if you can't find a way of avoiding taxes, don't cry on my shoulder."

"All right, John, I've got my controller here and we're ready to deal. We'll make you the same offer we made the Montezuma Automobile Company. We'll pay one hundred seventy-five million in cash for your tax losses and lease back to you a completely new plant in Ohio."

"Now you're making sense. That means neither you nor I will have to pay corporate taxes for the next five years."

"It's a sweetheart deal for both of us, John. Will you take it?"

"Sure, Hal. After all, what are friends for?"

"Great. How do you think Reagan's economic plan is going?"

"I think he's going to have to cut more fat out of the budget in order to get the deficit down. He's going to have to go after the welfare cheaters and the people who are always looking for a free lunch."

"You can say that again. When we were kids we worked for what we got. The only way Reagan is going to get this country back on its feet again is to stop giving everyone with a hard-luck story a handout."

Anybody Home?

I went over to see Harvey Dunlap during the Thanksgiving holidays and pay my respects to his kids, who were home from school.

Max was eating breakfast, Chris was eating lunch, and Dottie was holding hands with her boyfriend.

I'd never seen Dunlap so happy. "This is the first time since they've been home that we've had this many at the table at the same time."

"Who is that down at the end?"

"That's someone Dougie brought from school. I think

her name is Anna, and she's from Brazil. Do you speak Portuguese?"

"Sorry, no. Where's Dougie?"

"He's upstairs sleeping. I have an appointment to see him at five."

"An appointment?" I said.

"Yes. You see, Dougie said he would be so busy this weekend it would be best for me to make an appointment with him. He worked Edna and me in for five o'clock."

"That's damn decent of him," I said. "Most college kids aren't that thoughtful."

"Well, as you know, Dougie is studying to be a doctor, and he probably got the idea from that."

"You want to go to a movie?" I asked Dunlap.

"I'd like to, but I don't know what the kids are doing yet, and I can't walk out on them in case they decide to stay home."

"When will you know?"

"I'm not sure. They never can tell you until the last moment."

"Why don't you take a head count in the morning as to who will be eating dinner at night?" I suggested.

"We tried that yesterday. Everybody said they would be home for dinner, but as the day progressed they kept peeling off, because they had gotten a better offer. In the end there were only three of us—Edna, myself, and Anna."

"Dougie left Anna at home?"

"He had a date with his pals from high school, and told Anna she'd be bored."

"Max looks good," I said.

"Come to think of it, he does. This is the first time I've seen him since he got home."

"Wasn't he at your Thanksgiving dinner?"

"He was going to Florida with a friend, but at the last moment the friend decided to go to Aspen, so he drove home and missed our turkey by a day."

"How long is he going to stay?"

"He says either until tonight, tomorrow, or Monday, depending on some friends he's waiting to hear from in Vermont."

"It must be hard for you and Edna to make plans when no one is quite sure what they're up to. Where is Edna?"

"She's out in the kitchen cooking a roast beef just in case anyone decides to stay home."

"Has she seen the kids yet?"

"Yes and no. I believe they kissed her when they arrived, and she caught sight of two of them coming home this morning at seven o'clock. But I think the only extended conversation she had was when she asked who took her car keys."

"If I were you," I said, "I'd make them sign up on a schedule indicating when they were arriving, how many friends they were bringing home, how many meals they were planning to have, and when their flights were leaving. As a parent you have a right to know that much about your children."

"We had that information when they came—but no one stuck to the schedule."

"So forget about them and do what you want to do."

"We announced that yesterday, and Chris said, 'If all you and Mom are going to do is go out, I don't see why we came home in the first place.'"

A Question of
Civil Rights

There is a feeling by some people in the country that the present Justice Department is soft on civil rights, and is trying to turn back the clock on progress made in this field over the past twenty years.

This is not true. Just the other day a lawyer in the Justice Department went in to see his supervisor. "Sir, there seems to be a group of people in the South that is going to bring back slavery. I think we'd better get on it right away."

"What's the rush, Pettibone? There's no sense jumping into these things unless we know we're on solid legal ground. Now you say these people are going to bring back slavery. What side are you proposing the Justice Department take?"

"The antislavery side, sir. It's our duty to defend the Constitution which is the law of the land, and the Constitution says you can't have slaves."

"That's true, Pettibone, but there are other constitutional amendments which must be considered, such as states' rights. Now don't get me wrong. I'm not for slavery. I abhor it and always have. But I cannot allow my personal feelings to get involved in a sensitive matter such as this. The legal question we must ask is, would slavery violate the rights of those who are being enslaved?"

"Of course it would. A slave doesn't have any rights."

"Is there anything in this Civil Rights Bill that specifically forbids someone from owning a slave?"

"No, because there was no question of slavery at the time it was passed."

"Well, perhaps this is not our case then. After all, we can't go prosecuting people willy-nilly if it is not concerned with our division. We are short on lawyers as it is, because we inherited all those bleeding-heart civil rights cases from other administrations."

"But this is not just another civil rights case. This is the big enchilada. If we don't act immediately slavery could come back to the United States."

"I think you're overreacting, Pettibone. Every lawyer in Justice thinks his is the only case. But when you're sitting in this chair you have to be selective as to what cases the department should take, and what ones we should ignore. The one thing this administration has pledged to do is not clog up the courts with a lot of petty matters that could be settled through reason."

"What do you suggest?"

"Why don't you draft a letter to the people who are going to bring back slavery and indicate we are taking an interest and we're willing to work out a settlement which would be satisfactory to both sides?"

"What kind of settlement did you have in mind?"

"We would require them to justify their reasons for needing slaves. If, for example, they could prove it would have a favorable economic impact on their community, then we might look the other way. But if they just want slaves to do their dirty work for them, then we might consider making a case against them."

"I can't write a letter like that. It's unconstitutional."

"Pettibone, I don't believe it's the Department of Justice's job to decide what is unconstitutional and what isn't."

"What is our job?"

"To see that the laws of the land are carried out as long as they don't offend the people who elected President

Reagan. Can you imagine the political repercussions from the ultra-right wing if it got into the papers that we were thinking of suing people who wanted to bring back slavery?"

"If you don't do anything about this, I'll go to the papers myself."

"All right, Pettibone, if you feel that strongly about it, get the evidence together."

"And the department will prosecute?"

"I didn't say we'd prosecute, but we might submit a brief as a 'friend of the court.'"

Some Call It Art

The large doses of economic news we are all getting are not educating most Americans, but only confusing them.

Very few people understand them. Fortunately, I know someone who does. He is an economist named Alfred Daffy, and he endeared himself to the Reagan people with his economic theory that you can solve any problem if you throw enough Trojan horses at it.

When I first met Daffy he had constructed an economic model for unbelievable prosperity, full employment, and a surplus in the Treasury. It was a work of art, done in smooth clay without a line out of place. People from all over the country came to admire it; there was even talk Alfred might end up with a Nobel Prize.

I went to see Daffy at his studio the other day, and he had the model all torn apart.

"What are you doing?" I asked.

"I have to rework it," he said. "There are a few things I hadn't counted on." He took an enormous glob of clay and threw it at the side of the model.

"What's that?"

"The recession. On my original model I only allowed a little clay for a mild recession. Now we're in a real one and that puts my whole model out of kilter." He took another glob and put it on the other side. "There, that should balance it."

"What does that glob represent?"

"Unemployment. You can't have a large recession without large unemployment." He studied his model for a few moments, and then took some clay from the bottom and put it on the top.

"In my original model, I had interest rates down here. I never figured on them being up here."

"But they're falling," I said.

"Not for long," he said, grabbing a glob of clay in both hands and dumping it on top of the model. He took another glob and dumped that on top of the first one.

"What are you doing?" I cried.

Daffy said, "I'm adding a hundred-million-dollar deficit that wasn't in the first model."

"Why wasn't it there?"

"Because in my original model, everyone was going to get a tax cut which would spur the economy, and with more people working there would be more money going into the Treasury than the government was paying out, and we would have a surplus."

"What went wrong?"

Daffy kept throwing clay at his model indiscriminately. "The savings in government spending weren't there and the military budget jumped to over two hundred billion."

"That model is starting to look a mess," I said.

"I'm not through with it yet. Consumer spending is nil, our balance of payments is way out of whack, and the Gross National Product is down to zero."

"Are you sure you have enough clay?" I asked him.

There were tears in his eyes. "I created a masterpiece. Everything in the model was supposed to work. They were going to put it up in Rockefeller Center in place of the Christmas tree."

I tried to console him. "Alfred, you're being too hard on yourself. Economists aren't scientists—they're dreamers. And they translate their dreams into beautiful works of art such as your original model. President Reagan may not know much about art, but he knows what he likes. And he wouldn't have bought the other model if he didn't like it."

"Yeah, but what is he going to think of this one?"

"Well, to be honest, it may not be to his taste. But he paid for it, so he's going to have to live with it."

What Consultants Do?

Before Richard Allen became national security adviser, he was part-owner of a consulting firm, with a former adviser and speechwriter to President Reagan named Peter Hannaford. The firm was called Potomac International.

There is nothing wrong with this because Washington is full of consulting firms made up of both Republicans and Democrats. We in this city take them for granted. So I was thrown for a moment, when I was in Worcester. Massachusetts, and a lady in the audience asked, "What does a Washington consultant do?"

I promised her that as soon as I got back to Washington, I would find out and give her the answer.

I went to see a consultant I knew and said, "Charley, I know this is a stupid question, but what do you do?"

"I don't have to tell you," he said defensively.

"I'm not trying to get you in trouble," I said. "But a lady in Worcester asked me the question and I couldn't give her an answer. The Richard Allen business apparently has made people curious."

"Well, the best way to explain it is like this: Suppose you're having a problem with the government. You come to me."

"And you solve the problem?"

"No. I send you to the someone in the government who *can* solve the problem."

"Why can't I go and see the person myself?"

"Because you don't know who to see, and even if you did he wouldn't see you unless I asked him to. Consultants are like marriage brokers. We get a fee for bringing two people together. The bigger the problem the higher up you have to go in government to resolve it, and the larger the fee we have to charge you."

"That makes sense," I admitted. "How do you have access to the people who can solve my problems?"

"Through political connections. When the Democrats were in power, the Georgia crowd were the most sought-after consultants. Now that the Republicans are in charge, people are looking for a California connection."

"Will you plead a person's case for him, if the official doesn't feel he can do it?"

"Of course. But it will cost you more, because that means we have to leave the office and take a government official to lunch or dinner."

"It doesn't sound like hard work."

"That depends on how dedicated a consultant you are. Our business doesn't just depend on access to government and congressional figures. Many times we have to pretend we have access to them, even if we don't."

"How does that work?"

"Well, suppose you have a client from some South

American country and you want to impress him with the fact that you have clout in Washington. You take him to a restaurant where the White House crowd hangs out and you wave at them even if you don't know them.

"Let's say Ed Meese and Mike Deaver are at another table. You excuse yourself and go over to them and mutter something like 'You were great on *Meet the Press* last Sunday.' Meese and Deaver don't know who the hell you are, but since they meet so many people they pretend they do. You walk back to your table and say to your client, 'Those guys really drive you up the wall. Meese is mad at me because I didn't return his last telephone call.' I did that once with Ham Jordan during the Carter administration, and got Argentina on a fifty-thousand-dollar retainer for a year."

"That takes guts."

"You only resort to that kind of stuff when your people are out of office. If they're in, you don't have to fake it."

"Are you in or out right now?"

"I'm in like Flynn. Didn't you notice the picture on my desk?"

"Is that you eating raw fish in a Japanese sushi bar with Richard Allen?"

"One autographed photo in Washington is worth a thousand proposals. When the president of the Banzai Sewing Machine Company saw that picture, he signed up my firm for four years."

"I guess a consultant is the greatest thing you can be in Washington. It just about covers everything, and if you know the right people, you can make a lot of money."

"We don't do it for the money," Charlie said. "All we want to do is make people happy."

Fear of Tipping

Andy Rooney started it on CBS's *60 Minutes* by discussing one of America's greatest phobias, "Fear of Tipping." Rooney came out against tipping but he admitted he didn't have the nerve to lead an antitipping movement.

Coleman McCarthy, the columnist for *The Washington Post*, then wrote that Rooney didn't have to lead the antitipping movement in the United States because it already had leaders, including McCarthy, who not only "stiffs" waiters and cab drivers, but golf caddies as well.

I am happy to join in the discussion because in an earlier life, I worked as a bellboy. While Rooney and McCarthy can cry about the indignities heaped on the tippers, I can talk about the joys of being a "tippee."

First of all, for every defiant McCarthy willing to ignore the practice of tipping, there are ten Rooneys quaking in their boots because no matter what they've given as a gratuity, they're never sure if it was enough.

In my day, those of us who always had our hands out could spot a deadbeat like McCarthy before he even got out of the taxi. He was easy to identify because you could hear the cab driver cursing him as he drove away. Another clue was that a McCarthy type always tried to carry his own bag into the lobby, and after checking in, attempted to lug it by himself up to the room.

In the well-run bellhop corps to which I belonged, each man took his turn checking people in and out. The last man on the list was stuck with emptying the ashtrays in the lobby and attending to the needs of a McCarthy. You did these menial tasks because sooner or later you knew you would get an Andy Rooney.

When an Andy Rooney appeared at our resort hotel, and I was the lucky bellhop, I would rush out and say, "Good day, sir." Intimidated, he would immediately hand me a quarter. I would carry his bags and escort him smartly to the desk. After registering him, the desk clerk would ring a chime and give me a key, and I would say, "Please follow me, and don't worry, I have change for a ten-dollar bill."

An old bell captain, from whom I had learned the profession, told me, "When checking in a couple, there are two kinds you will be dealing with. The first will be married. Don't waste too much time on them, because the size of the tip has already been established in the husband's mind. But every once in a while you will luck out and get an unmarried couple. At this moment, money is no object for them to get into the room and to get you out. Stall for time, checking the windows, the closets, and the water in the bathroom. The longer you remain, the more nervous the man will become and finally in desperation, he'll shove a fistful of money in your hand if you just agree to leave."

"How will I know if the couple is married or not?"

"A married man usually flops on the bed first, and his wife always checks the closet to see if there are enough hangers."

"And an unmarried couple?"

"The unmarried woman usually starts combing her hair in front of the mirror, and the unmarried man always makes sure the bolt on the door is working."

My tutor gave me another piece of advice. "If the couple is unmarried, wait twenty minutes, and then bring them a bucket of ice. You'll earn the fastest five bucks you ever made in your life."

No need to go into other secrets of the trade, but suffice it to say that the Andy Rooneys of this world don't have a prayer against people who are used to being tipped for serving the public.

The next time you watch *60 Minutes* on television, take a close look at Andy Rooney, and you'll know why no one in the hotel, restaurant, or taxi business is afraid of him. All you have to do as a waiter is pour soup on him, and he'll shove a ten-spot in the palm of your hand.

Newspaper Sources

The White House is clamping down hard on any government employee who speaks to a member of the press. Originally they were concerned with "National Security" leaks from the State Department, Defense, the CIA, and the National Security Agency. But the rules are now being adopted by other departments, most of which have no state secrets.

On the surface, the Reagan administration cannot be faulted for wanting everyone in the government to speak with one voice (it seems to work very well in the Soviet Union).

But I believe there are inherent dangers in making it very difficult, if not impossible, for government officials to discuss anything of importance with the media.

What most people don't realize is that when a government official has lunch or a discreet meeting with a reporter, many times the official is trying to get more information out of the newspaperman than the newspaperman is trying to get out of the official.

For example, let us assume a Defense Department big shot is having lunch with a reporter from the *Daily Planet*.

The Defense Department man opens up the conversation.

"What have you heard?"

"The Navy is going to ask for two more nuclear carriers."

"Damn, where did you hear it?"

"A reliable source in naval plans."

"We haven't heard anything on that on our floor. How are they going to try and get them?"

"By going over your head direct to Congress. They figure if they ask for two, they'll get one."

"I better let the secretary know about it so he doesn't appear to be surprised. What else is going on in the Pentagon?"

"The Army is having more trouble with the M-one tank than they're admitting. But they're covering up because they are afraid you'll order them to stop building the tanks until the bugs are worked out."

"Is this straight?"

"I got it from the guy at *The Washington Post* who knows someone in the weapons testing department."

"This is good stuff," the Defense Department official says. "I'll get on it right away. You heard anything I should know about the MX missile?"

"*The Wall Street Journal* man says if you harden the present missile sites with more cement, the silos might not be able to handle the weight."

"How reliable is *The Wall Street Journal* on this?"

"The reporter's been working on the story for three months. I think he knows what he's talking about."

"How much time do we have before the story breaks?"

"Maybe two or three weeks."

"Our contractors haven't told us this."

"Why should they? They are hoping to sell you a lot of cement."

"Do you think I should tell the secretary of defense about it?"

"Yeah, but don't tell him where you got it. I don't want

The Wall Street Journal to give me a lie detector test to find out the source of the leak."

"Do you have anything on what Al Haig is up to these days?"

"Off the record? He's trying to get the autonomy talks between Israel and Egypt on the tracks. In order to do it, he may have to put the Golan Heights on the back burner."

"He hasn't mentioned his plan to Weinberger."

"He's going straight to the President with it, so Defense doesn't foul him up."

"You're really cooking today. Can I use it?"

"*The New York Times* man gave it to a White House aide, so I don't imagine it's classified."

"I appreciate this briefing and so does the secretary."

"Don't mention it. I believe that in a free society the people who work in government have a right to know what is going on in their own departments."

.

The Man's Story

I watched *Washington Mistress* on television recently. It added to the legend that sex, power, and politics are all we think about in the nation's capital.

In the show, the heroine is done wrong by an ambitious heel, a lobbyist who has political ambitions, but time to hop in bed with his "mistress" throughout the two hours, whenever he isn't having dinner with the vice-president of the United States or partying with the "right" people so he can become a Cabinet officer.

While everyone seems to dramatize the plight of the

bright young girl who comes to Washington, and is then victimized by some rat fink who just uses her as a doormat to power, no one ever talks to the young men who are seduced by the ambitious women here, intent on climbing up the ladder of success.

I interviewed one such man, who came to Washington starry-eyed only to discover that if he didn't play the game of sexual politics, he would remain a passport clerk for the rest of his life.

Here is Arnie's story:

"I was a kid from Warren, Pennsylvania, and all my life I dreamed of working for the government. After finishing college and earning a master's degree in international relations, I got a job in the passport division.

"One day a congresswoman came in for a new passport. Our eyes met as she handed me her two photographs and I could feel goose bumps go up and down my arms. As I pasted one of the photographs in her passport she said to me, 'How would you like to have dinner tonight?'

"I knew it was wrong, but there was something about her that made me say 'yes.' Besides, I was lonely in Washington and I saw no harm in just having dinner.

"That evening, as I was dressing, I told my roommates who was taking me out and they were flabbergasted.

"'Don't you know she's married?' my best friend Charlie said. 'You're asking for big trouble.'

"'Don't worry, it's just a dinner date, and I'm sick and tired of sitting home watching television every night. I can handle it. I wasn't born in Warren, Pennsylvania, for nothing.'"

Arnie, his hands fidgeting, continued his story.

"We had dinner at a fancy restaurant. 'Z' knew exactly what wines to order and I couldn't believe all the famous people she said hello to in the restaurant.

"After dinner she took me for a walk to the Lincoln Memorial. The moon was shining and there was a slight breeze blowing off the Mall. I stood with my head against a pillar and suddenly she took me in her arms and said,

'I want to make love to you.' I didn't know what to do. At first I tried to push her away, but suddenly I melted into her arms. I didn't care any more what happened. I was in love.

"What started out as an innocent one-night fling turned into an obsession. At work I could think of nothing else but 'Z.' I kept making mistakes such as stamping in people's passports 'Not good for travel in Switzerland,' or 'This passport is only valid in Albania.' My supervisor called me in and said, 'Arnie, I know what's going on. It's all over town you're having an affair with Congresswoman "Z." Believe me, she'll break your heart.'

"'How can you say that?' I cried. 'She promised she was going to divorce her husband and marry me.'

"'She'll never leave her husband. She is a very ambitious woman and wants to be chairman of the House Subcommittee on Student Loans. Her husband's family has the connections to get her the job. Do you think she'd give all that up to marry a passport clerk?'

"A few months later when we were in bed at the Twin-Marriott Motel, 'Z' told me, 'I'm going to have your baby.'

"I hugged her. 'Great, now we can get married.'

"'We can't right now. No one would ever accept a divorced woman as chairman of the House Subcommittee on Student Loans.'"

Arnie concluded, tears running down his cheeks, "I knew it was all over then. She would never marry me, because in Washington power is the name of the game, and except for issuing her a new passport without waiting in line, there was nothing I could do to further her congressional ambitions. It's no fun being a man in Washington—but then again, it's no fun being a man anywhere."

No Business Like CIA Business

One of the things the CIA does is run secret businesses known as proprietaries, to provide covers for agents to "wash" money for covert operations and for other clandestine operations.

Up until recently, these businesses have been very successful but lately many of them have been losing money. So "the Company" decided to call everyone back to Langley, Virginia, to see what was going wrong.

The director of covert business operations was in a foul temper.

He addressed the CIA agents who were charged with running the business covers.

"This is the worst year we've ever had," he said. "Our gross sales are down by twenty percent, and the CIA can no longer eat your losses. Now what the hell is going on?"

The agent, whose cover was president of the "Deutschland Music Box Company," said, "It's the fault of the Hong Kong station. They stole our designs and they're flooding the United States market with cheap imitations. I make the best music boxes in the world, but I can't compete on price."

"Isn't that tough?" the agent from Hong Kong, whose cover was chairman of the "Kowloon Toy Company," said. "If you can't compete, then get out of the music box business. I'm not making a dime on my boxes ever since the 'Taiwan CIA Company' started to undercut us."

The director said, "Why does everyone have to make

music boxes? Can't you come up with a new product like the Barbie doll?"

The agent running the "South Korean Novelty Company" said, "We put out a Nancy and Ronnie doll for Christmas and it laid an egg."

The director looked over his computer printouts. "What happened to you, Danfield? It says your 'New Delhi Exporting Company' dropped two million dollars in the last quarter."

"That wasn't my fault. I sent one million madras welcome mats through Donnegger's shipping company in Bombay, and his stupid people unloaded them in Pakistan. Anyone here ever try to sell a 'Made in India' welcome mat in Pakistan?"

Donnegger said, "Your company got the invoices all screwed up. You had the yak butter going to the United States and the welcome mats going to Pakistan. We're not mind readers."

"Oh, shut up," the director said. "Let's get to you, Brinkley. How do you explain the fact that you still have two hundred thousand Lapland ski boots in your warehouse in Helsinki?"

"I had an order from Harrod's in London for the whole lot, when the KGB's 'Finlandia Sporting Goods Company' got wind of it and made Harrod's an offer they couldn't refuse. I've asked covert operations to burn down the Finlandia factory three times, but they keep ignoring my request. How can I run a clandestine business if our people won't get tough with the competition?"

The director said, "I'll talk to the arson people later. Now we get to Biberman. I have a report that you used CIA covert funds to cover up your losses from the 'Mediterranean Fruit Fly Company.'"

"I'm suing Jerry Brown and the State of California. As soon as I win the case, I'll replace the money. I can prove every fruit fly we sent them was sterile."

The director said, "Biberman, you wouldn't know a sterile fruit fly from a gypsy moth. I see from this printout the only one who made a profit this year for 'the Company' was Tablestone. Let him tell the rest of you dunderheads how he did it."

"He isn't here, sir. He resigned last month and went into business for himself."

"What kind of business?"

"Selling submachine guns, bombs, and poison gas canisters to the Libyans. He said that as far as business was concerned, the CIA didn't offer him a future, and he'd rather strike out on his own."

"Where is he getting all his stuff?"

"The same people we get it from, sir."

"Do you mean to say he is telling people he is still working for the CIA?"

"No, just the opposite. He keeps telling them he isn't. But the more he insists he has nothing to do with us, the more our suppliers believe he does."

The director said, "You have to hand it to Tablestone. He always had a talent for making a buck. I wish I had a hundred more like him."

We Got Shortchanged

Did you know as an American citizen you own some of the most valuable oil and gas properties in the United States? They are located on public lands and are held in trust for you by the Department of the Interior.

Did you also know that the oil companies you leased the lands to shafted you out of an estimated $650 million in oil royalties for 1981, and probably billions of dollars in previous years by underreporting how much of your oil they took out of the ground?

Were you also aware that anywhere from two to six percent of all your gas and oil was just stolen from the oil fields and tank farms, and no one has done a thing about it?

I didn't know about it until I read a recent report by a Reagan commission which investigated fraud and mismanagement of the country's oil and gas reserves.

"What happened to my royalties?" you may be asking.

No one rightly knows, and if he or she does they're not making a big deal of it.

This apparently is how the system worked. Every once in a while when someone at the Interior Department had nothing better to do, they would call up one of the oil companies, which had a lease on public land, and say, "What's up?"

The oil company executive would say angrily, "What are you doing, checking up on us?"

"Of course not. I was just curious how much oil and gas you were taking out of the ground."

"We're lucky to get three cups a day," the oil company executive would reply. "It's really tough drilling on public land. You never know when you are going to hit a rock."

"The secretary was wondering if you could give him any idea how much royalties we can expect from your operation this year?"

"You mean to tell me with all the government has to do, you're bugging me for a few lousy royalty bucks? We'll tell you at the end of the year. The way things are you could owe us money."

"Don't you have any idea how much oil and gas you hope to take out of the ground?"

"Look, when we signed your lease, you put us on the 'honor system' and made each of us responsible for our own reporting. When we know how much oil and gas we took out, we'll tell you."

"Don't get mad. We're not questioning your figures.

But Congress says we're supposed to keep tabs on you people, and any figure you could give us is acceptable."

"I should hope so. The honor system is as sacred to the oil industry as it is to West Point."

"Just for my own information, how do you know how much oil and gas you take out of a well?"

"It's a very complicated procedure. We have a guy who sits on a stool next to the well and he counts how much oil or gas comes out, with a pocket calculator. Then he turns those figures over to the foreman who subtracts any oil that spilled onto the ground. The foreman sends these figures to the home office for verification."

"And what happens to them then?"

"The home office decides how much we should report to the government."

"That seems a fair way to do it. Are we allowed to audit your figures?"

"Sure you are, but that would mean you didn't trust us, and then the whole honor system would break down. Is that what you people want?"

"Of course not. We wouldn't be doing business with you guys if we didn't think you were honest."

"You got any other questions you want to ask?"

"No, you've satisfied me. Is there anything I can do for you?"

"Yeah, you could. Get the American Indians off our backs. They think they're not getting their fair share of royalties, and they want to do away with the honor system."

"That's unforgivable. I'll talk to the head of the Bureau of Indian Affairs right away."

Buy American

"There is only one way this country is going to get on its feet," said Baleful.

"How's that?" I asked, as we drank coffee in his office at the Baleful Refrigerator Company.

"The consumer has to start buying American," he said, slamming his fist down on the desk. "Every time an American buys a foreign refrigerator it costs one of my people his job. And every time one of my people is out of work it means he or she can't buy refrigerators."

"It's a vicious circle," I said.

Baleful's secretary came in, "Mr. Thompson, the steel broker, is on the phone."

My friend grabbed the receiver, "Thompson, where the hell is that steel shipment from Japan that was supposed to be in last weekend?...I don't care about bad weather. We're almost out of steel and I'll have to close down the assembly line next week. If you can't deliver when you promise, I'll find myself another broker."

"You get your steel from Japan?" I asked Baleful.

"Even with shipping costs, their price is still lower than steel made in Europe. We used to get all our sheets from Belgium, but the Japanese are now giving them a run for their money."

The buzzer on the phone alerted Baleful. He listened for a few moments and then said, "Excuse me, I have a call from Taiwan...Buster, how are you coming with those door-handles for the Mark Four? Look, R and D have designed a new push-button door handle and we're going to send the specs to you. Tell Mr. Chow if his people send us a sample of one and he can make it for us at the same price as the old handle, we'll give his company the order."

A man came in with a plastic container and said, "Mr. Baleful, you said you wanted to see one of these before we ordered them. They are the containers for the ice maker in the refrigerator."

Baleful inspected it carefully and banged it on the floor a couple of times. "What's the price on it?"

"Hong Kong can deliver at two dollars a tray and Don-Fu Plastics in South Korea said they can make it for one-seventy."

"It's just a plastic tray. Take the South Korean bid. We'll let Hong Kong supply us with the shelves for the freezer. Any word on the motors?"

"There's a German company in Brazil that just came out with a new motor and it's passed all our tests, so Johnson has ordered fifty thousand."

"Call Cleveland Motors and tell them we're sorry but the price they quoted us was just too high."

"Yes, sir," the man said and departed.

The secretary came in again and said, "Harry telephoned and wanted to let you know the defrosters just arrived from Finland. They're unloading the box cars now."

"Good. Any word on the wooden crates from Singapore?"

"They're at the dock in Hoboken."

"Thank heaven. Cancel our order from Boise Cascade."

"What excuse should I give them?"

"Tell them we made a mistake in our inventory or we're switching to fiberglass. I don't care what you tell them."

Baleful turned to me. "Where were we?"

"You were saying that if the consumer doesn't start buying American this country is going to be in a lot of trouble."

"Right. It's not only his patriotic duty, but his liveli-hood that's at stake. I'm going to Washington next week to tell the Senate Commerce Committee that if they don't get off the stick, there isn't going to be a domestic re-frigerator left in this country. We're not going to stay in business for our health."

"Pour it on them," I urged him.

Baleful said, "Come out with me through the show-room."

I followed him. He went to his latest model, and opened the door. "This is an American refrigerator made by the American worker, for the American consumer. What do you have to say to that?"

"It's beautiful," I said. "It puts the foreign imports to shame."

Tanks a Billion

As one who believes that the United States must have a strong defense at any cost, I decided to go out and buy a tank the other day. After listening to the testimony of the Pentagon experts and the secretary of defense, I decided the Chrysler M-1 tank was the best that money could buy. Besides, Lee Iacocca needs the business.

I went into the Chrysler tank showroom and a smiling businessman greeted me at the door.

"I'd like to buy an M-one tank," I said. "I understand it is superior to any armored vehicle in the world."

"We like to think so," the salesman said. He showed me the model on the floor. "It has the most sophisticated electronics equipment that man could devise. Why don't you jump in the turret and see for yourself?"

I inspected the interior. "How much is it?"

"It will cost you two million-five."

"I thought, when you announced you were going to build the M-one, it would be priced at five hundred thousand dollars."

"You must be joking, sir. You can't even get a Jeep for that price anymore."

"Well, I guess I better order one before the price goes up again," I said.

The salesman took me over to his desk and pulled a contract out of his drawer.

"I have to ask you a few questions. You are an American taxpayer, aren't you?"

"Yes."

"Good, that means we don't have to check your credit. Now you want one M-one tank. What color?"

"I think I'd like it green."

"Green. A very good choice. What options do you want on it?"

"What do you mean?"

"The tank costs two million-five, stripped. If you want it to perform right, I would strongly suggest the options."

"What kind of options?"

"Well, because it's so sophisticated it cannot do what other tanks in the past have done, such as dig itself in when it is prepared to fire its guns. You need a companion vehicle called an ACE which is a high-speed bulldozer to travel next to you."

"How much is the bulldozer?"

The salesman looked at the chart. "One million, one hundred thousand dollars."

"Do I really need it?"

"The M-one tank is no good without it. Now government regulations require me to tell you that the M-one is a gas guzzler and you'll also have to have a fuel truck behind you. We can supply you with one for six hundred and sixty thousand dollars."

"That was a little more than I wanted to spend. By the way, how far can I drive the M-one tank before it needs repairs?"

"About forty-three miles before it breaks down. I strongly recommend a service contract, which only costs three hundred thousand dollars a year. In the event the tank gets dirt on it and won't move, we'll send a team of Chrysler experts out within forty-eight hours."

"As a taxpayer, I was hoping you people could come up with a less expensive model."

"When it comes to combat effectiveness, you can't cut corners. This is the top of the line when it comes to tanks, and it's only for people who can afford it."

"Who can afford it?"

"The United States Army wants seven thousand of them. And the nice thing about the military is, they never haggle over price."

The Black Republican

The hardest thing for the Reagan administration to find is a "qualified" black person to appoint to an important position in the government. By "qualified," we mean somebody who is against busing, job-training programs, welfare, food stamps, government-subsidized housing, and equal-opportunity litigation.

But when the administration finds a black who's willing to buy the whole conservative package, he's welcomed into the government with open arms.

I don't want to brag, but I know one, and if all goes well he could become a rising star in the Republican party.

His name is Thomas Jefferson III, and I ran into him in Brooks Brothers where he was being fitted for a suit.

"How goes the civil rights battle?" I asked.

"I'm not into civil rights any more," Thomas told me. "Here's my new business." He handed me a card.

It read, "Thomas Jefferson III, Chairman, Black Citizens for the B-1 Bomber."

"That's a heavy title," I said. "What do you do?"

"Anything they ask me to."

"Who do you mean by they?"

"The Republican party."

"I thought you were a Democrat."

"I used to be until I decided there was no future in it. There are too many blacks in the Democratic party, and there's no opportunity there. But if you're a black Republican you can write your own ticket. There are so few of us that when they find one, they can't do enough for us."

"Such as?"

"Well, I'm particularly in demand for Republican fund-raisers. Not only don't I have to pay a thousand dollars for dinner, but they always sit me on the dais. When I was a Democrat, I was lucky to get a seat near the kitchen door. You know when they introduce the head table and the master of ceremonies asks everyone to hold their applause? Well, when they introduce me the audience can't contain themselves, and they start clapping right away. I get standing ovations for just taking a bow."

"That must be a great ego trip."

"You can't imagine how many people want to take me to lunch at the Metropolitan and University clubs. I turn down nine invitations for every one I accept. All my host has to say is 'This is Thomas Jefferson III—he's black,' and you'd think I was Robert Redford. I even get to play golf at the best country clubs. When I was a Democrat I had to wait hours to tee off at a public course."

"I can see you in demand as a guest," I said. "But how do you make a living?"

"Speaking at business meetings. You can't imagine how many corporations are desperate for a black speaker to fill out their program."

"What do you tell them?"

"Same old thing the white speakers do. I attack big government, welfare cheats, social programs, and regulations that are stifling business. The only difference is that when a black person says it they like it twice as much.

"When I was a Democrat, nobody asked me to speak. They were looking for a Jesse Jackson, or an Andy Young, or a Julian Bond, and the Democrats always expected them to speak for nothing. But Republicans know if they want a black speaker they have to pay for him."

"You're on to something, Tom," I said in admiration. "You found out, as a black, where the money is."

"I'm just killing time until I get the right government appointment. They're going to have to come to me soon because they've used up every black conservative they've got."

"I wonder why more blacks don't try to get on the Republican gravy train?"

"I hope they don't. If too many blacks join the party, the novelty will wear off and the Republicans won't treat us any better than the Democrats."

Foreclosing on Poland

I have not made up my mind yet whether or not I want to declare Poland in default on its loans. I've been wrestling with the problem ever since the Polish government declared martial law.

My first thought is that if we foreclose on them, it will teach them a lesson to pay their interest and principal on time. When I get a loan from the bank and put up my car or house for collateral and can't make the payments, the bank has no hesitation about taking them away. So I have always said, "What's good enough for me is good enough for Poland."

But apparently banks think differently about Poland than they do your average borrower.

Plummet, vice-president of the "I Love New York Bank and Trust Company," explained why. Although Poland owes his bank a billion dollars, the company chiefs have no intention of declaring the loan in default.

"If we put Poland into default, we would be admitting we made a bad loan to her, and people would start questioning our banking judgment. So we have to pretend the country isn't bankrupt."

"I can see the bank's reputation is at stake," I said, "but how do you stay in the loan business if you can't collect your money?"

"You have to understand international finance. All the Western banks have made loans to countries which are in almost as bad shape as Poland. If we foreclose on Poland, we would have to foreclose on other countries that can't pay back their debts. This would cause some of the largest banks in the world to go under. As long as we pretend they are still good loans, we can all stay afloat."

"But I thought the whole purpose of declaring Poland in default was to send a message to the present Polish government that we disapproved of their methods of squashing Solidarity."

"Banks are not concerned with political messages. We have to think of our money first. If we foreclose on Poland we have no hope of seeing any of it again. But if we can carry them, there is always the chance they may get back on their feet and start paying back their interest. As long as they're paying their interest, we can pretend they are good credit risks, and then no one can criticize us for making a bad loan."

"But in your heart you must know that's a pipe dream."

"International bankers live on pipe dreams. Let's assume we declared Poland in default. That would leave her no choice but to turn to the Soviet Union for financial help. The Western banks would be cut off from ever loaning Poland money again. Other countries would say we were heartless and money-grubbing institutions, and if we treated Poland like that, we would probably treat them the same way. Our reputation as benevolent money-lenders would be destroyed."

"So, what you're saying is that you would rather make a bad loan than no loan at all?"

"No bank likes to make a bad loan. But worse than making one is to admit you have. As long as we keep it on the books as a good loan, no one is going to question why we made it in the first place. But the moment you put the borrower into default, all hell breaks loose, and the people in the bank responsible for making the loan could lose their jobs."

"You don't feel that way about some poor sap who can't pay back his business loan, do you?"

"We would if he owed us a billion dollars. But if he

borrows fifty thousand dollars and doesn't pay us on time, we're not going to let him get away with it. When it comes to piddling sums we have to be tough or nobody would pay us back."

"Then as I see it, Poland has the Western banks over a barrel. They can't pay you, and you can't put them in default."

"That's the long and the short of it," Plummet said. "But for appearances' sake we still consider them one of our blue-chip clients."

Part Four

OUR TOWN

(With Apologies to Thornton Wilder)

OUR TOWN (WITH APOLOGIES TO THORNTON WILDER)

Our Town

(With Apologies to Thornton Wilder)

NEWS ITEM—The town of Kennesaw, Georgia, has just passed an ordinance requiring the head of every household to own a gun and ammunition. The law was prompted by a recent ordinance passed in Morton Grove, Illinois, banning the possession of handguns by all residents, except police officers and military personnel.

Stage Manager: "The name of the town is Kennesaw, Georgia. It's a nice town, y'know what I mean? Nobody remarkable ever came out of it s'far as we know. We're just plain simple folk here, we can't claim to be nothing more than just another town along Route Forty-one.

"I better show you around a bit. That large yellow house with the funeral wreath in front of it belongs to the Kettermans. Two days ago Hodding Ketterman shot his son, Junior, who was trying to sneak in the window at three o'clock in the morning and Hodding thought he was a thief. The town feels terrible about it, but everyone says Junior should have known better.

"There's one of our leading citizens, Jeffrey Bean, on his way down to the Sears Roebuck parking lot to have a shootout with Abel Grimstead. It seems Jeffrey's dog knocked over all of Abel's garbage, and this made Abel real mad and he took his Smith and Wesson and pumped the dog full of lead. Most folks in town think Abel overreacted, but Abel says that's what guns are for, and there's nothing on the books says you can't shoot a dog on your property.

"Here comes Doc Lafferty. He looks a little peaked. He's been at the hospital all night removing a bullet from Hart Doubleday, who was practicing drawing his gun in front of the mirror and shot himself in the leg.

"Over there is the courthouse. There's lots of excitement there because Betty Bentley is on trial for emptying her .45 into Lorelei Lee, who she suspected was playing around with her husband, Charles. Betty says it was an accident, and the gun went off while she was showing Lorelei how she won a silver cup at the Kennesaw Handgun church picnic last month.

"Here comes Hiram Dollop, who's become the village idiot because he refused to have a pistol in his house on religious grounds. Everyone thinks he's crazy, but he's harmless and except for the kids throwing mud at him because he doesn't own a gun, we leave him alone.

"Don't get nervous about those shots you just heard. That's eighty-year-old Sam Francis. Every time the postman forgets to bring Sam his Social Security check, Sam starts shooting at the mail truck.

"Well, it's getting on to bedtime. The Putnams are having a party to celebrate the opening of a new pistol range they built in their basement. Outside of that, most of the people in our town are tucked into bed, their guns under their pillows, sleeping sweet dreams after another eventful day. Good night all."

Eight Out of Ten Doctors

The good news for hypochondriacs these days is that the Food and Drug Administration has now given permission to companies to advertise prescription drugs directly to the public.

There is no law on the books preventing pharmaceutical people from advertising prescription-type drugs to patients, but they refrained from doing it in the past, figuring the doctor might be a better judge of what a patient needed.

But business is business, and the companies now feel if a patient is educated in the efficacy of a certain prescription drug, sales will soar, and it will give the doctors less work to do.

I have not made up the above item. It is a fact, and according to *The New York Times* it has been encouraged by Dr. Arthur Hull Hayes, Jr., the commissioner of food and drugs.

The only ones who are not thrilled by the pharmaceutical companies' drumbeating their prescription drugs are doctors. The fear is that most people bombarded by commercials may believe the actors on TV, rather than their physicians.

There is no reason *not* to believe that this scene may soon be playing in your local doctor's office:

The M.D., after examining the patient: "You appear to have a chest infection. I'm going to give you a prescription. Take four a day, six hours apart."

"What are you giving me?"

"Dundemycin. I've had very good results with it for chest infections."

"But eight out of ten doctors are prescribing Carraflex for people with chest problems."

"Where did you hear that?"

"Orson Welles said it on television during a commercial last night. I think it was Orson Welles—but it could have been Robert Young or Ricardo Montalban."

"With all due respect to those fine actors, I don't believe they know much about chest infections."

"Maybe so, but whoever it was held up a test tube of bronchial bacteria and then showed how Carraflex killed them twice as fast as Dundemycin."

"The reason I don't prescribe Carraflex is that it tends to have side effects such as nausea and palpitations of the heart, and can even cause severe kidney damage."

"They didn't say anything about that in the commercial."

"They wouldn't. If they had to read all the side effects of Carraflex, they couldn't afford the TV time. Please take Dundemycin. I'm sure it will clear it up."

"I don't know, Doc. I respect you, but Orson Welles knows a lot about medicine. And Robert Young has played a doctor on TV for years. And as far as Ricardo Montalban goes, I'm not one of those people who think a guy is a lousy M.D. just because he speaks with an accent. Besides, Carraflex sponsors the LA Dodgers baseball team and I want to show my gratitude."

"You're going to have to get another doctor if you want a different prescription."

"That's what they said in the TV commercial. 'If your M.D. is not clued in on the miraculous medical benefits of Carraflex, find yourself a doctor who is!' Then they gave a toll-free number for people to call to find the name of the doctor nearest them who is willing to prescribe Carraflex. No hard feelings, Doc?"

"Of course not. Miss Denna, send in the next patient. Mr. Rubin, what seems to be wrong?"

"You gave me a sleeping pill prescription for Lahdee-dah."

"I remember. You said it was satisfactory."

"Yes, but that's before I heard about Blissnatabs. Apparently they're the only pills on the market that make you dream of Brooke Shields."

"Who told you that?"

"Brooke Shields. She did a commercial on it last night."

"Frankly, with your blood pressure I don't think you're up to dreaming about Brooke Shields. Besides, Blissnatabs are twice as expensive as Lahdeedah, because of this particular advertising campaign."

"You doctors are all alike. You resent your patients' knowing as much about medicine as you do."

Ask Not

President Reagan is asking the private sector to pick up the slack in all the government social programs he's axed. He wants companies to fill the void by supporting charities, universities, medical research, and the arts.

He couldn't have asked business to step in at a worse time.

I went to see the president of the Sludge Automobile Company to make a personal appeal for my alma mater.

His showroom was jammed with people, from directors of day-care centers to society women ready to plead for their symphony orchestras.

After a four-hour wait, I finally got in to see him.

"Hi, Jake," I said.

"The answer is no," he said.

"I haven't even made my pitch," I protested. "My school is having a ten-million-dollar drive to make up for federal scholarship funds we've lost, and President Reagan and I thought—"

"Don't mention that man's name to me. If he thinks he can throw his social problems in my lap, he's crazier than his budget."

"Jake, I thought you were a big Reagan man."

"You saw my showroom. Everyone is out there wanting a handout. My phone hasn't stopped ringing since Reagan said business has to take up the burden caused by his budget cuts. Hasn't he heard of the recession? Our profits are down by eighty percent. We may have to close several dealerships in the first quarter. And you want me to give money to your alma mater?"

"But, Jake, we can't get it from the government, so we have to appeal to the private sector. What better place to start than the auto companies?"

Jake cried, "I haven't sold a car in a month. You want blood? Go to the Red Cross."

"But if the business community doesn't take over the areas where the government can't help anymore, where can we go for money?"

"The same place I'm going—to the bankruptcy court. Look, I run a business. When things are good, I give. When things are bad, I can't give. The reason the government can't give anymore is things are lousy. If it was good for them, they wouldn't tell you to come to me. What makes them think things are good for the private sector, if it's lousy for them?"

"Corporate America can't ignore its social responsibilities, just because you're not making any money," I said. "If Reaganomics ever has a prayer of working, you people have to suffer pain. What is more painful than giving money to programs that the government can no longer afford?"

"Trying to make your payroll for one," Jake said. "Going out of business for another."

"I guess Reagan has more faith in private enterprise than you do. He would have never cut out the funds to my alma mater if he didn't believe you were ready to take up the torch."

"Well he can have the torch back. I'm not the keeper of the flame. Why don't you go to the oil companies?"

"I did, but now that there is an oil glut, they have no guilt money to hand out anymore."

Jake was almost in tears. "My wife's on the board of a hospital, my daughter works for a senior citizens' lunch program, the only guy who bought a car from me this year made me buy a table for the Kidney Foundation dinner. How the hell can I give to you when I've already been wiped out by giving to them?"

"I can only give you one answer, Jake."

"What's that?"

"Your President wants you to."

And Now, Here's Juanie

"Good evening, ladies and gentlemen, welcome to the hit television show, *Guerrilla of the Week*, brought to you direct from the State Department, by a grant from the Central Intelligence Agency. Ed, will you bring out our latest guerrilla."

"Dean, this is Hernandez Juan Pico, a Cuban-trained Nicaraguan, who was captured in the jungles of El Salvador after making a parachute drop from Ethiopia into Honduras, carrying a Soviet-made bazooka."

"It's good to have you on the show, Juan. They say

you're a real tough Marxist hombre. Tell us, Juan, how long have you been a Commie guerrilla?"

"I am not a guerrilla. I am a raisin picker from Juarez, Mexico."

"Ha, ha, that's a good one, Juan. It says right here that you are the leader of the First of May Che Guevara Brigade, and fought in Angola with the Fifth of October Fidel Castro Ski Troops."

"That's not me. I am a raisin picker. See, I filled out all the papers."

"Then what are you doing on this show?"

"I don't know, Señor. I came to the State Department to apply for a green card, so I could pick raisins, and the lady sent me in here. I promise, sir, I will go home as soon as the raisin season is over."

"Are you trying to tell me that you were not trained by the Cubans in Ethiopia with Soviet weapons to overthrow the legal government in El Salvador?"

"Si, Señor. I have never been out of Juarez. But I have a cousin who lives in Fresno, and he will guarantee me a job if you would just give me a green card."

"All right, let's knock off the play-acting, Juan. Just tell us how you hate the gringoes in America and what the KGB told you about the United States."

"I love the United States, Señor, from sea to shining sea. This land was made for you and me. I am a Yankee doodle dandy, a Yankee doodle do or die. Please, sir, can I have a green card and catch a bus for Fresno?"

"Juan, we don't give out green cards on Guerrilla of the Week."

"That's too bad. This is the fourth office they've sent me to. Maybe you know someone who will let me pick raisins in Fresno. I will light a candle for the secretary of state every day."

"There seems to be a mix-up somewhere, ladies and gentlemen. Don't turn your dial...Ed, where the hell is the real Pico?"

"I just checked with the CIA, Dean. Someone issued him a green card while he was waiting in the Blue Room, and the last anyone saw of him, he had a job driving a taxi at National Airport."

Chatting with Eastern

Because of the stiff air competition these days, Eastern Airlines has asked its flight attendants to initiate conversations with passengers before and after they get on the plane. Frank Borman has requested that flight crews start conversations with at least two passengers in the terminal and three in the air, as a way of showing that Eastern is friendlier in the skies than United. According to Rudy Maxa of *The Washington Post*, Eastern inspectors are spot-checking their employees to make sure the directive is being carried out.

I thought it was just a publicity gimmick until I took an Eastern flight to Florida not long ago. I was sitting in the terminal, reading a book, when a comely stewardess came up to me and said, "Hi, I'm Nancy. You going to Miami?"

I looked up in surprise. "Yes, and my name's Art."

"Business or pleasure?" she asked.

"Sort of business. Would you like to have dinner with me?"

"Sorry, I'm happily married," she retorted.

This got me sore and I said, "Then why did you start talking to me?"

"I'm supposed to talk to two people in the terminal

before we take off, and three people in the air, or I'll lose my job."

"You stewardesses are all alike," I complained bitterly. "You string a guy along so he'll fly Eastern Airlines, and then when push comes to shove, you tell him you're happily married."

"It's not my fault," she said almost in tears. "But there could be an inspector watching me right now."

"Okay, Nancy, no hard feelings. It's just that no stewardess ever started a conversation with me in a terminal, and I guess I got overexcited."

I went back to my book until they announced we could board the plane. When I took my assigned seat, a stewardess, whose name tag said Eileen, asked me if I wanted to hang up my coat.

"You're just trying to start a conversation with me," I told her.

"No, I'm not. It doesn't count if I ask a passenger if he or she wants to hang up a coat. It doesn't even count when I ask you to fasten your seatbelt. Our orders are we have to initiate conversations that have nothing to do with our jobs. I'll come back and talk to you later."

"Nancy already talked to me in the terminal," I warned her.

"That's okay, as long as she didn't talk to you in the air," Eileen said.

I gave her my coat and went back to my book.

An hour later a stewardess wearing the name Alice stopped by my seat and said, "Would you like to chat?"

"I'd love to," I told her. "But I promised Eileen I would talk to her after she hung up my coat."

"She's already talked to three people, and I haven't talked to anyone."

"I don't know what to say," I said. "She indicated she needed me."

"She tells that to all the passengers," Alice said bitterly.

At that moment Eileen came up and said, "This one belongs to me."

Not wanting to cause any trouble I said, "Couldn't I talk to both of you, and then you'll each get credit for initiating a conversation?"

Alice said, "I don't know. I'll ask the captain." She returned in a few minutes and said, "It's all right with him as long as we don't make a habit out of it."

"Good," I told them. "Would either of you like to have dinner with me tonight?"

"I have a date," Eileen said.

"I'm going to bed," Alice said. "Are you enjoying your book?"

"Yes," I replied, "I like to read on airplanes."

That was it. Both Eileen and Alice left me. But a half hour later a steward named Jack came up and said, "I hear you're looking for someone to have dinner with tonight."

"Buzz off," I told him angrily. "I'm a happily married man."

Half a War
Is Better than None

The big debate over defense expenditure is how many wars the United States should be prepared to fight at the same time.

When you ask to spend a trillion and a half dollars over five years, there are always a few sourpusses in America who want to know where the money is going.

Every President sees it differently. President Eisenhower believed nuclear weapons were enough of a deterrent to stop the Soviets, and he was for the "big-bang-one-war" theory.

John F. Kennedy was a two-and-a-half-war man and wanted us to be prepared to fight the Russians, the Chinese, and some Third World country, all at the same time. Then, as luck would have it, the Soviets and the Chinese had a falling out, so he scaled down our military strategy to fighting only one-and-a-half wars.

Lyndon Johnson was also for one-and-a-half wars (the big one with the Russians, and the half one against the Vietnamese).

But before you could say "bang," the half-a-war turned into a whole one in Indochina, and the military started having doubts that you could fight half-a-war without escalating it into something bigger.

People who know about these things say Nixon's defense strategy after the Vietnam war ended was to also prepare us for one large war and one small war, not necessarily in the same area.

President Carter came along, and while his critics say he only was interested in fighting one big war, he did start building up the military to fight two, though there was some question as to whether we could even fight one with a volunteer Army.

Now we have President Reagan, who insists we must prepare for a "nuclear war," a "conventional war," and a "protracted war," and that's why it's going to cost us one trillion and a half big ones.

His predecessors talked in terms of the number of wars we should be able to handle at the same time, but the President and his defense secretary are thinking in other terms.

At the minimum we must have a three-ocean Navy, and prepare for "horizontal escalation," which means rather than confront the enemy at the target of his choosing, we should attack him or his client state at a place where he is weak. All this is predicated on the assumption that only non-nuclear weapons are put into play.

The Reagan strategists have also added a new deterrent which ups the defensive ante, which is that we must also prepare ourselves for a "protracted war," rather than the short one that other administrations were counting on. The reason for this, according to an article written by Richard Halloran of *The New York Times* (from which I stole most of this information), is the Reagan people don't want the enemy misled into thinking he could outlast us in a conventional war.

Although the Defense Department is certain how much money it needs to get us even with the Soviets, it has not explained where it will get the troops to fight a horizontal war, a protracted war, and possibly a nuclear war all at the same time. But I'm sure once they get the weapons they'll be able to find the people.

If you think I'm crazy discussing what defense options are open to us these days, you should talk to the people in Washington who are thinking them up for us.

Smoking and Research

Despite the overwhelming evidence that smoking can cause cancer, heart disease, and other fatal illnesses, there are still some physicians in the United States who maintain that all the facts are not in, and the medical profession is overreacting. Most of these doctors are employed by the tobacco interests, and some people are skeptical about their research.

I don't happen to be one of them. I believe that the

fact that a doctor is on the tobacco industry's payroll doesn't mean he is not as objective about smoking as someone who isn't.

Take my friend Dr. Heinrich Applebaum, who gets one hundred thousand dollars a year to defend the cigarette manufacturers' interests. He took me through his lab the other day.

There were hundreds of white rats in cages, jumping about and playing and munching on tobacco leaves.

"Have you ever seen happier rats in your life?" he asked me.

"Never," I admitted. "Do they all smoke?"

"A pack a day," he said proudly. "They don't get anything to eat unless they smoke first."

"And none of them contract cancer or heart disease?"

"They better not. If one of our rats gets sick, we throw it out of the program."

"But how do you know if smoking was not the cause of its illness if you throw it away?"

"It's a question of priorities. When you're looking for scientific answers to medical problems, you don't waste your time on sick rats."

A lab assistant came up and showed Dr. Applebaum a rat that seemed to be expiring.

"What do you think, Doctor?"

"Get it out of here. It could have yellow fever."

"It doesn't appear to have yellow fever."

"Then maybe it's typhus."

"Should I do an autopsy on it?"

"Who do you think you are, Dr. Noguchi? We're running a laboratory here, not a coroner's office."

The lab assistant disappeared.

Dr. Applebaum seemed upset. "I run into that all day long. Every time a rat comes down with something, some smart aleck tries to find out if it was caused by cigarettes. Nobody ever wants to leave well enough alone."

"Maybe they're just being thorough?" I suggested.

"Haven't you ever found a rat that died from a smoking-related disease?"

"Not since I've been working for the tobacco industry. When I took this job, they gave me carte blanche to find out all the facts, plus a bonus of twenty-five dollars for every rat I could prove died of natural causes. I also get one thousand dollars every time I go on television to attack the surgeon general's report on smoking. So I call them as I see them, because my scientific reputation is at stake."

"Then why is the entire medical establishment against you?"

"It's simple. If they blame smoking for somebody's heart attack they won't be sued for malpractice."

"Doctor, will you come over to cage Two hundred thirty? None of the rats seem to be moving," a lab assistant said.

We walked over. Dr. Applebaum said, "What have you been feeding them?"

"Milk and cheese," the assistant replied.

"Just as I suspected. Look for calcium kidney stones."

"Suppose I don't find any?"

"Then you can get yourself another job."

Tora! Tora! Tora!

Every time Secretary of Defense "Cap" Weinberger goes abroad, I get the willies. The success of every mission seems to be based on how much American military equipment he can give or sell to the country he visits, as

well as his ability to persuade the head of the state he is
drinking tea with to build up his armed forces.

I don't mind when Weinberger does a selling job on a
Third World power, but I start shaking when he puts
pressure on a country like Japan to get its military act
together.

This is what Secretary Weinberger did recently on a
trip to Tokyo. He wants the Japanese to rearm and become a military power to be reckoned with.

To those of us who served in World War II, memories
die hard when it comes to allowing a powerful Japanese
military establishment. And the way things are going eco-
nomically for them and us, we're taking a big chance
letting them return to their old ways.

For argument's sake, let's assume that the Japanese
buy the Weinberger proposal, and, with their fierce com-
petitive spirit, technological robots, and dedication to
quality control, they manage in a few years to build the
biggest and best army, navy and air force in the Far East.

At first, the Pentagon is overjoyed, as the Japanese
relieve them of the financial burden of keeping American
troops in Korea, Japan, and Okinawa.

Now a new President of the United States is elected,
and under great pressure from American manufacturers
decides to embargo all Toyota automobiles and Sony TV
sets. A summit meeting between the President of the
United States and the premier of Japan on Guadalcanal
produces harsh words.

The President warns the premier that he has ordered
United States submarines to sink any Japanese ship loaded
down with Toyotas, on sight, and not to pick up any
surviving spare parts.

The Japanese premier tells the President the well-being
of his country depends on shipping automobiles and TV
sets to the United States and future shipments will be
escorted by warships.

The President returns from his trip and orders all Seiko

watches sold on the West Coast to be rounded up and sent to internment camps in Utah.

The premier of Japan disbands his cabinet and puts a new military clique in charge of the government. He orders them to start flooding the Philippines, Singapore, Hong Kong, and Burma with jogging shoes and sweat bands.

United States intelligence manages to break the Japanese naval code and discovers that the Japanese also have plans to land one hundred thousand Toyotas and fifty thousand Sony Betamax machines on Okinawa. They also intend to invade the United States Army PX there with thousands of Japanese instant cameras that could destroy the Polaroid and Eastman Kodak companies overnight.

The President calls in the Japanese ambassador to the United States and warns him that if the Japanese plant as much as one computer chip on Okinawa it will mean war.

The Japanese ambassador assures the President that his country has no intention of invading Okinawa with its products, but at the same time says that unless the United States lifts its embargo, his government intends to dump ten thousand Honda motorcycles on Wake Island, and sell them to the United States Marines.

After the Japanese ambassador leaves, the President turns to his most trusted counselor and says, "He's lying through his teeth. What is today?"

"Saturday, sir."

"Then tomorrow could be a 'Day of Infamy.' Damn, Weinberger. Why couldn't he have left well enough alone?"

Meanwhile, back at Pearl Harbor they're holding a dance at the officers' club, Burt Lancaster is making love to Deborah Kerr in the ocean, and two hundred miles offshore Admiral Yamamoto is standing on the bridge of his carrier looking through his binoculars towards the lights of Hawaii.

He sighs and says to his aide, "Americans never learn. Tora, Tora, Tora."

Enchilada Wins a Victory

Flounder rushed into Bass's office at the State Department and cried, "The secretary wants a slide presentation on the elections in Enchilada to show to the American people."

"I anticipated that," said Bass. "I've been putting one together. Sit down.

"This is the Garcia family, which lives in Miami and which financed the Liberal Peasant Assassination party of Miguel Tortilla."

"Who is Tortilla?"

"He is known as 'The Hammer' because his people like to beat on opposition politicians with hammers. In 1971 we called him Enchilada's 'Criminal of the Year.' But he got twenty-five percent of the vote."

"Wow, it's going to be hard for us to support him."

"Not necessarily. We found a slide of Tortilla giving blood to the Red Cross. Next."

"That looks like Beverly Hills."

"It is. The Gomez family, which owns all the vanilla plantations in Enchilada, resides there."

"Who takes care of their affairs back home?"

"The Sambico Death Squads, led by Heraldo Destino. The Sambicos claim to have wiped out twenty villages in the Ole Mountains. They're policemen by day, and work for the Gomez family at night. Destino ran on the National Unity and Freedom party under the political slogan 'Land Reform Sucks.' He got eighteen percent of the vote."

"Can we deal with him?"

"We're going to have to because he's formed a coalition with Tortilla. Next slide."

"I don't recognize that fellow."

"That's the 'Gorilla of Cuevas,' who represents the United Papillon Front, a group that splintered off from Destino because the National Unity and Freedom party gave up the use of machetes to frighten the Indians during the election. His money comes from the Diego family, which lives in Palm Springs. He got twenty percent of the vote. He's willing to form a government with Destino and Tortilla, provided they go back to using machetes against the Indians."

"How do we explain him to the American people?"

"As an Enchilada freedom fighter who has read every book on Thomas Jefferson. Here is that crumb Jiminez Tipperillo, the loser we supported in the elections. Even with CIA help and a fifty-million-dollar military slush fund he couldn't pull it off."

"We're going to have to back away from him."

"We have already. We put out the word he sleeps with a picture of Fidel Castro under his pillow."

"What are the rest of the slides?"

"Photos of the Enchilada Marxist guerrillas raping and pillaging the country."

"How did we get them?"

"We took them in Uganda, but who the hell is going to know the difference?"

"It looks like a pretty convincing slide show to me. Of course if we continue our military aid the President is going to have to certify that the new government believes in human rights."

"That's no problem. I spoke to Tortilla on the phone this morning and he assured me that anyone who opposes the new government's human rights policy will be shot in the knees."

Trouble in the Schools

Linda Peeples was giving the dinner. When dessert was finished, she said, "I have some exciting news for all of you."

"So tell us already," someone said.

"My son George just read his first book."

We all raised our wine glasses to toast the occasion.

"How old is George?" Reilly asked.

"He'll be eighteen next month," Linda said.

"That's fantastic," Rowan said. "My son is twenty-one and he hasn't read a book yet."

"George has always been a bright student," Linda bragged.

"What book did he read?" Frannie Huff wanted to know.

"J. D. Salinger's *Catcher in the Rye*."

There was an embarrassed silence at the table.

"What's wrong?" Linda wanted to know.

"*Catcher in the Rye* is a dirty book," I said. "Where did he get his hands on such filthy literature?"

"He found it in the school library," Linda said.

Exstrom was outraged. "You ought to report the librarian to the school board. They probably don't even know it's there."

"But George seemed to enjoy it," Linda said defensively.

"Sure he enjoyed it," Reilly said. "It's full of sex and bad words. But it doesn't belong in a high-school library. The next thing you know, George will be reading *Huckleberry Finn* and Kurt Vonnegut's *Slaughterhouse Five*."

"Or Studs Terkel's *Working*," I said.

"Not to mention Somerset Maugham's *Of Human Bondage*," Frannie Huff said.

"Are they all bad books?" Linda asked.

"The worst. They've ruined kids for life," I said.

"But we've been trying to get George to read a book since he was twelve years old. *Catcher in the Rye* was a breakthrough, and it would break his heart if we told him he couldn't read any more like it."

"There are books and there are books," Exstrom said. "My daughter came home from her English class with William Faulkner's *Sanctuary*, and I told her if she ever brought anything like that into the house again, I'd throw it in the furnace. I also reported her teacher to the principal."

I said, "If more parents took an interest in what their kids were reading we wouldn't have such a rotten society."

"Well, it's too late now," Linda said. "George has already read *Catcher in the Rye*. What do I do?"

"Watch him closely," Frannie Huff said. "Search his room, If you find a book by John Steinbeck or James Baldwin under his bed, then you know he's in real trouble and I would take his library card away from him."

"I wish I had kept a closer eye on my son. I let him read Hemingway's *The Sun Also Rises* when he was fifteen years old, and the next thing I knew he checked out Malamud's *The Fixer*," Exstrom said.

"Where do you find out what books are bad for children's minds?" Linda wanted to know.

"There are organizations all over the country that will

supply you with lists," I said. "We get our guidance from a couple who censors books in Texas."

"What's George reading now?" Reilly asked.

Linda said, "Voltaire's *Candide*."

"I hate to tell you this," Frannie Huff said, "but you have a sick kid on your hands."

Riffing

Riffing, or what is known in the government parlance as "reduction in force," is taking its toll on Washington. By law, those with seniority cannot be fired from a department if there is another job available, even if it is a much lower one. The person has to be kept on for two years before he can be let go. Many overqualified people are taking menial jobs just so they can stay in the government and collect their pensions, or hope that someone will put them back where they belong.

One of these happens to be Delbeck, who has a Ph.D. in geology, and formerly worked with the United States Geological Survey studying moon rocks.

I went to see Delbeck out in Reston, Virginia. Instead of being directed to his laboratory I was told I would find him in the mail room.

"Dr. Delbeck, what are you doing here?" I asked him.

"Sorting mail. It was the only job open when we had our last riff."

"What a comedown!"

"It's actually not a bad job as soon as you learn the alphabet. You see, you ignore the first name and only look at the initial of the last name. Then you put the letter in the box corresponding to the letter on the envelope. When I get the letters all sorted out, I give them to Dr. Fromm and he marks the room numbers on them."

"Dr. Fromm?"

"Yes, he used to head the mineral exploration division, and he's a whiz at knowing room numbers without having to look them up in the directory."

"What happens after Dr. Fromm puts the room numbers on them?"

"Then Dr. Lasker takes them and puts them in a supermarket basket and delivers them to the various offices."

"What did Dr. Lasker do before he took that job?"

"He was in charge of studying earthquake faults around the world. He was working on a new way of predicting them in advance, until the OMB decided it was a waste of money."

"He must be very bitter."

"He was until the head of the mail room explained it to him that delivering people's mail on time was just as important as figuring where the next earthquake would take place. Sometimes while Lasker is waiting for us to sort out the mail, he sneaks off in a corner with his calculator and predicts earthquakes just for the hell of it. But he has to be careful no one sees him, because there's talk they may lay off someone in the mail room and he has less seniority than Dr. Fromm and myself."

"Do you ever examine moon rocks any more?"

"No, but if it's a light day I might take out my microscope and analyze what kind of ink they used to print a postage stamp. I like to keep my hand in just in case something opens up upstairs."

"I can't believe the government would be so stupid as to allow three scientists like yourselves to work in a mail room."

"We're lucky. Dr. Ridgwell, who was just about to figure out a way of measuring ultraviolet rays by a laser beam, is now operating a paper-shredding machine in the boiler room. She was riffed out of a Nobel Prize."

The head of the mail room came over to us. "Delbeck, go down to the cafeteria and bring me up a coffee and Danish."

"Yes, sir," said Dr. Delbeck. "Cream and sugar?"

"You know I like it black, dummy," the head said as he walked away.

"Do you let him talk to you like that?"

"As long as they pay us fifty thousand dollars a year, what choice do I have?

"Look, I'm not going to stay in the mail room forever. Dr. Billington, who discovered titanium deposits on the ocean floor in the Gulf of Mexico, is retiring in a couple of months, and when he leaves he's going to recommend me for his job."

"What does he do now?"

"He works in the motor pool as a night watchman."

Let It All Hang Out

If we are sincere about deterring the Soviets from starting aggression, I can't think of a better way to scare the hell out of them than by piping in a local radio talk show from any town in America. Nothing would convince the Russians more how much we mean business.

"Hi, folks, Jerry Dodge here and welcome to another four hours of *Let It All Hang Out*. Tonight we're going to deal with the question I am sure has been bothering most of you this week, and that is, 'Should the United

States freeze its nuclear missiles or should we continue our arms buildup until we're certain we can zap every Commie in the world?' Let's hear from our first caller."

"Jerry, my name is David Umansky and my wife, Adrienne, thinks it would be real dumb to freeze our missiles now because we're on our own twenty-yard line, and it's third down and if we don't come up with the big play, that means we'll lose the ball, and put the Russians in field-goal range. At this stage, we can't afford to let them get three points on the board."

"How do you feel about giving up our first-strike nuclear capability, David?"

"Sick. Life is an Atari game. Once you've put in your quarter, you've committed yourself. And even if you know you're going to be wiped out, you still want to take as many asteroids with you as you possibly can."

"Thanks, David. Hello there, you're on *Let It All Hang Out*."

"Jerry, this is Louise Royal of Princeton, and first I'd like to tell you how much I enjoyed your program yesterday advocating the death penalty for people who are late in filing their income tax returns."

"Thanks, Louise. How do you feel about nuclear disarmament?"

"My car pool is against it, except for Bobbie Fletcher, who thinks that there are too many nuclear weapons now. But no one pays any attention to her because she believes nuclear war is unwinnable."

"What makes her think that?"

"She said she read somewhere that if we had a war, everyone would be blown to bits so it doesn't make any difference who starts it."

"Have you tried to straighten her out?"

"No, we just laugh at her."

"Thank heavens Bobbie is not in the government. Let's take another call. You're on the air."

"Jerry, this is Anne Kohlmeier. I have a brother-in-law named Marty and he says if you dig a hole five feet deep and cover it with a green garbage bag and then put a foot of peat moss over it, you can protect yourself against an atomic attack. The garbage bag and peat moss keep the radioactivity from penetrating the hole."

"That's a good tip for our listeners. Why hasn't the government told the people about it?"

"They're afraid there would be a run on green garbage bags. But my brother-in-law says the civil defense people have been stockpiling them and will make the bags available as soon as the whistle blows."

"That's good news. Hello, you're on the air."

"Jerry, I'd just like to say that I think all the people calling in and talking about nuclear war are nuts."

"What do you do for a living, sir?"

"I'm a doctor and we predict one hundred million people will be killed in the first twenty minutes if these weapons are used."

"Doctors have been known to be wrong."

"Maybe so. But if people think we're going to be around to make house calls after a nuclear holocaust they're kidding themselves."

"I'm sorry to cut you off, Doc, but you're not making any sense. Sorry about that last caller, folks, but every once in a while we get an idiot on the show, and there is nothing we can do about it. We've got the time for one more call, and let's hope he can add something more intelligent to our discussion."

"Jerry, this is Fred from Finster. I listen to your program every night. In case we MARV the Soviets and then they MIRV us, will your show still be on the air?"

"It better be. If the balloon goes up, newspapers will be the first to go and our sponsors are going to need radio spots more than ever."

Youthful Job Training

Most of the telephone calls I've been receiving these days go something like this:

"Hi, it's Phil."

"Hello, Phil, how are you?"

"Never mind the small talk. My kid is graduating from college this year and he wants a job."

"This is a bad time to get a job in Washington."

"That's why I'm calling you. I figured you would know somebody."

"I know a lot of people, but I don't know anybody who can give him a job."

"What about all those senators and congressmen you're always writing about?"

"I haven't had any luck with them. I called a senator the other day about a job for my nephew, and he asked me for a job for his niece. It was a standoff. Neither one of us could do anything for the other."

"You know Ben Bradlee?"

"Of course I know Ben Bradlee."

"Good, get my kid a job with *The Washington Post*."

"I can't do that. Bradlee had to get a job for his godson, so he called up Otis Chandler at the *Los Angeles Times*. Chandler said he'd give the kid a job if Bradlee hired his godson to work on the *Post*. Bradlee had to use up his last draft choice in the trade with Chandler."

"What about the White House? My kid is willing to start anywhere."

"I can't ask the White House for a favor because if

they give your kid a job, they'll expect me to go in the tank for them in exchange."

"What about the State Department?"

"I don't know anybody in the State Department. Besides, any job there is offered first to the kids of big Republican contributors. You have to understand. I have nothing to trade with anybody. I can't just call up and ask for a job for your kid in this town, if I can't get one for his."

"So what you're saying is I should tell my kid you won't get him a job in Washington."

"That's unfair. I like your kid, but I have forty-five resumés from sons and daughters on my desk right now, and I can't even get them into the Marine Corps."

"How about calling up your friends at Public Television?"

"I don't have any friends at Public Television any more. They were all laid off."

"My kid isn't proud, he'll even work for a lawyer."

"Look, Phil, I'd love to help you but I don't have any clout with lawyers. The word is out on the street that I can't get their kids a job in this town, so they have no interest in interviewing anyone I send them."

"You turned out to be one helluva friend. All I ask you for is one little lousy favor and you give me the brush."

"Has your kid come to Washington and tried to get a job for himself?"

"I told him he didn't have to because I knew you. It's pretty late in the game to tell him he has to find his own job. It will break his heart that his uncle Artie wouldn't even help him fulfill his lifetime dream."

"Why didn't you call me first before you told him I could get him a job?"

"Because if you said you couldn't, he would lose all respect for me."

"Okay, I'll make a few calls. Maybe I can get lucky."

"That's more like it. Who are you going to call?"

"I have a friend in the NBC bureau here, who is looking

for a job for his kid at CBS. I know a guy at ABC who is looking for a job for his kid at NBC. If I can swing that, then the guy at ABC will owe me one, and I can get him to interview your kid."

"Great. I'll tell my kid."

"Hold it! The whole deal hinges on me getting a job for Bill Paley's granddaughter in cable television."

A Question of Shrinks

One of the things I can never understand is why learned psychiatrists, who are hired by the government and the defense in a major crime case, can arrive at such different opinions when it comes to the sanity or insanity of a defendant.

I asked a defense lawyer why it was impossible for opposing psychiatrists, when testifying, to agree on the mental condition of the accused at the time he committed the crime.

"Doesn't it confuse the jury?" I asked.

"I guess it does. So, as a lawyer, I have to be very careful when selecting a shrink that he looks and sounds as if he knows what he's talking about. When you're going for an insanity plea you don't want your expert to look like a quack."

"Suppose you hire a psychiatrist to examine your client and he decides the person was sane at the time he committed the crime."

"I fire him. Obviously he is not sufficiently qualified to be a defense witness. You waste a lot of money when you hire a psychiatrist with an open mind. I've had cases where five shrinks have examined my client before I could get one to say he was crazy."

"And that was the one you called to the stand?"

"If I called the other four, I could have been sued for malpractice."

"How do you find your medical experts?"

"We have lists of shrinks who believe anyone who commits a major crime is crazy, just as the government has lists of doctors who are willing to testify that anyone involved in one was sane. We don't use their lists and they don't use ours."

"Besides the lists you work from, what else do you look for in a psychiatrist for the defense?"

"Appearance counts for everything with a jury, so you want your shrink to look more psychiatric than their shrink. I personally prefer one with a beard and glasses so he will remind the jurors of Sigmund Freud. If I can't get a guy with a beard, I'll settle for one that looks like Alan Alda. People believe in the medical opinions of an Alan Alda. If my expert has a tweed suit I always ask him to wear it. I don't want my doctor to look too rich, or the jury will suspect he's in the testifying business for the money."

"I imagine the prosecutors prefer their experts to look the same way."

"Yes. Sometimes it's hard for the jurors to distinguish which shrink has testified for the defense and which one was a witness for the state. That's why it's better to have a psychiatrist with a German name, and preferably an accent.

"I always insist that my man testifies in language that will not overwhelm the layperson. But I want him to use enough medical jargon to show he isn't just some doctor who walked in off the street.

"The most important thing of course is that my shrink does not become rattled in cross-examination by the prosecution. I don't want him to lose his cool when they start questioning him about his childhood."

"How do you cross-examine the government's psychiatrist?" I asked.

"Ruthlessly. I must make the jury believe the government's expert should never have been granted his medical degree.

"The trick is to trip him up so badly he starts behaving on the stand like Captain Queeg in the Caine Mutiny trial. I might even raise the question of his sanity before I get finished with him."

"One final question. What type of psychiatrist is willing to spend all his days in court and put up with this kind of abuse?"

"Mostly one who is tired of listening to people's dreams."

Part Five

WHY JOHNNY CAN'T EAT

WHY JOHNNY CAN'T EAT

Why Johnny Can't Eat

"The class will please come to order. Today, children, we will talk about American agriculture. The United States produces more meat, grain, corn, dairy products, vegetables, and fruit than any country on earth. Thanks to our farmers, food is one of our largest exports and we are able to feed people all over the world.

"Now, Johnny, can you name a meat that comes from an American farm?"

"Tofu."

"No, Johnny. Tofu is not a meat. It looks like meat, but it is made from soybean curd."

"Lady in the cafeteria said it was meat."

"I'm sure she didn't say it was meat. What she must have said was that you are entitled under the Department of Agriculture regulations to have a delicious tofu instead of a hamburger."

"It tasted lousy."

"Now, Johnny, you must understand tofu is an acquired taste. Does anyone know what an acquired taste is?"

"Something that tastes lousy?"

"Now, I'll have no more of that kind of talk in this sixth-grade class. An acquired taste is something you have to get used to. When I was a little girl I didn't like spinach. But as I grew up I acquired a taste for it, and now I eat it once a week."

"You ever acquire a taste for tofu?"

"We didn't have tofu when I was a little girl."

165

"You're lucky. It really tastes lousy."

"Now let's talk about other things farmers raise. Edna, name something a farmer produces."

"Milk."

"Very good. Milk and other dairy products are some of the most important foods for young growing bodies because they contain calcium which your bones need to make you strong. How many glasses of milk should a young person drink a day?"

"A half a cup."

"No, Johnny. A half a cup is certainly not enough milk for someone your age."

"The lady in the cafeteria said that's all I could have."

"She was just following federal regulations concerning school lunches."

"What's federal regulations?"

"Those are the rules the President and his advisers decide the people must live by. He had to cut down on your milk allowance to save money for the country."

"What does he do with all the milk we ain't allowed to drink?"

"It's made into butter and cheese and stored in warehouses all over America, until it gets rotten and then they throw it away."

"You're kidding."

"No, Johnny. That's the only way we can encourage farmers to produce milk. By buying up their surplus they're guaranteed a profit on their milk. Shall we move on to vegetables? What kind of vegetables do our American farmers raise?"

"I know the answer to that one. Catsup."

"Catsup is not a vegetable, Johnny."

"Lady in the cafeteria said it was a vegetable. She said I was entitled to two vegetables; potatoes and catsup."

"Well, it's true that the Department of Agriculture declared the other day that catsup was a vegetable, but farmers don't raise it. They raise tomatoes and afterwards they are squashed up and put into bottles as catsup. Then people like yourselves put the catsup on your hamburgers to make them taste better."

"Lady in the cafeteria wouldn't give me no hamburger."

"Well, then, you can put catsup on your tofu."

"I did, but it still tasted lousy."

"Johnny, you have disrupted this class enough today. You will stay after school and write one hundred times on the blackboard, 'America produces more food than any country in the world today.'"

Dinner at the White House

One of the main concerns of the White House is that President Reagan has been perceived by the media as being insensitive to the poor. The matter came to a head when CBS's Bill Moyers produced a documentary titled, "People Like Us," which showed people who purportedly were not enjoying Reaganomics.

Although the show had a very low rating, the President happened to see it and told his people something had to be done about his image.

A high-level meeting of advisers was called the following morning to discuss ways of counteracting the "insensitivity" issue.

"The President is sick and tired of being portrayed as a bad guy when it comes to poor people. We have to come up with an idea to turn this perception around," a top aide said.

"How about this? Why doesn't the President give a black-tie dinner for the poor people at the White House?"

"That's not bad. Does anybody know any poor people we can invite?"

There was silence in the room.

"Let's call the Republican National Committee," someone suggested. "They must have a list."

An aide picked up the hot line to Republican headquarters. "We need two hundred poor people to invite to dinner at the White House.... Never mind why. Just give us the names.... You don't have any?"

The aide hung up. "They said they don't keep names of poor people because they never give to the party."

"What about the Department of Human Resources? They must have a list of disenfranchised citizens in their computers," someone else suggested.

The same aide picked up the phone and got a deputy secretary of human resources on the phone. "We need the names of two hundred poor people to invite to a dinner at the White House.... Just a minute, he wants to know how poor?"

"Real poor. People who are feeling the pain of the recession and have nowhere to turn," the chief White House aide said.

The man on the phone told the deputy secretary, "Scrape the bottom of the barrel. Unmarried mothers on welfare, senior citizens who have lost their homes, people who have been unemployed for more than a year, and a few who went bankrupt and are now existing on food stamps. Get the names over here by three o'clock, so we can run a poverty check on them."

"Okay," someone said. "Now that we've got the guest list, let's talk about the menu. What do poor people like to eat?"

"I know they like cheddar cheese. Every time we give it away, they stand in line for hours to get a block of it."

"Good, we'll serve cheddar cheese soufflé."

"Wait a minute," someone said. "How do we get them to the White House?"

"That's their problem," an aide said.

"Hold it," a communications expert said. "These people don't have money to come to Washington. If we have a dinner for them and no one shows up, the whole thing will blow up in our faces. We'll have to pay to bring them in."

"But if we do that, they might decide to cash in their tickets and pocket the fares instead."

"Are you trying to tell me that someone would rather have the airfare than dine at the White House?"

"Poor people have been known to do crazy things. That's why we have to keep a safety net under them."

The Airline Price War

The airlines are in one of the most brutal price wars in history. They're all being killed, but no one will surrender.

It's gotten so that when you go to the airport, you never know anymore how much you're going to pay for the trip.

I went to National Airport the other day to take a plane to Miami, Florida. The lady wrote out my ticket. "That will be fifty dollars."

"It seems like a lot of money," I said.

"Ah, yes, but it also entitles you to fly on to Karachi, Pakistan, for the same price."

"I don't want to go to Karachi," I told her.

"Well, for five dollars more you can go to Hong Kong, and stay at a hotel for three nights."

I was about to pay for the ticket, when I noticed the

person at the next counter from another airline put up a sign.

It read, "Fly to Miami with us for $40 and have the use of a rental car for one week."

I told the lady to forget it, and I got in the other line.

While I was waiting, a man came up to me in a red jacket and whispered, "Can I talk to you for a moment?"

"I'll lose my place in line."

"You won't be sorry," he said. "Follow me around the corner." When we got out of sight of the counter, he said, "We'll take you to Miami for twenty-five dollars and your family can go for free."

"My wife and children are at home," I said.

"We'll send a limousine for them and hold the plane."

It seemed like a pretty good deal, and I was about to take it, when a very attractive lady in a blue uniform came by and dropped her purse. I picked it up and handed it to her.

"Don't do anything until I talk to you in the bar," she said.

I excused myself from the man in the red jacket and followed her. We found a table and she took my hand in hers.

"I overheard you saying you were going to Miami," she purred.

"Yes," I said, as I nervously looked around.

"Why don't you fly with Snail Darter Airlines?"

"How much is it?" I asked.

"How much would you like to pay?"

"I hadn't thought about it," I admitted. "Would fifteen dollars be enough?"

"We can put you in first class for that. Here's a coupon. Go to our ticket counter and tell them Sally sent you."

"Thanks a lot. Can I pay for the drinks?"

"Of course not! When you fly first class, they're on the house."

I picked up my suitcase and started heading for the Snail Darter Airline counter. It was at the end of the terminal, and as I was walking there, a young man, his head shaved, wearing a saffron robe, came up and stuck a carnation in my suit lapel hole.

"I gave to the Hare Krishnas at the office," I told him.

"I'm not a Hare Krishna. I'm marketing vice-president of Camelot Airlines. We're willing to make a deal."

"Do you fly to Miami?" I asked.

"Not usually, but in your case we'll make an exception."

"Snail Darter will fly me there for fifteen dollars first class," I warned him.

He said, "For ten dollars we'll take you there and wait for you until you're ready to come back."

"First class or tourist?"

"If you hurry, you can sit in the copilot's seat!"

Under the circumstances it seemed like the best I could do so I gave him my credit card. He took a computer from underneath his robe and punched out my ticket.

"What about my luggage?" I asked him.

"Don't worry," he said, giving me a tag. "Frank Borman will deliver it to your hotel personally."

My Latest Nightmare

I'll tell you what I'm frightened about at the moment. The next big war is not going to be started by two countries, but by an anchorman from one of the major TV networks.

I've been watching all the news shows concerning the Falkland Islands, and I'm getting the feeling that everyone interviewing the leaders involved is pushing the sides into a corner they can't get out of.

This is my nightmare:

The anchorman is seated behind his desk and behind him is a large screen. He says to the audience, "In a moment we will be talking to the Argentinian minister of war. Mr. Rodriguez, do you see any way out of this situation, except going to war?"

"Argentina has always said it was willing to negotiate an honorable solution."

"But suppose the British sink one of your ships?"

"Then we will attack them with everything in our arsenal."

"Thank you, sir. And now from London, we have in our studio Devlin Person, undersecretary for foreign affairs. Mr. Person, as you just heard, the Argentinian minister of war said he plans to hit the British fleet with everything he has, and we must assume from that he means bombers and submarines. What does Great Britain plan to do about this?"

"I'm quite sure we can handle any situation that we are faced with. Her Majesty's government is willing to discuss the dispute peacefully and no one wants to go to war. But at the same time our honor is at stake."

"I understand that, sir. But assuming the Argentinians will not sit down with you, are you prepared to use nuclear weapons to make your point?"

"I don't think that this is the time or place to discuss whether we would resort to nuclear weapons."

"Why not?"

"We prefer not to escalate the war talk any more than it has been already."

"Forgive me for pressing you on this, but are you saying that if Argentina sinks a British aircraft carrier you would not nuke Buenos Aires?"

"We are keeping all our options open."

"Thank you, sir. And now to New York to talk to the Argentinian ambassador to the United Nations. Mr. Ambassador, as you just heard, the British might use nuclear weapons against your cities, if you don't pull your troops out of the Falkland Islands. How will you respond to such an attack?"

"We doubt if this will happen. But in case it did, we would call on a non-NATO major power to retaliate against the British much closer to their home."

"Obviously you're talking about the Soviet Union. Has your government been in touch with Moscow?"

"I would rather not say at this time."

"Thank you, sir. Let's go now to the State Department here in Washington and talk to Undersecretary Robert Dobson. Mr. Dobson, does the State Department have any contingency plans in case the Soviets supply atomic weapons to Argentina?"

"We are working on a peaceful solution to the crisis, and trying to get both sides to sit down and talk to each other."

"I don't think you answered my question. I want to know if the United States is willing to go to war with the Soviets, if they introduce their missiles into the Western Hemisphere."

"No comment."

"Thank you, sir. I'm sorry, our time has run out for this evening. Tune in tomorrow for an update on another possible Cuban missile crisis between the United States and the Soviet Union. Good night and pleasant dreams."

School Prayers

It is to the President's credit that with all the things on his plate, including unemployment, a tough budget fight, the Falkland crisis, and his efforts to try to close the "Window of Vulnerability," he would take time to propose a constitutional amendment to permit prayers in school.

Critics have accused Mr. Reagan of raising the issue at this moment as a sop to his right-wing supporters, who feel the President has been spending too much time on the country's financial problems and not enough energy on the real issues facing the nation, of which school prayer is one with the highest priority.

Whether a constitutional amendment is a solution is up for debate. I believe we should try some other remedies first to satisfy everybody.

The administration has come down strongly on the side of giving tax credits to parents who send their children to parochial schools. It seems to me if this law is passed, a compromise solution to the problem would be to permit children attending public schools to be bused to a religious school of their choosing in the morning, say their prayers, and then get back on the bus and go to their public school to do their work. In this way you would give American children an opportunity to pray, but you would also keep religion off state property. Those on the bus who didn't want to pray could remain in their seats and hit each other over the heads with books.

The proprayer people say the constitutional amendment is voluntary and a child will not have to pray if he doesn't want to. The antiprayer people maintain that peer pressure as well as teacher pressure will force a kid to pray whether he has the choice or not.

The latter group sees this kind of scenario:

"All right, children, we will now open with a morning prayer. Those sinners who don't believe in God can either stand in the back of the room with their faces to the wall, or hide in the clothes closet.

"Come, you little Bolsheviks, hurry it up so the rest of us can get on with seeking divine guidance. Where are you going, Tony?"

"I'm going to the back of the room. I already prayed at home this morning."

"And you think that's enough?"

"It's enough for me."

"Look at Tony, children. He is a perfect example of a secular humanist. He'd rather stand in the back of the room than pray to the Lord. Does anyone know where Tony is going to wind up with his attitude?"

"In Hell."

"Very good, Charles. And who will he find in Hell?"

"Satan."

"And what will Satan make him do?"

"He'll make him feed the flames of a fiery furnace, and Tony will have to wear a tail, and he'll be screaming all the time and fighting off snakes, but it won't do him any good."

"That's absolutely right, Enid. Who knows what else will happen to him?"

"Blackbirds will peck his eyes out, and he'll have a stomachache all the time and his toes will drop off."

"Very good, Everett. Well, what do you have to say to that, Tony?"

"I'd still rather stand in the back of the room."

"Are there any other Communists in the class who would like to join him? All right, Tony, you seem to be the only one. Go to the back and I don't want to see your ugly face until I tell you to take your seat. Now, class, let us bow our heads and pray for Tony's soul! Heavenly Father, there is always one rotten apple in the barrel. . . ."

A Dry Run

Unlike most people, I take Civil Defense very seriously. While the evacuation plan for Washington hasn't been fully worked out, I know what we're supposed to do. When the sirens go off, we're all to get in our automobiles, grab our credit cards, and head for Lickety Split, West Virginia.

The other evening around five o'clock I decided to take a dry run. I came home and told my wife, who was in her housecoat and curlers.

"Get in the car, we're going to have a practice evacuation drill."

"Let me get dressed first."

"You don't have time. Do you think when the real thing happens, the Russians are going to wait for you to get all gussied up? Grab the credit cards and let's go."

"What credit cards should I take?" she asked.

"American Express, Visa, Master Charge, and Diner's Club," I told her. "If we use up our credit line on one, we can switch to another."

"Do you have gas in the car?" she wanted to know.

"I have half a tank."

"That won't get us to Lickety Split."

"I'm sure if the real thing happens, the Civil Defense people will have emergency gasoline trucks all along the highway. After all, they can't expect us to evacuate Washington during an atomic bomb attack and not supply the petrol. Now stop talking and get in the car. We have to pretend this is not a drill."

As soon as we got near Key Bridge, we found cars bumper to bumper. We moved ten feet every five minutes.

"What's going on?" my wife wanted to know.

"It's normal rush hour traffic," I explained.

"If it's like this now, what's it going to be like when they try to evacuate the entire city?"

"They'll have National Guardsmen on every corner to move the traffic along," I said. "It wouldn't surprise me if they emptied Washington in twenty minutes. The Soviets are in for a shocker when their missiles hit Ground Zero and find nobody there."

We made it over the Key Bridge in forty-five minutes and moved smoothly along the George Washington Parkway at twenty-five miles an hour until we hit the Beltway and were slowed down to fifteen.

"I guess you didn't get out of town as fast as you had hoped," my wife said.

"That's because this is just a drill. When people know they're racing against a Soviet ICBM, they'll be doing eighty miles an hour."

"How do we get to Lickety Split?" my wife asked.

"I guess the Civil Defense people haven't put up their signs yet. Where's the map?"

"We don't have a map of West Virginia."

"I told you to always keep a map of West Virginia in the car. You never listen to anything I tell you."

She started to cry. "Let's go back."

"We can't go back until the Civil Defense people tell us it's safe. Washington, as far as this drill is concerned, has been completely vaporized."

By asking directions from forty people, we finally got to Lickety Split six hours later.

It was dark, and no one was on the streets. We knocked

on the door of a farmhouse. A man carrying a shotgun answered it.

"Hi," I said, "we're from Washington, D.C., and we were told to come to Lickety Split in case of an atomic attack. We thought we'd arrive early and look the place over just to see where we'd be the most comfortable."

"You got one minute to get off my farm."

"Don't shoot. Haven't you heard from the federal Civil Defense people? You're supposed to open your homes to us until they can rebuild the capital."

"Thirty seconds."

"We'll sleep in the barn," I pleaded. "We're not proud."

"Fifteen seconds."

My wife pulled me away from the door towards the car.

"I'm reporting you to the Federal Emergency Management Administration," I yelled at him. "You're making their atomic war evacuation plan into a farce."

Poor-Mouthing Defense

Frederenko, my KGB contact, and I dine about once a month and exchange information on each other's country's defenses.

"Haig told me the Soviets have missile superiority to the United States," I said.

"Is big liar," said Frederenko angrily. "By claiming nuclear inferiority, American military is able to spend billions of dollars on new weapons. The USSR is not going to let you say you are inferior when whole world knows you more powerful than we are."

"You are a victim of your own propaganda, Frederenko," I told him. "The truth is your missiles are much larger and have more throw-weight. Ours are smaller and more vulnerable to a first-strike attack. Soviet know-how is forcing us into an arms race we can't afford."

Frederenko was getting red in the face. "You only know about our successes. You don't know about our failures. If we have to use our ICBM missiles, half of them would fall into the sea."

"Don't try to plant disinformation on me," I warned him. "We are aware your submarine cruise missiles are targeted on every city in the United States."

"And what about your B-fifty-two bombers with hydrogen smart bombs that can wipe out all of Russia?"

"We haven't tested one in years. For all we know none of them will even explode."

"Our Backfire bombers are a joke," said Frederenko. "We only built them to use as a chip in the SALT II talks."

"We're not too thrilled with our nuclear aircraft carriers. Rickover says in case of war they won't last more than six days."

"You must not tell anyone," Frederenko said in a low voice. "But the cameras on our spy satellites take everything out of focus."

"Since you have told me that, I will tell you something. Our AWACs break down after only twenty-five hours of flying time."

"We can't even fight a war in Afghanistan."

"We couldn't even rescue fifty hostages from Iran."

"We're not even sure the Warsaw Pact countries will be on our side."

"NATO is a paper army," I told him. "In a conventional war, you could capture all of Western Europe in ten days."

Frederenko said, "You are just saying that to trick us. We know how many tactical nuclear weapons you have planted all over West Germany. You could wipe us out in no time."

"I've seen studies of our war games, my friend. We've lost to the Soviets every time."

"I spit on your war games. We have to keep millions of troops on the Chinese border. We're spread so thin now we can't even defend Moscow."

"And what about our window of vulnerability in the United States? Unless we close it, you could blackmail us into a political defeat in any part of the world."

"Reagan made up the window of vulnerability to scare Congress into giving him the biggest defense budget in history."

"Frederenko, you must take my word for it. We are no longer a superpower. Here is a copy of the Joint Chiefs of Staff testimony to the Senate Armed Services Committee. It proves you are superior to us in every military area."

"And here are the microfilmed minutes of the last Politburo meeting. The minister of defense says we are outgunned and outmissiled on land and sea, and in the air."

We exchanged secret papers of the various failures of our defense systems and said goodbye.

When I reported back to my CIA superior in Langley, he said, "Did Frederenko buy it?"

"I don't think so. He kept poor-mouthing Soviet military superiority."

"We'll have to send Haig back up the Hill again to testify how weak we really are. Under no conditions can we afford to let the President discuss disarmament with the Soviets from a position of strength."

Acrimony Payments

The latest census has revealed that there are still more people who are married than there are divorced. The only surprise was how many people are still married, but are not living together.

I know one named Marylou. She is a friend, and she told me at lunch the other day that she and Archie had been separated for seven years, but had never been divorced.

"How come?"

"Because if he gets a divorce he won't have any excuse not to marry the floozie he's living with."

"Do you mean to tell me Archie is using you to protect himself from having to marry somebody else?"

"That is exactly what he's doing. I heard from friends that he keeps telling everyone that I won't give him a divorce. He portrays me as some kind of vengeful ogress who refuses to give him his freedom."

"And he doesn't pay you for that?"

"Pay me?"

"Of course. He's using you so he doesn't have to make another permanent commitment, and you should be compensated for it."

"How do I do that?"

"You have to ask for Acrimony."

"Is there such a thing?"

"Well, the courts don't recognize it, but that doesn't mean you can't ask for it. I should think you would be entitled to fifteen hundred dollars a month from Archie in Acrimony payments, as long as you stay married to him. That's a cheap price for him to save himself from another marriage."

"How do I get him to pay it?"

"You go to him and say, 'Archie, unless you pay me Acrimony I'm going to tell your girlfriend I'm willing to get a divorce any time you want it.'"

"He'll blow his top," Marylou said.

"Let him. But when he cools down he'll realize it's cheaper to pay you than to get a divorce and marry somebody else. Don't you see where Archie is coming from now? He has the best of both worlds. I'll bet you every time he tells his girl what an obstinate dragon lady you really are, he's laughing all the way to the bed."

"Do you think fifteen hundred dollars is enough?"

"You could make a deal with him. For fifteen hundred dollars you'll just keep silent. But if Archie wants insurance, you could ask for two thousand dollars a month, in which case you'll promise to go around and tell everyone that you'll only give Archie a divorce if you want to get married again. And if he wants to pay the full Acrimony fee of twenty-five hundred dollars, you could announce you were converting to Catholicism and Archie could only get a divorce over your dead body."

"He'll accuse me of blackmailing him."

"It's not blackmail. It's marital support. If he wants to keep you as a wife for his own nefarious purposes, he has to support you as a wife."

"Suppose he misses an Acrimony payment?"

"Then you put out the word that you are going to start divorce proceedings. If he really doesn't want to get married again, he'll beg, borrow or steal the money to keep you from going through with your threat."

"Do you know anybody who is collecting Acrimony now?"

"I know at least half a dozen women. They were all treated as doormats until they asked for Acrimony. One lady I know gets three thousand dollars a month, and all she has to do is send her husband a registered letter every thirty days telling him that under no conditions will she grant him a divorce. It's one of the happiest separations I've ever seen.

"The only thing you have to be careful of is when you get a visit from the 'other woman' and she begs you to give your husband up. I know one wife who gave in, and instead of getting two thousand dollars a month in Acrimony, she was only awarded seven hundred fifty dollars a month in alimony, and since her husband had to marry the other woman he claims he can't even afford that."

The Gates' Syndrome

It seems that Los Angeles Police Chief Daryl Gates has been under fire because so many blacks have been dying from a vicious "chokehold" the police use to cut off the supply of blood to the brain.

Gates said in defense of the LA force that he had a "hunch" that blacks are more susceptible to neck injuries because more blacks are harmed with this hold than whites.

"We may be finding that in some blacks when it [the chokehold] is applied, the veins or arteries do not open as fast as they do on normal people," he told the *Los Angeles Times*. "There may be something arresting the ability of the blood to flow again [after the hold]. We're going to look at that very carefully."

What Gates doesn't know is that a lot of work has been done in the field of black mortality by Professor Ku at the University of Kluxclan.

Ku is the one who discovered that more young black

than white suspects were killed by police bullets, and thus arrived at the conclusion that there is something in blacks that will not fight lead poisoning. In another study, he postulated that more black suspects in handcuffs were injured in police cars on the way to station houses than white, which he attributes to a metabolic defect in blacks who lose their balance when being roughed up in the backseats of automobiles.

In his most recent paper titled "Racial Weaknesses as Applied to the Gates' Syndrome," just published in the *Police Gazette*, Professor Ku writes:

"With regard to chokeholds in the United States, three times as many blacks as whites suffer severe injuries to themselves before being booked at the police station. For reasons that cannot yet be medically explained, blacks require twice as much oxygen when being choked as whites. This phenomenon, known as 'Gates' Syndrome,' has doctors perplexed, particularly because a black's arteries cannot deliver sufficient blood to the brain.

"A normal white person can withstand being choked for at least three minutes without passing out. In tests at several Los Angeles police stations, black volunteers passed out in less than two minutes. One theory expounded by visiting Professor Bother of the University of South Africa is that, when arrested, a black's fear of the police causes his veins to contract at the moment he is being choked. When the hold is released the trauma remains and it is impossible for the blood to go to the head.

"Professor Lembeck, of the National Police Institute of Houston, disagrees with Bother on his trauma theory and maintains that the 'Gates' Syndrome' can be attributed to a vitamin deficiency caused by a black person's diet. Lembeck says, 'Cutting off a normal victim's windpipe for a reasonable amount of time should not cause undue damage, unless the victim is lacking Vitamin F, which is essential for breathing. Therefore it is recommended that the arresting officer use a chokehold only

after he has been given training in mouth-to-mouth re-
suscitation.'

"There is not enough data available at this time to
accept either Bother's or Lembeck's theory. The racial
connection has been established as a cause of 'Gates'
Syndrome' but the 'why' is still a question mark.

"Unfortunately, Civil Rights organizations in Los Angeles are trying to cut off research work in this important
area by demanding the chokehold be abolished before the
medical cure for 'Gates' Syndrome' can be found.

"I submit that this would be a great mistake for black
people everywhere. The circulatory system of blacks has
tremendous scientific importance for the justice system
of the country. Until we find out why they can't tolerate
choking as easily as normal white people, the mystery of
black fatalities in Los Angeles will never be solved."

The High Cost of Messages

One of the problems with everyone's foreign policy
these days is that countries have decided to send more
and more expensive messages to each other. In bygone
years, an ambassador delivered a message to a foreign
government in a leather briefcase. The foreign secretary
would then call in the ambassador and hand him his government's reply. It was all neat and tidy and a very cheap
way of keeping in touch with each other.

But now the price of messages has gone sky high.

This is how governments are communicating with each
other:

The President calls in his secretary of state: "I want

to send a message to the Soviet Union that they better stay out of Central America. Give the El Salvador government five million dollars in arms."

"Yes, sir."

A few days later the President calls the secretary. "Have we had a reply to our message to the Soviets?"

"It just came in. The Soviets have delivered fifty MiGs to Cuba, as well as new ground-to-air missiles."

"Get off a tough message to Cuba right away. Send a squadron of Huey helicopter gunships to Honduras, and make sure they know we're going to give Guatemala anything they ask for. Sign my name to them so they know we mean business."

"Right, sir. By the way, we just got a message from France. They're supporting the Sandinista regime in Nicaragua by selling them one hundred Mirages. What is our reply?"

"Give the government of Trinidad two submarines and a missile cruiser to inform Mitterrand we disapprove of the sale."

A week later the President is being briefed by his national security adviser. "Libya is protesting our vote in the United Nations on Israel and has sent us a message by supplying the PLO with Russian-made heavy artillery."

"What kind of reply do you suggest we send?"

"We could give Sudan two hundred United States-made tanks. I think that would be loud and clear."

"I don't think that's strong enough. Why don't we send a hundred F-sixteens to Egypt?"

"Then we would have to give a hundred F-eighteens to Israel."

"Let's do it. That would also be a message to Iran. I've been wanting to send them one for some time."

"Haig has reported that he got nowhere with Gromyko on Poland."

"We're going to have to send the Russians another

message. Have Defense Secretary Weinberger arrange to place a thousand cruise missiles in West Germany."

"Is that in response to their message of putting a hundred SS-twenties in the Warsaw Pact countries?"

"I hope they read it that way. We must get through to them that we mean business."

"What about developing new chemical warfare weapons that would destroy the world? They might get that message."

"It's worth a try. Tell the Pentagon boys to get on it right away and leak it to the press. Anything else?"

"Did you want to send a message to the People's Republic of China by giving Taiwan a new shipment of planes?"

"We better hold off on that for the moment, as China might get the wrong message that we don't need them in the Cold War with Russia."

"That seems to do it for today. I'll get these messages off right away. Oh, one other thing, sir. Our ambassador in Moscow has just sent a cable that he needs a Cadillac limousine, because the small car we gave him is giving a message to the Russian people that capitalism doesn't work."

"I didn't know we had an ambassador in Moscow."

"We don't use him. But we keep him there just in case you want him to deliver a message to the Kremlin."

"Why would I want to do that when there are so many easier ways of communicating with the Soviets?"

Catch-22

"Mrs. Consumer, may I speak to you for a few minutes?"

"Sure, I'm not going anywhere."

"When are you going to start spending money again so the economy can get on its feet?"

"When George lets me. He says we have to hunker down until the recession is over."

"But the recession will continue if you don't start spending money."

"George is afraid he'll lose his job. He doesn't want us to get into any more debt than we are already."

"Can I speak to George?"

"Go ahead. He's sitting in a chair over there watching television."

"Hi, George, can I join you?"

"Sure, hunker down in a chair."

"You thinking about buying a new car soon?"

"Not really. They sure look nice on television, but my old one runs okay. We'll stick with the one we got until things start looking up."

"When do you expect that to happen?"

"Reagan said either this spring or summer."

"You know they won't start looking up unless you go out and buy a new car."

"Can't do it with those interest rates. I'm not going to buy a new car until they come down."

"They won't come down if the economy doesn't look

up, because business is not going to invest if they don't think you are ready to spend some money.

"I don't imagine you're planning on buying a new house this year."

"You have to be kidding. I can't even afford to paint this one."

"George won't even let me recover the furniture. I was lucky to get the money to buy braces for our daughter."

"Doesn't it bother you, Mrs. Consumer, that you can no longer keep up with the Joneses?"

"Haven't you heard? Jones went bankrupt a few months ago. They took everything including his house. No one wants to keep up with him any more."

"This is a very serious state of affairs. If no one is trying to keep up with the Joneses, then how do we get out of the recession?"

"Don't worry, Reagan will get us out of it with his tax cut."

"What are you going to do with your tax cut, George?"

"Use it to pay my real estate taxes. The city really socked me this year, because they lost all their federal funds for education. I'm going to have to give them my federal tax cut plus a couple of thousand more, which I don't have."

"George, if you're not going to buy a house and you're not going to buy a car, and you're not going to buy any paint, the recession is going to continue indefinitely."

"I'd like to do my share, but I have to send my son to college this year. Have you any idea what that is going to cost?"

"Isn't there anything you want to buy immediately as an impulse item?"

"I could use a new TV set to watch the World Series."

"But they're all made in Japan. That's not going to help the American economy."

"I can't help that. It's the only entertainment we can afford during the recession."

"May I tell both of you that your attitude is counter

to all the expectations of the economists, and as long as you persist in this frugality, we will never get out of the economic crisis we're in. You are not part of the problem any more. You ARE the problem. If you don't start spending money, who will?"

"Reagan will. Have you seen his budget for next year?"

Paris Under Mitterrand

PARIS—I hadn't seen my friend Dupont in six years. We chanced to bump into each other on the Avenue des Champs Elysées. The last time we met he was the most dapper Frenchman I knew. He openly bragged about his penthouse in Paris, his villa in the country, his yacht on the Mediterranean, horses in Deauville, and a mistress between the sixth and eighth arrondissements. When he showed me his Porsche double-parked on the Avenue Foch, he said, "President Giscard has been good to me."

I couldn't believe it was the same man this time. The lapels and cuffs on his suit were frayed, his tie had soup stains on it, he had just come out of the Metro station, and his eyes were adjusting to the light.

"How goes it, Dupont?" I asked.

He looked around nervously. "Shh, I could be taxed for talking to an American."

"How could that be?"

"Mitterrand is taxing everything. If the finance people see me talking to you, they will think I'm trying to get my money out of France."

"Speaking of money, how is your penthouse in Paris, your villa in the country, your mistress between the sixth and eighth arrondissements, and your Porsche double-parked on the Avenue Foch?"

"I don't want to talk about them," Dupont said.

"But that's all you did want to talk about when I saw you the last time. You haven't lost them, have you?"

"No, but I can't talk about them. The Socialists are taxing everything I own. Nobody in France brags anymore about what he owns."

"Mitterrand is really going after the rich, then?"

"If your entire worth is more than five hundred thousand dollars, they put your name into a computer. Once your name is in it, you can't get out. You have to declare everything you own, including your wife's jewelry. I spend all my time trying to knock down everything I have."

"That must be hard to do with your race horses."

"What race horses? They are milk horses."

"And the yacht?"

"It's no longer a yacht. It is now a sinking rowboat."

"And the villa in the country?"

"Are you talking about my broken-down farmhouse without a roof on it?"

"What happened to the Porsche that was double-parked on the Avenue Foch?"

"A junk heap, which I couldn't sell if I wanted to."

"You had a wonderful maid. Do you still have her?"

"Are you talking about the cousin that lives with us until she can find an apartment?"

"I see what you're doing, Dupont. But it can't be much fun to own the good things in life and not talk about them."

"What choice do I have? Mitterrand is taking everything away from the rich and giving it to the poor, and the economy is the worst it's ever been."

"That's odd," I said. "Ronald Reagan is doing just the opposite, and our economy isn't doing any better than yours."

"But at least the rich aren't suffering in America."

"Reagan isn't out to get them, if that's what you mean.

But then again he never was too big on soaking people just because they have money."

"Reagan is a good man," Dupont said. "I wish he was president of France."

"Some people in the United States wish he was, too. I have an idea, Dupont. Mitterrand worries about the poor people in France, and Reagan worries about the rich in the United States. Why don't we send France our poor people, and you could send us your rich people, and then everybody would be happy?"

"It is forbidden to take any of our money out of France so we can only be rich here," Dupont said. "If we went to America and our fortunes stayed here, we would be poor."

"I'm sure the French are smart enough to figure how to get money out of France."

Dupont's eyes lit up. "Perhaps. How would you like to buy the most beautiful villa in the French countryside? I'll throw in my cousin who works as a maid in the deal."

New French Souvenirs

PARIS—The French have always been noted for their perfume and their beautiful clothes. But recently they have become famous for their ground-to-air missiles.

I went to a high-class shop on the Rue Royale the other day to buy one souvenir.

The clerk said, "Can I help you, *Monsieur*?"

"I was looking for an Exocet cruise missile as a gift."

"Alas," he said. "We are all out of stock. Peru bought the last ones."

"What about the one in the window?"

"It is sold to Saudi Arabia."

"How long would I have to wait to get one?"

"We have orders from all over the world. Everyone wants an Exocet, even Libya."

"Well, is there something else particularly Parisian?"

"How about a new Mirage two thousand fighter? They can shoot down anything in the sky."

"Can I get it on the plane?"

"We'll wrap it for you in bubble paper so it won't break."

"If I can't get an Exocet, what would you suggest I put on it?"

"Perhaps the Super Matra missile. It's the top-of-the-line rocket and can be launched at anything from a plane to a tank. It has a delayed fuse and doesn't explode until it's in the target. The Egyptians are very happy with it."

"Do you have anything smaller?"

"We're now making a helicopter with rocket launchers that is perfect for destroying buildings."

"How much is it?"

"Less than a million dollars. If you don't want it with rocket launchers, we can sell it to you for seven hundred fifty thousand dollars and since you live in the United States you don't have to pay French sales tax."

"I don't know. Do you have anything else that says *France* all over it?"

"What about a torpedo boat? The Nicaraguans are very pleased with them. Our torpedoes are sound-activated and can home in on another ship's motors at ten miles."

"That's nice. What else are you selling?"

"We sell everything, *Monsieur*. We are the third-largest suppliers of military equipment in the world. Perhaps you would like a French tank? It comes equipped with a laser that follows its target by day or night."

"I don't think my friend would like a tank."

"Perhaps an automatic French machine gun, made in

France under license from the Israelis. It's automatic and can spray anything within sixty yards."

"That's not a bad idea. How do I get it into the United States?"

"We can ship it to you through French Canada."

"Do you take American Express credit cards?"

"Of course, *Monsieur*. How many did you want?"

"Maybe a dozen."

"Ah, *Monsieur*, we don't sell them by the dozen. Our minimum order is five thousand. If we sell a few of them they could get into the wrong hands."

"I see your point. What's that stuff that looks like Silly Putty?"

"Plastique. You just stick it on to anything and insert this fuse and everything goes BOOM! We've had it for years but it is still very popular in Third World countries, where everything goes BOOM all the time."

"Well, I must say for a souvenir shop you're very well stocked. You don't have any perfume, do you?"

"You mean that can be sprayed with bacteria?"

"No, I just mean perfume that you could smell."

"You must be crazy. What kind of a French store do you think this is?"

"I Love a Parade"

"Do you know what the trouble with the anti-nuke war movement is?" David Emge asked me.

"I have no idea," I said.

"They lack discipline."

"How so?"

"Well, for one thing, when they're parading down an avenue they never keep in step. They straggle along, as if they're all marching to a different drummer. Do you know why they march like that?"

I said I didn't.

"Because they don't have any drummers. You can't have a decent parade if you don't have a band playing martial music for you."

"But they have guitars."

"No one can keep in step to guitar music. I'll tell you what else is wrong with their demonstrations. They don't have uniforms. Everyone wears anything they damn well please. When people come out for a parade, they want to see a plethora of uniforms."

"Probably the reason they don't wear uniforms," I suggested, "is that they have to sit on the ground a lot. If they wore uniforms they'd get them all dirty."

"That's not good enough," said David. "Nobody enjoys watching scruffy people in a parade."

"What kind of uniforms would you suggest?"

"Real sharp military ones with shiny boots, snappy headgear, brass buttons and lots of gold on the epaulets."

"But if it's an antiwar parade, wouldn't uniforms make the participants look militaristic?"

"So what? The main purpose of a demonstration is to win over people to your cause. What better way than to put on a good show with bands, uniforms, flags flying, and thousands of people on the sidewalks cheering them on?"

"I'll admit the idea has merit, but what you're describing is against everything the anti-nuclear war people stand for."

"It's the end results that count. Once you've got the people in a patriotic fervor, they'll go along with anything you suggest. Right now no one comes out for an anti-nuclear parade because there is nothing to see. What attracts people to a parade is that they never know what's coming next."

"You're not suggesting the protestors also pass by with missiles, are you?"

"Why not? They could have mock-ups of nuclear weapons, and drive them past, pointing them toward the sky. Kids love that."

"The next thing I know you're going to suggest a flyby with airplanes."

"That's not bad. All you need is two jets with colored smoke coming out of their tails."

"I can't put my finger on it, David, but there is something crazy about your whole idea."

"I may not know anything about nuclear war, but I do know what makes a good parade," he assured me.

"But there's more to an anti-nuke rally than a parade. There are speeches, and protest songs, and praying," I said.

"Right. But without a good parade all the people are doing is talking to the converted. The ones you want to reach won't follow your parade if you don't give them a decent show. And the only way you're going to do that is by slapping your rifles sharply when you pass the reviewing stand."

"You're suggesting the anti-nuclear protestors carry rifles?"

"With fixed bayonets, gleaming off the sun. If you do it right, you'll have everyone on the sidelines waving an American flag, from the first color guard that goes by to the last tank bringing up the rear."

"It would be a different anti-nuclear protest," I admitted.

"And a peaceful one, because the police would never arrest a person in uniform."

Who Needs College?

"Hey, Dad, guess what? I've been accepted by Harvard, Yale, Princeton, Cornell, and Stanford."

"That's just wonderful, son. But are you really sure you want to go to college?"

"Gosh, Dad, you always said the one thing everyone needed in life was a college education."

"I was making conversation. I know a lot of people who are big wheels in their fields who never had a university diploma. You know my friend Sam Steg in Boston? He not only never went to college, he never even saw an Ivy League football game. He is one of the most successful men I know.

"And Eddie Aaronson of Rockville, Maryland, made a decision that he could educate himself much better than any school could do it for him. The man can buy and sell anybody who went to the Wharton School of Business."

"But you went to college."

"If I knew then what I know now, I would have never done it. I wasted four of the best years of my life studying for exams. I could have been driving a taxi then, instead of throwing my parents' money away on books and courses and dates. But just because I made a mistake is no reason you have to make the same one."

"Gee, Dad, you never told me how unhappy you were at Dartmouth."

"I didn't want you to know, because I was afraid you would think less of me. All fathers have skeletons in their closets that they try to keep from their children. Now that you're a man I feel I can level with you. The only reason I went to college was to stay out of the Army."

"I thought you would be pleased that I was accepted by five of the best schools in the country."

"I am, son. But just because they accepted you is no reason you have to go to any of them. You've got a brilliant mind, and I hate to see them load it down with a lot of intellectual nonsense that could mess you up for the rest of your life. Besides, every college that has accepted you is part of the elitist establishment. By the time you graduate, you'll think that you are better than everybody else. Worse still, everybody else will think the same thing. Once you get a degree from a top-flight school, you'll be a marked man for the rest of your days."

"Mom wants me to go to a good college."

"All mothers want their sons to go to a good college. But that doesn't mean it's right. They think because you've been accepted in some fancy school it reflects favorably on them. It's not important what Mom wants for you. It's what you want for yourself."

"I want to go to a good school."

"You say that now because you've never been to one. You're young and idealistic and you believe that all you need to get ahead is an education. But as you grow older you'll discover it isn't the college but the man that matters. I can introduce you to graduates of every university you have been accepted at, who will tell you they would have been happier being male disco dancers."

"What do you want me to do, Dad?"

"It's your decision, son. I don't want to influence you one way or the other. But if I were your age, I'd buy a backpack and hitchhike across the country. You'll learn a lot more than you will in some Ivy League institution."

"Dad, can I ask you a question?"

"Yes, son."

"Are we broke?"

"We're not broke. But we will be if you go to one of those five schools."

"Okay, then I'll go to the University of Maryland. It always was my first choice."

"Thanks, son. You just saved the old plantation."

The Computer Widow

For every home computer sold in America, there is a computer widow somewhere.

I dropped over to see the Bengals the other night. Mrs. Bengal offered me a drink.

"Where's Walter?" I asked Adele.

"Where he always is these nights. He's in the library talking to his home computer."

"He talks to a computer?"

"All the time. It's taken the place of television, conversation and foreplay," she said bitterly.

"I didn't know Walter was into computers."

"That's all he's into. As soon as he finishes dinner, he leaves the table and says, 'Well, I've got to go in and program a new household fiscal budget for next year.'"

"At least he's working to save you money."

"He *says* he's working on a new budget, but I walked in last night and he was playing 'Star Wars.' He told me he was just checking out his floppy disk drive. I've never felt so alone in my life. At least when he watched football I could sit next to him. But now that he has a home computer he says he has to be alone with his software."

"You poor kid. Maybe he'll tire of it."

"No way. He reads computer magazines the way he

used to read *Playboy*. His idea of a centerfold now is a sixty-four-K Ram Micro-Computer that will expand to one hundred twenty-eight bytes and produce a six-color high graphic screen resolution."

"Has he told you this?"

"No, but he talks in his sleep."

"Well, at least he's not dreaming about another woman," I said.

"I could compete with another woman," Adele said, "but I can't compete with a computer. We have no communication any more. The only language he uses is BASIC, COBOL, and FORTRAN. I'm at my wits' end."

"You're not thinking of leaving him?"

"I threatened to last week and he said to hold off until he could program all the variables, and come up with a modified alternative."

"Have you ever thought about getting your own home computer and plugging into his? Perhaps you could talk that way."

"I'm not interested in interfacing with him through a terminal. After all, we are in the same house."

"Maybe I should talk to him," I suggested.

"You can try, but I doubt if it will do any good."

I went into the library and found Walter hunched over his keyboard. "Hi, Walter. Am I disturbing you?"

"No," he said, squinting at me. "I was only justifying my margins."

"How's life?" I asked.

"Fine. I was having a problem with my cursor for a while, but I straightened it out by adding a protocol."

"You have to be careful with cursors," I said. "What news of Adele?"

"Wait a minute," he said, "I'll find out."

He put in a disk, pushed a code key, and typed on the screen ADELE. Then he hit his RETURN button.

"Here it is," he said. "She's either in the kitchen, the bath, her bedroom, or went to a baseball game."

"A baseball game?"

Walter looked worried. "That doesn't look right. But it's no problem. All I have to do is hit this DELETE button."

"Adele thinks she's losing you to a floppy disk retrieval system," I told him.

"That's ridiculous," Walter said. "All I'm trying to do is store and index data that will be able to forecast how we can enjoy the September years of our life."

"We've been friends for years, so I'm going to ask you a very personal question, Walter. How much do you love Adele?"

Walter, without saying a word, inserted a disk, and started hitting the keyboard.

"What are you doing?" I asked.

"I'm counting the ways. It's much faster to do it on a computer."

Part Six

MAKE ME AN OFFER

MAKE ME AN OFFER

Make Me an Offer

You can't imagine what disarray the oil-producing nations are in until you visit an open market oil bazaar and see for yourself. I went to one recently to buy a barrel for a birthday gift.

A sheik from Kuwait was singing, "Oil for sale, oil for sale. Sweet crude oil for sale."

"How much is it?" I asked.

"Thirty-four dollars a barrel. But since it's a birthday gift, I'll let you have it for thirty-two."

I was about to taste it when a man grabbed my arm and pulled me into his tent. "That man is a thief. Here, try this delicious Libyan oil." He handed me a tin cup.

"Very tasty," I said. "How much for a barrel?"

He smiled. "Thirty dollars. We're having a Kadafi Day Founders' Sale."

"I'll be back," I promised him.

I walked along the dusty streets of the bazaar as Nigerians, Saudi Arabians, and oil merchants from Qatar all implored me to buy their products.

A man wearing a straw hat said, "*Señor*, please, would you like to buy this 1983 vintage which just came out of an offshore well off the coast of Venezuela?"

"Is 1983 a good year for oil?" I asked him.

"It's nouveau oil. The weather was just right for pumping it out of the sea. You can refine it today."

"How much is it?" I asked.

"If you promise not to tell anyone I will sell you a barrel for twenty-nine dollars," he said.

"That's five dollars below the OPEC price."

"I spit on OPEC. They are all double-crossers, and are undercutting me all over the bazaar. I have a family to feed and that's why I am sacrificing my oil at cost."

"I'd like to think about it," I said.

As I walked farther down, a man in a sombrero standing in an alley called to me. "Psst, *amigo*, are you looking for some fast action?"

"It all depends on what you have to offer."

He showed me a photograph of a barrel of Mexican oil.

"I give you her for twenty-seven dollars and will throw in the transportation for free."

"She's very beautiful," I said. "But how do I know she's the real stuff?"

"He will guarantee that you won't be disappointed," said the Mexican merchant, pointing to a nervous man wearing a pin-striped suit, a white shirt, and a Harvard School of Business tie.

"Tell him, Thomas, how great my oil is."

"She's everything he says she is," the pin-stripe assured me.

"Who are you?" I asked.

"I am from the Chase Manhattan Bank, and this man is into me for six billion dollars. Buy his damned oil and give me a break."

"I really didn't want to spend that much," I said.

"I say, old chap," a fellow in a morning coat who looked like a floorwalker at Harrod's said, "I'd be very careful of those Latin cutthroats. Could I interest you in some very fine British petroleum from the North Sea? It's certified by the royal family."

"How much?"

The British never haggle over price when it comes to oil. "Twenty-five dollars—take it or leave it."

"Twenty-three dollars," I said.

"I'll make it twenty-four dollars and arrange to have your picture taken with Princess Diana's baby."

"I guess I can't do better than that."

"Yes, you can," an Iranian oil merchant said, pulling me into his hut.

"What's your price?"

"Are you American?"

"Of course," I said.

"Then I will give you this barrel for twenty dollars."

"Why so cheap?" I asked.

He put his arm around my shoulder and whispered, "We Iranians and Americans have to stick together."

Invasion of Privacy

"All right, class, Journalism one-oh-five will come to order. Today we will deal with invasion of privacy, which is one of the most important lessons you will have to learn if you wish to succeed in your profession. First, why should the media invade someone's privacy?"

"Because everybody likes to read about it, or see it on TV."

"I can see why you would arrive at that answer, but it is not necessarily the correct one. We invade someone's privacy because their conduct may affect the public good. Does anyone have any examples where the press has contributed to the people's right to know?"

"I do, sir. When Elizabeth Taylor separated from John Warner."

"That's a good example. Why was this an important story?"

"Because John Warner was a United States senator, and Miss Taylor's departure could have affected Mr. Warner's performance as a member of the Senate Armed Services Committee."

"Correct. If Miss Taylor had separated from singer Eddie Fisher to marry actor Richard Burton, would it have been a news story?"

"No, sir. That would be considered gossip and no one would want to read about it."

"Fine. Now let us take the case of Sophia Loren, who went to jail in Naples for not paying her taxes. Why was this newsworthy?"

"It showed the Italian people that no one was above the law."

"Then the idea of Miss Loren, one of the most beautiful women in the world, going to jail was not a news story in itself."

"No, sir. It only became a public matter when her taxes were involved."

"Now let's deal with a hypothetical case. Someone is giving a lavish party to honor Mrs. Jackie Onassis. The hostess announces that the press will not be allowed to cover it. What do you do?"

"You try to crash it?"

"What a beastly idea, Waters. The ethical thing to do is to stand on the sidewalk and hope that someone leaving the party will talk to you. If this doesn't work, you go back to your editor and tell him you can't write anything about the party."

"Won't he get mad at me?"

"He may for the moment. But in the long run, he'll respect you for not going to a party where you were not invited."

"Professor, suppose I have a hot story and the guy I'm after won't talk to me on the phone. Do I climb into his window and try to catch him unawares?"

"You do not. A man's home is his castle, and if he doesn't want to talk about his troubles you owe him a 'No comment.'"

"I have a question, sir. I'm planning to go into photography. Suppose I see Bo Derek topless on the beach, and I have a telescopic lens. Do I shoot the picture?"

"No. That would be invading her privacy. What you should do is shout to her that you have film in your camera, and ask her to cover herself up so you won't embarrass her."

"Suppose I'm working in TV and I'm ordered to stake out the house of someone who has just been indicted for a big white-collar crime. What do I do if he refuses to be interviewed on television?"

"You turn off your cameras and report to your producer that the person did not want to be questioned."

"Shouldn't I film his neighbors and his wife?"

"That would not be cricket, as people who are not directly involved tend to exaggerate and make things up."

"Professor, have you ever worked on a newspaper or for television?"

"I can't say that I have. I much prefer to teach journalism so I can prepare students for the time when they go out into the real world."

Psychological Baggage

"This is ridiculous," said Tabash, as he read *The New York Times* on the beach. "It says here that the toughest time for couples is when they go on vacation. The reason seems to be that the couple is together for an uninterrupted block of time. The husband and wife have fantasies of what it will be like to be together, and many times these fantasies don't come true, so they get angry and pick fights with each other over little things. One doctor in the article calls it 'psychological baggage.'"

Fenton laughed. "Barbara and I don't feel that way."

Fenton's wife sat up angrily and said, "My name isn't Barbara. It's Bernice."

"Barbara—Bernice, what's the big deal?" Fenton asked.

"After fifteen years of marriage you could get my name right."

"Now you're getting picky," Fenton said. "Barbara is my secretary, and every once in a while I get them mixed up," he explained to the rest of us.

"It's an honest mistake," I agreed. "A guy can't remember his wife's name *all* the time. That's why I call mine 'honey.'"

"What else does the article say?" Fenton wanted to know.

Tabash referred to his paper. "People who take vacations are full of guilt. They feel guilty about not working. They feel guilty about taking a vacation their parents can't afford. Guilt leads to disharmony in the couple and ultimately spoils their vacation."

"I don't feel guilty about not working," said Dobler. "I'm enjoying every moment of it."

"Then why are you on the phone to the office every day?" Astrid Dobler asked.

"Because I have to know what is going on," Dobler replied bitterly. "You can't have a good time if you have no idea what they're doing in the shop while you're away. My clients don't pay me to sit on the beach all day long. I notice you call the house-sitters every day."

"That's different. It's my house, and if they don't hear from me daily, they'll think I don't care what they do to the place," Astrid retorted.

Dobler turned to all of us. "I couldn't go on vacation if I didn't check in with the office. One lousy call a day doesn't make you a workaholic."

"You've never known how to take a vacation, because your parents never took one," Astrid said.

"They never had the money to take one," Dobler shouted. "Right now they're stuck in an apartment in Brooklyn all summer. It gives me heartburn every time I think about it."

Astrid said, "I'm not responsible because you're having a guilt trip about your parents."

"Keep reading, Tabash," I told him. "I think you're making our summer."

Tabash continued, "The article says they did a study at the University of Minnesota and found more couples fought with each other during the summer than at any other time in the year."

"It figures," I said. "That's when they're stuck with each other's neuroses for the longest period of time."

"What neuroses?" my wife wanted to know.

"I'm not talking about us," I said. "Besides, I thought you were sleeping."

She threw a bluefish at me.

"What am I supposed to do with this?" I sputtered.

"Stuff it in your psychological baggage."

It's All in the Waist

As everyone is aware, many of the clothes that you find in stores are now made in Taiwan, Hong Kong or South Korea. While they are not lacking in quality, there are problems with sizes.

For example, I bought a pair of shorts the other day marked LARGE. When I attempted to put them on, I discovered they did not fit. My first fear was that through bracket creep I had become X-LARGE. But before I panicked, I asked my son, who is MEDIUM, to try them on. They fitted him perfectly. It was obvious the people in Hong Kong had made a mistake. Fortunately, there was a slip included with the shorts which said, "Anything wrong with garment please refer to Inspector 7."

I immediately telephoned information, located the factory in Hong Kong, and called. Inspector 7 was not there but I got someone in charge who spoke English. I explained the problem of the sizes.

He said Inspector 7 was a very reliable man and had worked in the factory for fifteen years. This was the first time they had had a complaint about him. He even admitted that it was the first time they had had a telephone call from the United States about any of their inspectors.

I told him I didn't want to make trouble for Inspector 7, but I was just curious about how they inspected their shorts that were exported to the United States. I mentioned that many of my friends were also having difficulty with the sizes of Hong Kong shorts.

"What do you want to know about Inspector seven?" he asked.

"Well, for one thing—how tall is he?"

"I believe he is four feet eleven inches," the man said.

"And how much does he weigh?" I wanted to know.

"We never weigh our inspectors," the man said. "But I would guess about ninety-five pounds."

"Then that could be your trouble. Are most of your inspectors about that height and weight?"

"Yes, but I don't see what this has to do with your shorts."

"It's quite clear. To them a MEDIUM looks like a LARGE size, a LARGE looks like an X-LARGE, and EXTRA-LARGE is too much for them. They are thinking in terms of themselves when they're inspecting your shorts. Do they ever try them on?"

"Once in a while."

"There you are. Inspector seven puts on the shorts,

and on the basis of his height and weight is down-sizing all your garments. He has probably never seen a truly LARGE or an EXTRA-LARGE waist in his life."

There was a pause on the other end of the line followed by some fast chatter in Chinese. Finally, the man came back on the phone and said, "We will be happy to make a pair of shorts to your size if you will give us your measurements."

"That's very kind of you," I told him. "But I'm calling not only for myself, but for all the large-sized men in America."

"All our employees are small," the man said.

"Then in order to maintain your credibility in the United States, I suggest that you invite some portly American tourists to come into the factory and show your inspectors what is a LARGE size in shorts and what is X-LARGE."

"But if we do that, Inspector seven will lose face."

"He will either have to lose face or put on weight. If you people in Hong Kong want to flood our stores with clothes, you're going to have to start thinking BIG."

Business Is Good

War and destruction in the Falklands and Lebanon may be bad for people, but it has certainly helped the arms business.

I went over to see "Madman" Rangell, who runs a weapons discount bazaar across the street from the Pentagon, and he was writing up orders like mad.

"Everyone used to want surface ships," he complained. "Now all they want is submarines. You can't

predict people's tastes. I've got a warehouse of frigates
I can't give away ever since the French missiles sank the
British ones."

"Who are your best customers now, Madman?" I asked.

"The Third World countries. They used to come in and
buy a few used tanks and maybe a broken-down artillery
piece. Now they want F-sixteen fighter jets, missile
launchers, radar-controlled antiaircraft guns. I don't know
where they get the money, but if it isn't top of the line,
they're not interested."

"They're probably spending more on defense than they
are on food, housing, and creating jobs in their countries."

"I don't ask questions. If their people can't eat it's not
my problem."

"Obviously you're not being hurt by the recession."

"You have to be kidding. Whoever heard of a recession
stopping arms sales? A general from a Third World country came in the other day; nice guy, beautifully dressed
in a new uniform; wanted a gross of heat-seeking missiles
that could shoot down F-five fighter planes.

"While he was waiting to have them packed, I showed
him our latest electrically controlled land mines. The guy
went nuts for them and ordered fifty gross. Then he asked
me if I had any howitzers. I took him in the back and
showed him a 1982 model and he was like a kid with a
new bicycle. He took two dozen."

"Where did he get the money to pay for the stuff?"

"He went across the street to the Pentagon and explained he wanted it to kick the hell out of the Soviets.
They wrote him out a check on the spot."

"You have a great location," I told Madman.

"The best in Washington. Now here's the funny part.
As soon as that general left, another general came in from
the Third World country that borders the first general's.
I told him what the other guy purchased and sold him an
entire system to fool the heat-seeking missiles the first
guy bought. Then I talked him into buying a thousand
mine detectors that could blow up the mines. I also sold

the second general a long artillery piece that could knock out the 1982 howitzer. It was an eighty-million-dollar order."

"You have a good business here," I told Madman.

"I make a living. The beauty of it is that no country considers itself safe anymore. The Reagan administration has cut down on economic aid to the Third World because you don't get a bang for it. But they're upping military aid to win the hearts and minds of their people."

An Israeli military attaché came in.

"I have sixty-five million dollars' worth of Syrian and PLO weapons in my pickup outside, and I was wondering if you want to buy them."

Madman Rangell went outside. "It's all junk. There's no market for this stuff. I'll give you two hundred fifty dollars on a trade-in, and that's just because I'm a nice guy. What do you want to buy?"

The attaché took out his list. "Forty planeloads of cluster bombs, ten thousand artillery shells, and six AWACs."

"Speak slower. I can't write it down that fast."

The attaché said he had some other errands and would pick up the order in the afternoon.

"What are you going to do with all the Syrian and PLO used goods you bought?" I asked him.

"I'll probably sell them to Bangladesh. I don't want them cluttering up my yard."

Letters from Jim Watt

Interior Secretary James Watt has been very busy lately drumming up support for Reagan's strip-mining and oil-drilling plans for America. In his now-famous letter to the Israeli ambassador to the United States, Watt warned that opposition to the administration's energy program by American Jewish liberals would weaken this nation's "ability to be a good friend of Israel."

While the White House disavowed the letter, even though it was written on Interior stationery, Watt defended it, and said he was not threatening anyone. He claimed he was appealing for support from every identifiable group in America—from "unions, the black community, Catholics, Protestants, Jews and Gentiles."

This means Watt's going to have to write an awful lot of letters to prove he doesn't just have it in for American Jewish liberals.

I can see him in his office right now.

"Miss Bloomsbury, take this letter to the Nigerian ambassador to the United States: . . . 'Dear Mr. Ambassador: As you know, the Reagan energy policy is very close to my heart as it is to the President's. Unfortunately there are many liberal blacks in this country who are opposing us. The conservative blacks are for us, but the others are making our life difficult. Therefore I must inform you that unless you can persuade American blacks to back our program, relations between the United States and Nigeria could go very badly. Please do not take this as a threat, but a fact of life.'

"Okay, who's next?"

"The Catholics. Do you want to write to the ambassador of Ireland, or Italy?"

"I think I'll send this directly to the pope. Start with 'Your Holiness: Forgive me for intruding on your time, but I believe that you should be aware that there are many Catholics in this country who are trying to preserve the environment and keep us from becoming self-sufficient in coal and oil. This administration will not stand by and allow any religious group to interfere with our energy policies. Relations with the Vatican, up until now, have been good. But the Catholic liberals in this country must be made to realize that when they don't support the President, they are making it impossible for him to support you.' I don't think that's too strong, do you?"

"No, sir. I think it's all right. Shall we write to the Protestants?"

"Send the same letter to Queen Elizabeth. If we mail it to the archbishop of Canterbury he'll throw it in the wastepaper basket. Does that take care of all the religious liberals?"

"I think so, unless you want to write to Khomeini."

"Let's skip that for a moment, and deal with the ethnic groups that have been opposing us. How about one to Indira Gandhi warning her if she doesn't get the liberal American Indians to stop opposing us, we'll cut off all food shipments to Bombay?"

A Barrel of Laughs

People are constantly asking me, "Who is the man with the most humor in the Reagan administration?" They are surprised when my response is "Cap" Weinberger, our secretary of defense. "Cap" says things with a straight face that make you want to roll on the floor.

Just the other day he told newspapermen he is for a "protracted nuclear war." He doesn't want one of these hair-trigger wars which last thirty or forty minutes. "Cap" said he has ordered everyone at the Pentagon to figure out not only how to keep a nuclear war going, but how to make sure the United States wins one when the missiles start flying.

Half the people in the Pentagon took "Cap" seriously. But those who knew what a deadpan comic "Cap" is just laughed and went back to doing the crossword puzzle.

The material for "Cap's" "prolonged nuclear war" came out of a routine he did when he first took charge of the Defense Department and came up with a comic version on "limited nuclear war."

He tried this one out in front of an armed services committee last year and had everyone in stitches. "Cap," without cracking a smile, said he thought a "limited nuclear war" with the Soviets was not only feasible, but essential so the United States would have time to fight a conventional war.

"Cap" said if we let the Russians know that we were only going to fight a "limited nuclear war" then they would agree not to use their big stuff to attack us.

The only ones who didn't laugh were our NATO allies, who figured out if a "limited nuclear war" was going to be waged, it would be on their turf, and even after Al Haig tried to explain to the Europeans that "Cap" was only joking, they still didn't find the secretary of defense's war routine very funny.

So "Cap" got his writers together and said, "I think my jokes are losing something in the translation. We're going to have to come up with a new monologue, and throw the 'limited nuclear war' stuff out."

One of the writers said, "I got it! What if you just stand up at the microphone and say you're no longer for a 'limited nuclear war,' but you've opted for a 'protracted' one instead? Say we're going to build offensive weapons that will make the United States prevail no matter what the Russians throw at us."

"That's pretty funny," "Cap" said. "Let's work on it. But keep it quiet or Johnny Carson will hear about it, and use it on his *Tonight* show first."

The writers all went to work and came up with some memorable lines.

One was, "You show me a secretary of defense who is not preparing to win a nuclear war, and I'll show you a secretary of defense who should be impeached."

Another one which was a real crowd pleaser: When he was asked if a nuclear war was winnable, "Cap" replied, again with a straight face, "I just don't have any idea; I don't know that anybody has any idea. But we're certainly going to give the armed forces everything they need to win one."

These are just a few samples of "Cap" Weinberger's humor. They may not sound as funny on paper, but when you see him standing up in front of the mike, looking like Woody Allen, delivering them, you could die laughing.

Copping a Plea

There is a lot of plea-bargaining going on in our courts these days. The prosecutors keep saying they have to deal with criminals to avoid expensive trials and also to get the little fish to testify against the big fish.

The only problem with the second argument is that so many little fish get off the hook to catch the big fish, that many times no one is caught.

This is how it works:

"All right, Trout, we know you blew off Barracuda's head in New Jersey, because he wasn't kicking back on the guns he sold to Libya. If you testify against Mackerel to the Grand Jury we'll drop your murder charge down to driving without a license."

Trout goes for the offer, and the prosecutors soon get a visit from Mackerel's attorneys. "If you let Mackerel off," his attorneys say, "on a vagrancy charge, he'll be the star witness against Sharkey, who is the biggest dope dealer south of Miami."

The Justice Department has been after Sharkey for years, so they say, "You've got a deal."

Sharkey is arrested on Mackerel's testimony and held on ten million dollars' bail.

After a week in the slammer, Sharkey tells a government attorney, "I was just a courier in the dope business. If you really want some big fish, lower my bail to five thousand dollars and I'll deliver whoever you want."

"Can you give us Bass?" the government attorney asks.

"I'll hand you his head on a platter."

The Justice people go to the judge and tell him Sharkey is a key witness in a case they're building against Bass and has to be bailed out.

Sure enough, two months later Justice has Bass nailed to the wall for running the largest white slavery business in America. But he's hiding in Brazil. He sends word that he's willing to come back and blow the whistle on Whale, the most notorious labor racketeer in the country, but only if they drop the felony charges, and prosecute him for spitting in the subway.

Justice says they can't make that kind of deal. But if Bass is willing to turn state's evidence they might reduce the hundred white slavery counts to one count of selling liquor to a minor.

Bass goes for it and lo and behold Whale has been arrested for the first time in his life.

Justice is preparing the prosecution when Whale drops a bomb on them. If they overlook the labor racket and extortion charges, Whale says he can implicate a United States congressman in a Brinks robbery.

The FBI checks out Whale's story and finds that it's true. They promise Whale if he testifies to everything he knows, they'll give him a new identity, a job, and a condominium in Palm Beach, Florida.

Whale starts singing and the United States congressman is a dead duck. So the congressman offers to testify against one of the "highest" officials in America, who has been getting regular payoffs from Fidel Castro.

The Justice Department lets the congressman plea-bargain his way down to "malicious parking," and start their case against the "high" government official.

But just before they're ready to go into court they get a visit from the CIA who tells them the high government official really works for them. They warn the Justice people that if the official is tried, the entire United States espionage effort against Cuba will be destroyed.

Justice drops the case, and with no big fish to fry, they go back to finding out if they can get a better deal from the courts for breaking up the telephone company.

The Human Comedy

The lady came in to see Senator Jesse Beenbag the other day. She was carrying a baby in her arms.

Beenbag immediately called in the Senate photographer to have his picture taken with it.

"It's mighty kind of you to stop by," the senator said, trying to usher her out of his office after the picture-taking.

"I didn't come to have my picture taken," the woman said.

"Then why did you come here?"

"You're leading the fight against abortion, and I thought you could help me with this unwanted baby."

"You mean you don't want this baby?"

"No, sir. I have five more at home and I can't afford to feed them. I figured since you are so interested in human life, you could tell me where I could get some help to raise this one."

"My interest in human life starts at conception and ends with the fetus. Once the baby is born, you're on your own."

"That's what I was afraid of. How come if the Reagan government is so concerned about preventing people from having abortions, they keep cutting back on all the services for unwanted children?"

"The government cannot afford to take care of children after they're born. We can't fund every screwball social program for unwanted children, or we'll never have a balanced budget."

"So what do I do with the child?"

"Madame, I have no idea what you should do with it. But if you think the antiabortion forces are going to support it from the cradle to the grave, you're sadly mistaken. The federal government has to get out of the child-rearing business."

"Since you're so concerned about the value of human life, why don't you take the kid?"

"What would I do with a child?"

"That's a question I keep asking myself."

"Have you gone to the local child services office?"

"They closed it because the government cut off all their funds. The local charities have no money, and all the food programs are going out of business."

"Then get a job," Beenbag said impatiently.

"I'm trying to. But even if I found one I couldn't afford the day-care center. I decided to come to you as a last resort because of your interest in a baby's right to life."

"You came to the wrong person," Beenbag said angrily. "My bill makes it a federal crime *not* to have a baby. But it doesn't provide continuing services for people who have one. Why is your kid crying?"

"I guess he's hungry," the lady said. "Unwanted children cry a lot."

"You're not going to change my stand on abortions just because your baby is crying," Beenbag warned. "Were you sent here by the Planned Parenthood people?"

"No. It was my idea. I saw you on television a while back saying it was a mortal sin for a pregnant woman to abort, so I had my baby. Since you were so adamant on the subject I thought you or President Reagan might have some ideas as to what I do now."

"Madame, I'm a very busy person. I'm trying to get prayers back in school, protect the tobacco industry, and fight the handgun control lobby. I don't have time to worry about your child's welfare."

The lady put the baby on Beenbag's desk.

"What are you doing?" Beenbag screamed.

"I'm changing his diaper. You don't have a large handkerchief to spare, do you?"

"Get out of my office, and take that bawling kid with you," Beenbag said.

"If you support the right to life," the lady said, "you have to support right-to-life functions."

"But he just did it all over the President's letter of support for my bill," Beenbag cried.

The lady smiled, and said, "Naughty boy."

Smart Bombs and Dumb Kids

According to Barbara Bush, the vice-president's wife, the United States is having an illiteracy epidemic. In the 1950s we ranked eighteenth among the United Nations in literacy. Now this country ranks forty-ninth. It is estimated that there are sixty million people in this country who are considered illiterate or functionally illiterate.

This poses a major problem for this country's future, and I broached it with someone in the administration.

"What are we going to do if we have a nation of dummies, and you people keep cutting back on education in the federal budget?"

"We have to make some hard choices," he said. "We

can either afford smart weapons and dumb kids, or dumb weapons and smart kids."

"But how can a dumb kid fire a smart weapon?"

"Because they're built so anybody can fire them."

"Isn't a nation's security based on the brains of its people?"

"It used to be. But now with the new hi-tech computers it's not that essential. As long as you have a few good programmers you don't need a lot of people with college degrees."

"How can a super power rate forty-ninth in literacy and still maintain its position in the world?"

"It's not easy," he admitted, "but so far we've managed to do it. Naturally we'd like more of our citizens to be able to read and write. On the other hand, if you have to cut federal programs it's easier to do it in education than it is in defense."

"It doesn't make any sense. What is the country going to do with sixty million illiterate people?"

"We're going to have to make an effort to improve the school systems and upgrade the salaries of our teachers."

"How do you do that if the government won't provide the necessary funds to pay them?"

"We start by allowing voluntary prayers in school."

"How would that improve the school system in the country?"

"It would give children an opportunity to pray for a better education. Teachers could pray for better pay. And school supervisors could pray for better teachers."

"So the administration believes praying is the solution to the country's illiteracy epidemic?"

"It's not the whole solution, but it would certainly go a long way to solve the problem. Do you remember when the Soviets sent up Sputnik and everyone in this country suddenly felt that our schools had let us down? We prayed that we could come up with a space program that would put the Russians to shame, and when we landed men on the moon, our prayers were answered."

"We also put a lot of our money into education at the same time," I reminded him.

"Those were the days when we could afford prayers and butter. Now we can only afford prayers, and that's why the President is working so hard for the school prayer amendment."

"There are some people who say the school prayer amendment is just a smoke screen to make parents forget their kids aren't learning how to read and write."

"They're wrong. You don't solve illiteracy problems by just throwing money at them. Once we put God back into the schools, we're going to see a tremendous improvement in the education of our children, and it won't cost the taxpayers a dime."

"I'll pray you're right," I said. "Because if you're not, the next generation of Americans will turn out to be a bunch of real dumbbells."

"We know we're right. A nation under God is the only kind that can afford to cut its education budget to ribbons."

Moscow Hot Line

Good news from Moscow! The Soviet Telephone Company, according to news reports, now has a twenty-four-hour working number where you can call for counseling and psychiatric advice. The phones are manned by professional personnel from the National Center for the Study and Prevention of Extreme Conditions.

What kind of calls are coming through? Here's my best guess:

"This is the Moscow Confidential Telephone. I am listening."

"I want to leave the Soviet Union. The police say I'm crazy."

"Why do you want to leave the motherland?"

"Because my father went to California, and he said it was a much better place to live, and he wants me to join him."

"Do you always do what your father tells you?"

"Not always. But this time I think he has a pretty good idea."

"You shouldn't make big decisions when you're depressed."

"I'm only depressed because they won't give me an exit visa to go to California. I don't want to spend another winter in Moscow."

"You can't solve your personal problems by moving some place else. You will only take them with you."

"That's what you think, boychik. Just get me on a plane to California and I won't have a problem in the world."

"You're not in any condition to talk about getting on a plane. Come to the institute tomorrow and we'll talk about it some more."

"That's what the police told me."

"Listen to them. They know more than your father."

"Hello, is this the Confidential Telephone?"

"You sound angry."

"I am angry. How come the people in the USSR don't have enough to eat?"

"You think we don't have enough to eat?"

"I know we don't have enough to eat. Have you been to the market this week?"

"Do you always get angry when you don't have enough to eat?"

"No, sometimes I do a dance and sing the 'Volga Boatman.' Why shouldn't I get angry when I don't have enough to eat?"

"Anger is dangerous if you don't know how to channel it. Who are you angry at?"

"The stupid officials in the government who don't know how to feed the people."

"You shouldn't get angry at them."

"Then who should I get angry at?"

"You can get angry at me."

"Why should I get angry at you? You don't have anything to do with collective farm planning, do you?"

"No. But on the other hand, I don't have the authority to send you away to Siberia for twenty years either."

"This is your Confidential Telephone. Do you have a problem?"

"No, I'm as happy as can be. I have a two-room apartment I share with four other families, my son was captured in Afghanistan, I work two shifts at the steel factory, but only get paid for one, and my daughter has just been thrown out of the university for reading a book by Boris Pasternak. I've never been more content in my life."

"So why did you call?"

"Don't I sound nuts to you?"

"No. You sound as if you're going through a midlife crisis. It happens to anyone when he thinks he's achieved the Soviet dream."

Unnecessary Roughness

"Negative Political Ad Agency, may I help you?"

"This is Chaps Dunbar. I'm running for senator this November and I was calling to inquire about your negative political ad campaigns."

"Just a minute. You want to speak to Mr. Slinger."

"Slinger, my campaign seems to be in a little bit of trouble and I was hoping your people could come up with a few dirty TV commercials to help me get well in the polls again. I was very impressed with the one I saw the other night for Bill Damadun, in which you filmed an actor who looked like his opponent, Horace Lager, pushing an old lady down the stairs in her wheelchair and a voice said, 'That is Horace Lager's answer to Social Security.'"

"Yes. We're very proud of that one ourselves. We had to use six old ladies before we got it right. Thank God for Medicare or we would have gone over budget. Do you know we had more protests on it than any negative commercial we've ever done? But our surveys indicate that eighty-seven percent of the people now believe Lager pushes old ladies down the stairs."

"What can you do for me?"

"Give me a little background on your opponent."

"He's a former congressman named Flap who has been traveling around the state promising the people jobs, prosperity, and an honest government—the usual stuff. Trouble is, he looks like a young Jimmy Stewart and the people think he can do it."

"You got any dirt on him we can use in a TV commercial?"

"He played left tackle at college, and was once penalized fifteen yards for unnecessary roughness."

"What else?"

"We couldn't find too much stuff on him after that."

"Okay, we'll take the testimonial approach. We won't show Flap in your commercials. But we'll show people who support him."

"What's so dirty about that?"

"We'll get a clip of Fidel Castro ranting and raving and waving his hands. Then underneath we'll run subtitles of what he's supposed to be saying—something like, 'If Americans elect Congressman Flap to the Senate, you will make me the happiest dictator in the world.'"

"That seems pretty negative. I'll tell you what's a big issue here—crime in the streets."

"We can hang that one on Flap. We'll show a guy being mugged in the park, and then we'll show a clip of Flap smiling and shaking hands with workers as they leave the gate of a factory. Our announcer will intone, 'Congressman Flap cares more about freeing criminals than he does about protecting the victims of crime.'"

"I don't get it."

"Most factories look like prisons, and nobody will know the people he is shaking hands with aren't inmates."

"That is about as dirty as you can get," Chaps chuckled.

Slinger said, "Did you see the mean one we ran last week, in which we used the ex-wife of Dick Tanquery, who is running for Congress, and she said into the camera, 'I lived with him for twenty years, now you people can live with him for two'?"

"I loved it. Particularly when she showed the bruises on her arms. You people are real experts when it comes to slinging mud."

"Any candidate who thinks he can win an election these days by being affirmative is crazy."

"How much do you charge?"

"Our standard sixty-second smear is fifteen thousand dollars. If you want us to film a look-alike of your opponent sticking up a Brinks truck, or running over a dog, it will be five grand extra."

"I'm willing to spend the extra money. No one will ever say when Chaps Dunbar ran for office he didn't go first class."

Takeover Lane

It isn't easy to explain what happened in the bloody takeover battle involving four giant conglomerates, Bendix, Martin Marietta, United Technologies, and Allied Corporation.

One fine day some time ago, Charlie Bendix, flush with cash, was taking a stroll down Takeover Lane, when he stopped in front of Marty Marietta's house.

"Nice house you got there," Charlie said to Marty, who was mowing his lawn. "How much you want for it?"

Marty said, "Buzz off, Charlie. My house is not for sale."

"I happen to know your relatives would sell it in a minute if the price was right. If you won't turn it over to me in a friendly manner, I'll make them an offer they can't refuse."

"Oh yeah, wise guy?" Marty said. "If you try to buy my house, I'll buy your house. How do you like that?"

Charlie laughed at him because he knew Marty didn't have the money to buy the Bendix house.

The next day Charlie ran an ad in the newspaper saying

he would pay twice as much for Marty's house as it was worth.

Marty ran an ad the following morning saying he would buy out anyone who had an interest in Charlie's house.

The price on both houses went soaring, and Charlie and Marty had to go to the banks to borrow large sums of money to try to purchase each other's homes.

Charlie had done a lot of homework, and he knew in a real estate war he could outlast Marty.

His information was correct, up to a point.

Marty had a pal named Hugh Nighted, who loved to dabble in real estate, and anything else that caught his eye. Marty went to Hugh and said, "Charlie Bendix is trying to buy my house and to defend myself I'm trying to buy his house. Right now he's got me against the wall because I don't have enough money to swing my end of the deal."

"Tell you what I'll do," Hugh said. "I'll buy Charlie's house with you. All I want is the kitchen, one bathroom and the living room. You can have the basement and the upper floor. We'll split the dining room between us."

Marty was relieved because with Hugh's backing he now had a chance to save his own house.

When it was announced that Hugh Nighted was behind Marty, Charlie Bendix should have backed out of the deal. But Charlie was a proud man and he didn't want everyone in the neighborhood saying he didn't know how to buy another guy's house. So Charlie upped the ante again for Marty's place, and before long both Marty's and Charlie's homes had the most inflated real estate prices ever seen on Takeover Lane.

For a while it looked as if Charlie would wind up owning Marty's house and Marty would wind up owning Charlie's house at ten times what each had paid for them.

At this point, an acquaintance of Charlie's, named Al Eyed, came to Bendix and said, "I want to buy your house."

"So do Marty Marietta and Hugh Nighted," Charlie said.

"The only difference," Al said, "is if I buy it, I'll let you live in it for a while. If those guys buy it they'll kick your tail out in the gutter."

Charlie Bendix was in tears. "All I tried to do was buy Marty's house, and now I have to sell mine. Is that fair?"

"It's dog eat dog on Takeover Lane. If it will make you feel any better, Marty almost went broke trying to stop you from buying his home. He'll be in debt for ten years. Well, do you and I have a deal?"

"What choice do I have?"

"None. So just sign here. By the way, what are you going to tell your wife?" Al asked.

"I don't have to tell her anything," Charlie replied. "It was her idea in the first place."

A Great Sport

I hadn't been on a golf course since I was a kid. The reason was that in my youth I was a caddy, and after carrying around heavy bags filled with irons and woods every weekend, I vowed when I grew up I would never step on a fairway again.

But the other day, a friend named Riley, who plays every week, persuaded me to go out with him. "You'll love it," he said. "It's great exercise and the most relaxing sport in the world."

"I'll go along with you," I said, "but I won't play."

So the next morning we showed up at the golf course.

"The first thing we have to do," Riley said, "is rent an electric golf cart."

"Why do we need a golf cart?"

"Because they won't let you play here on the weekend unless you drive around the course. If people walk they slow up the game."

"But if you drive around the eighteen holes, how do you get any exercise?"

"Looking for your ball. They permit you to get out of the cart to look for it. But they don't want you to look too long because the people behind you will get sore."

"How long do they let you look for your ball?"

"Three minutes."

"That long?"

"It gives you just enough time to stretch your legs, but at the same time, it doesn't tire you out. Here come the other three guys we're playing with." I was introduced to Hal, Chris, and George. They each had their own golf cart.

"Why do you each need a golf cart?" I asked.

"We like to race one another up and down the hills," Hal said. "And besides, if you have your own golf cart you can block the view of your ball and kick it to a better lie."

Chris said, "Sometimes if one of the other players gets a real good shot and you can get to his ball first, you can run over it, so he can't find it."

"Frankly," said George, "I find golf cart racing is far more fun than playing the game. It gives the average guy a chance to drive like Evel Knievel."

The foursome teed off and then we all got into our carts and raced to our respective balls. Since I wasn't playing. Riley let me drive his vehicle. "Park as close to the ball as possible," he told me, "so that I don't have to walk."

Riley hit his second shot into a sand trap and started cursing. "I knew I should have used a seven iron instead of a five."

"Relax, Riley," I told him. "It's only a game."

It took him three shots to get out of the sand trap, two to get on the green, and three to putt into the hole.

He slammed the bag with his putter, as Hal, Chris, and George laughed at him.

"I don't care which one you hit," Riley muttered, "but I want you to ram one of their golf carts."

"But we could hurt somebody seriously."

"So?"

"Look, Riley, I haven't been on a course in many years and I just remembered why. Golf is the most frustrating game in the world. I've never seen anyone on a course who had fun while he was playing."

"Shut up and drive," he said.

The next seventeen holes went about the same way, with all the players cussing and gritting their teeth after they hit the ball. But for the most part, we just kept driving from one shot to another. I figured that if you counted how many steps they took to measure their ball to the flag, each player had actually walked the equivalent of two city blocks for the entire eighteen holes. The rest of the exercise came from carrying their golf bags from their cars to the locker room.

I'm not trying to put down golf because I know millions of people play it. Actually it's a great contact sport. It's like auto racing, and it takes a heck of a lot more skill than driving the bumper cars on the Boardwalk at Atlantic City.

Filling the Tubes

A bunch of sports executives at Zenith Network were sitting around the conference table trying to come up with some programming to replace the NFL football games. It was the eighth week of the strike and they had tried everything from lacrosse to ladies' mud wrestling, but for some reason they just couldn't attract the audiences to warrant the $250,000 a minute they were charging for the time.

"I think I've got it," said Dexter. "The Girls' Latin School of Boston is playing Our Lady of Victory's field hockey team on Sunday. It's a grudge match that goes back fifty years. With proper promos I think we could get people to tune in."

"Who knows anything about women's field hockey?"

"I'll bet you Howard does. Let's call him in."

Five minutes later: "Howard, we're thinking of putting on the Girls' Latin–Our Lady of Victory field hockey match this Sunday, to keep the crowd that likes pro football. Could you handle the color?"

Howard smirked. "That is a silly question. Girls' Latin in Boston has a lifetime record of three hundred forty-five wins against one hundred sixty-five losses. Under the famed, but very underrated Mary McGrory, they had four undefeated years, a record that has never been surpassed in the New England Regional Conference. Regrettably, and I must be candid about it, the team has not been living up to the high expectations we all had for it at the beginning of the year.

"Nikki Harris, probably one of the most astute and skilled field hockey coaches since Carry 'The Stick' Renfrew, who led Katherine Gibbs to a ten-and-oh record in 1924, told me that the locker-room problems earlier this year between Roz Rogers and Hilda Marton had been sorted out, and she believed the team was up for an Our Lady of Victory defeat.

"Which brings me to a story about Francie Barnard. Francie, as you know, had been offered a scholarship to Georgetown Visitation, and Dumbarton Oaks. Her mother had played for Visitation in 1956 and made All-American. But Francie had developed a knee injury on a skateboard and doctors had told her she would never play field hockey again. She went to an orthopedic specialist named Alice McKelvie, who put in an artificial knee. Alice McKelvie was a friend of Nikki Harris and told her Francie could play. Nikki arranged for a full scholarship for Francie and that is why Francie is now playing for Girls' Latin instead of Georgetown Visitation."

"Thanks, Howard, you seem to know your field hockey."

"Our Lady of Victory had its greatest years under Sister Mary Therese Botticelli, between 1941 and 1953. Sister Mary used to smash a player's wrist with a hockey stick every time the player hit the ball. In 1965 Victory's Mother Superior, Dorothy Tubridy, decided to de-emphasize field hockey after Eunice Shriver bought her daughter Maria a Mustang convertible for scoring three goals against Madeira.

"Fortunately, the alumnae rebelled, as field hockey was the only reason most parents sent their daughters to Our Lady of Victory, and now they are back in the big time. If I may interject a personal note, I remember that afternoon on October sixth, 1971, when Mary Healy in the classic contest with Potomac Normal..."

"That's enough, Howard, you've convinced us."

"Well are you going to go with the Girls' Latin game next week or not?" Howard asked.

"Either that or a horseshoe-pitching match between the Flatbush Odd Fellows Home and the Sun City Bulldogs."

"I'll never forget watching the Flatbush Odd Fellows defeat the Calgary Nursing Home in an overtime, in that memorable series in Anchorage, Alaska, on January fourth, 1947. Flatbush had a one-armed thrower named Skippy Danziger, and Skippy had left his favorite horseshoe on the train. So he saw this Canadian Mounted Policeman and he—"

"Okay, Howard, we'll get back to you as soon as we make our decision."

"I'm sorry, gentlemen, but I have to tell it the way it is."

Splat!

"Did you hear the good news?" Colt, a handgun-loving friend of mine, asked.

"What's that?"

"They now have ammunition that can penetrate any lightweight bulletproof vest. It's called the KTW and it's coated with Teflon."

"Fantastic," I said. "That's the same stuff the vests are made of."

"That's right. An ammunition company figured out if a Teflon vest was strong enough to stop an ordinary bullet, then a Teflon-coated bullet could penetrate one."

"You have to hand it to the person who thought up that one. He must be a genius. Wait a minute. Don't law enforcement officers and public officials wear Teflon vests to protect themselves? Won't they be endangered by the KTW?"

"Of course not. The KTW costs a dollar-fifty a round, and the price is much too high for your run-of-the-mill trigger man. Besides, it's only sold by better gun dealers."

"The police can't be too happy about the KTW."

"They aren't, but you can't just stop selling ammunition because it can penetrate soft body armor."

"Why not?"

Colt said angrily, "Because when you start talking about armor-piercing ammunition you're getting yourself into a very complex and subjective area. There is no simple dividing line between bullets that will go through Teflon vests and those that will go through a deer, an antelope, or an elk. If you ban something like the KTW, you have to also ban other ammunition that is used for hunting and target practice."

"Who would try to ban a bullet that could go through a policeman's vest?" I asked.

"Congressman Mario Biaggi of New York, for one. He has proposed a bill that would ban all soft armor-piercing ammunition."

"What does he hope to gain by that?"

"Who knows? But it's bottled up in committee, and I doubt if the NRA will let it get out. Even the Justice Department thinks it's a lousy bill."

"What's their objection?"

"There are a lot of other kinds of handgun bullets that can go through a Teflon vest, and they feel the Biaggi bill is so broad it would hurt the sale of them as well."

"Maybe instead of worrying about ammunition, Congress should concentrate on developing a safer garment for policemen to wear," I suggested.

"That's the way we feel about it. It's the responsibility of the bulletproof vest people to keep up with the times. The KTW is alive and well and you don't solve the problems by banning it, just because it can splat through Teflon."

"I imagine the handgun-control nuts are supporting Biaggi."

"Of course they are. They figure if they can ban bullets that kill policemen, they'll eventually be able to ban all ammunition used in handguns."

"But that would hurt the law-abiding people who use armor-piercing bullets for sport and target shooting."

"That's why we're making such a big issue of it. Let me read you this letter from Wayne Lapierre, the NRA lobbyist, which was sent to all congressmen. 'The most clear and present danger to law enforcement and public officials is not the presence of one type of bullet. Rather it is from the unwarranted and irresponsible publicity surrounding this or other means of defeating soft body armor.'"

"That says it all," I told Colt. "It's the media and not the KTW which is threatening the lives of our policemen. Biaggi would be doing a much better service to the country if he proposed a bill forbidding the press from talking about ammunition that can blast through Teflon. By the way, why would somebody want to buy a KTW bullet in the first place?"

"Because," Colt said. "It's there."

The Hazards of EPA

"Environmental Protection Agency. May I help you?"

"Yes, somebody is pouring toxic sludge in my back yard."

"I'll connect you with Mr. Digging in our mudslide division."

"I don't want to talk about mudslides, I want to talk about toxic substances."

"We've combined toxic wastes, mudslides and killer ants in one department, as an economy measure. Mr. Digging is on the line."

"Digging, I want you to know that someone is dumping toxic sludge in my back yard."

"So?"

"So what is the Environmental Protection Agency going to do about it?"

"How much waste is being dumped?"

"Three truckloads and the driver says he's going back for more."

"Well, it has to be dumped *somewhere*."

"I thought your job was to see that the citizen was protected against the dumping of toxic substances in residential areas."

"It is. Where do you live?"

"In North Carolina."

"Did you call the Denver office to lodge a complaint?"

"Why should I call Denver?"

"It handles all poison waste complaints for North Carolina. At least it did until we shut it down for economic reasons."

"Then what good would it have done for me to call Denver?"

"You would have gotten a telephone recording referring you to one of our other regional offices."

"Well, since I've got you on the phone and Denver is closed, where do I call?"

"Let me see. St. Paul, Minnesota, is closed; Portland, Oregon, is closed; Albuquerque is closed. Here's one that is still open—in Baton Rouge, Louisiana."

"Give me their number."

"You'll waste a call. They only deal in waivers for dirty coal furnaces."

"What do you people do in Washington?"

"We're involved in getting the government off people's backs. We weigh the price of environmental protection against the price to industry and then decide, cost-wise, whether we should enforce the regulations or not."

"I thought you were mandated to protect the environmental health of the country."

"We are, but we have priorities."

"What kind of priorities?"

"The Clean Water Act, for onc. We've lowered the pollution levels permitted by communities that discharge sewage into lakes and streams by fifty percent. This will save the taxpayers over two billion dollars, at no hazard to the people."

"Who says so?"

"Our new studies indicate water will absorb a lot more pollutants than scientists originally believed."

"What about acid rain?"

"The jury is still out on acid rain. There are rumors it stunts trees and kills wildlife, but we only have the word of people who live in the Midwest, Northeast, and Canada for that. We're not going to go on a fishing expedition just because the water in Maine tastes like shaving lotion."

"Okay, let's get back to my problem. What are you going to do about the toxic waste they're dumping in my back yard?"

"Have you thought about selling your house?"

"Yeah, but who is going to buy it with poison all over it?"

"If you don't report it to the EPA, who will ever know?"

The DeLoreans Are Selling

I went into a DeLorean sports car showroom the other day. The place was jammed with eager buyers.

I finally got the attention of a sales manager, who was deliriously happy. "They said our car wouldn't sell. Now you have to wait in line to get one."

"How do you explain the sudden surge of interest in the DeLorean?" I asked him.

"We changed our advertising campaign. Mr. De-Lorean's been on television every night, and now that they have seen him, people know they can trust him to make a good car."

"It's true," I admitted. "I wouldn't have thought of visiting a DeLorean showroom myself until I saw him on the evening news."

"Mr. DeLorean's a natural salesman," the manager said. "Did you like the commercial where he handcuffed himself to the steering wheel of his car and said, 'If I can drive a DeLorean with one hand, so can you'?"

"That was a good one. I also enjoyed the one on the Dan Rather show where his lawyer said, 'When you buy a DeLorean product you'll go on a trip you'll never forget.'"

"How about the one where DeLorean is walking down the halls of the LA County Courthouse with his hands behind his back and he says to reporters, 'I'd give five million dollars to be driving a DeLorean to Brazil right now'?"

"I didn't see it," I admitted. "But the advertising cam-

paign must be working or you wouldn't have all these
people in the showroom today. By the way, how much
is a DeLorean?"

"You want our price or the street price?"

"What's the difference?"

"Our Silver Spoon model is twenty-five thousand dollars. But when you cut it up and put it on the street, a
pure DeLorean package could go for as much as twenty-
four million dollars."

"I didn't realize there was such a mark-up in sports
cars. Could I see one?"

"Sure. This one comes with snow-white tires. They're
imported from Colombia, South America."

"They're gorgeous."

"Let me show you the trunk space. You can put five
valises or two hundred twenty kilos of anything you want
in here."

"That's a big haul."

"Would you like to sniff the carburetor?" he asked me.

"Why not?" I said.

He opened up the back hood and I sniffed.

"Not that way, stupid," he said. "Hold one nostril and
sniff with the other. Then you'll get the full power of it."

I did what he told me and started giggling.

"Sit inside and put your head back on the seat and
relax," he said. "Have you ever felt better?"

"It's like being on cloud nine," I told him. "They don't
make cars like this in Detroit any more."

"I'll tell you a secret," he said. "The government is
very interested in this car. The Drug Enforcement Administration has offered to go into partnership with
DeLorean."

"You've got to be kidding! Why would the DEA want
to go into the automobile business?"

"Because the DEA knows a good business investment
when they see one. They've been meeting with DeLorean
secretly in hotel rooms all around the country discussing
the deal. If it goes through, DeLorean will be flying high."

"I can't believe the DEA is interested in bailing DeLorean out of his financial troubles."

"If the government did it for Chrysler, why shouldn't they do it for DeLorean?"

"Suppose the DEA financing deal falls through?" I asked.

The manager shrugged his shoulders. "Then I guess DeLorean will have to take a powder."

Our Election Endorsements

It is now time for this column to endorse certain political candidates for public office. We have studied all the issues and arrived at our conclusions by comparing not only who our choices are running against, but also how they stack up to what we've got already.

For United States Senator—Plato Syracuse. We support Plato because he was the only political candidate this year who did not have his picture taken with an unemployed automobile worker. When this was pointed out by his opponent in their final debate, Syracuse defended himself by saying, "I couldn't do anything to get the man his job back, and he knew it and I knew it, so why use up a lot of my time for a lousy two minutes on the evening news?"

For Congress—Walter Rosebud. Our reason for choosing Rosebud over his opponent is that Rosebud, although a multimillionaire, refused to use a cent of his own money to finance his election. He was quoted on *Meet the Press* as saying, "I worked hard for my fortune, and I have no intention of blowing it on an election when I can get thirteen percent on tax-exempt municipal bonds. If the special-interest political action committees don't want to buy my vote, then I don't think I want the job."

For governor—Hayden Dunkerman. This was a tough choice because Dunkerman's opponent has a much prettier wife. But Dunkerman has two more children than his rival. Dunkerman also was an all-state running back in college, while his opponent, because of a bad knee, wouldn't go out for the team. Dunkerman's other qualification for making a better governor is that, in his state, which has a twenty-percent Hispanic population, his whole family professes to be crazy about Mexican food.

For lieutenant governor—Ramsay Wilder gets our nod. Wilder disagrees with almost every stand Hayden Dunkerman has taken. Therefore, since neither one of them could work with the other, it's unlikely that Dunkerman would dare leave the state during his four years in office. Although Wilder has no executive experience, we still endorse him because a lieutenant governor doesn't need any for this nothing job.

For state attorney general—Dallas Reisling would probably make a better attorney general than Arnie Burchett. He has been more forthright in answering the tough questions posed to him by the media. Last week in a televised debate with WTWIT's hard-hitting Reg Smiley as moderator, Dallas was asked where he stood on the death penalty and he replied, "It's none of your damn business." Smiley's follow-up question on how Dallas would deal with white-collar crime brought this answer: "I didn't come here to discuss my personal life." Smiley then tried to pin Dallas down on what stand he would take on prayer in public schools. Dallas replied, "I have made it a rule never to talk about the Constitution when appearing on television."

For making Smiley look like a fool, we have to endorse Reisling over Arnie Burchett, whose makeup on the show made him look terrible.

For mayor—the incumbent, Charles Bledsoe, has done

a good job and deserves another term. The fact that he gave the garbage contract for the city to his brother-in-law and received a free trip to Tokyo from the company that sold the city two hundred buses that have been recalled for faulty brakes does not detract from our opinion that Bledsoe is probably one of the most popular machine mayors the city has ever had. We endorse Bledsoe because he is beholden to no one, thanks to a blind trust fund in the Bahamas set up by his close friends in the school contracting business.

For City Council president—Sarah Evans gets our overwhelming endorsement, because she's a woman.

As for the various propositions on the ballot: We favor all the odd-numbered ones and are against the even ones, with the exception of Proposition 82, which reads, "The people of this state believe that in the event of a nuclear attack, no alternate parking will be permitted at ground zero."

Part Seven

100 NEEDIEST FAMILIES

100 Neediest Families

Under the title "100 Neediest Families," we are asking everyone who can possibly do it to take in one MX missile this Christmas. A cruel and unyielding House of Representatives has made MX missiles homeless during the holiday season. Originally they were supposed to be sheltered in a dense pack twenty miles long and a mile wide near Cheyenne, Wyoming, in concrete silos. But the plan was vetoed and now the MX missile has no place to go.

The MX missile will not give you any trouble if you take it into your home. You can put it in your attic and just visit it once a day to see if it needs any fuel or water. It has ten nuclear warheads on it, but you don't have to touch them, because they've already been targeted for someplace in the Soviet Union.

You might ask, "Why should I take an MX missile into my home?"

The reason is that the MX is a deterrent against first-strike aggression, and President Reagan says we need it as a chip in the nuclear arms talks in Geneva. Those of us who are blessed with so much should show the MX missile family that they are not alone during the happiest season of the year. How can anyone in this country enjoy the Christmas holidays when they are aware that there are hundreds of missiles who have no place to celebrate, and no one to turn to on what should be a festive occasion?

We took an MX into our home last week. At first there was apprehension in the family. My wife asked nervously,

"Suppose it goes off while we're having Christmas dinner?"

I assured her the missile would not go off unless someone in the White House pushed a button.

"I'll feel uncomfortable having a stranger in the attic," she protested.

"It may be a stranger when it first arrives, but before long it will be part of the family. You'll learn to love it. Besides, how can you enjoy your Christmas when you know there is an MX missile with tiny nuclear warheads to feed somewhere out there in the cold?"

The kids were very excited when I told them we were taking in an MX for Christmas.

"Can we play with it?" my son wanted to know.

"No, it's not a toy. It's the real thing."

"Does it have a joy stick on it?" my daughter asked.

"I'm not sure," I told her. "But even if it does, I don't think you should fool with it until I read the instructions."

"How do we get one?"

"I'm going to call the United States Air Force now," I said.

I placed a call to the Pentagon and told a colonel, "We'd like to take in an MX missile for Christmas, as we understand you have many who do not have homes."

"Bless you," the colonel said. "We've had a hard time placing them during the holidays. We were afraid we'd have to keep them on the base. We'll have one delivered to your house tomorrow morning."

The next morning a two-ton Air Force truck arrived and the service personnel gingerly carried our MX guest up to the attic and positioned it so it would be aimed towards Europe.

"We'll come back for it after the holidays," the colonel said, "as we still haven't tested it. If you know anyone else who wants one for Christmas just give us a call."

I assured him I would.

After they were gone we all went up into the attic.

My daughter put a quilt on it because she was afraid

it would get cold. My other daughter petted its nose. My son put warm milk next to it "in case the ten nuclear warheads got hungry." My wife got into the spirit of things and decorated its fins with holly leaves.

The MX didn't respond in any way and seemed to be contentedly sleeping.

My daughter asked me, "Do MX missiles dream?"

"I'm sure they do," I told her. "I wouldn't be surprised if at this very moment it was dreaming of blowing up Leningrad."

We all tiptoed quietly downstairs filled with the spirit of peace and good cheer. By taking in a homeless MX missile during this holiday season we all had learned the true lesson of what Christmas is really about.

The Woman Behind the Woman

Behind every liberated woman, there is another woman who has to do the dirty work for her.

I discovered this talking to Lila Peabody. Lila works for a law firm from nine to five, or six, or seven, depending on what case she is involved in.

Lila told me she couldn't do it if it wasn't for Juanita.

"Who is Juanita?" I wanted to know.

"Juanita takes care of the house and the children, and cooks our meals. I couldn't work if it weren't for her, and the fact the Safeway stays open until nine."

"You pay her?"

"Of course I pay her," Lila said. "Half my salary goes to Juanita."

"You mean your husband doesn't contribute to her wages?"

"No. He insists if I want to work I have to pay somebody to do the things I had to give up when I took my job."

"That doesn't seem fair. I should think he would be proud of you for being a lawyer and making it in a man's world."

"He is, as long as there is somebody at home. Frankly, I think he's more proud of Juanita. She always knows where his shirts are."

"I didn't know there was such a high price for women's liberation."

"There is if you're married and have to keep a house. For every liberated woman you see in an office, there is another woman behind her providing the support system for the marriage. If the woman is divorced and has children it's even more costly, because no ex-husband is going to pay for his wife and also the woman who has to take care of his kids."

"But at least you're a person in your own right," I said.

"I am as long as Juanita doesn't quit. It isn't easy to find someone who will be housekeeper and take care of the kids, and wait until you get home at night. I've been through three Juanitas in two years. One came from El Salvador, another from Ecuador, and this one is from Bolivia."

"Your Spanish must be very good by now."

"It's perfect, but frankly we're all getting a little tired of fried beans."

"It seems ironic that in order to be free, a woman must find another woman to replace her."

"There's no choice. A husband is willing to go along with a liberated wife as long as things are running smoothly at home. But one breakdown in the support system and then he starts screaming he didn't marry a woman who would ignore her house and children."

"But every magazine you read in the supermarket features husbands of working wives sharing the household duties."

"The magazines are the only place you see them. The American male is prepared to accept that his wife should be free to do her own thing, as long as everything else is done as well. When we go to parties, my husband introduces me proudly to everyone as 'my wife the lawyer.' When we get home at night, he wants to know why there are no clean sheets on the bed."

"It's funny," I said. "Until I talked to you, I thought every liberated woman had it made. I always saw you as someone who had the best of both worlds. Now it turns out that without Juanita mopping floors, you wouldn't be liberated at all."

"You've got the picture," Lila said. "Any married woman who wants to be liberated better have a good pal in a Latin American employment agency."

"What happens when your support system gets sick?"

"I stay home and everyone in the law firm says, 'We knew this would happen if we hired a *woman* lawyer.'"

Gas Lighting the Consumer

The price of natural gas will go up between twenty and forty percent this winter for the consumer. There is a very good reason for this. But for the life of me I couldn't find out what it was.

I first went to my local gas company, and talked to a very friendly man who anticipated the question.

"It's not our fault," he said. "We just buy the gas from the wholesaler and have to pay whatever he wants to charge us. If he raises his price we have to pass it on to the customer. If you want to know why the price has gone up, talk to the people who sell us the gas." He gave me a free book titled *Cooking With Gas* and showed me to the door.

I went to see a vice-president of a wholesale gas company in Houston. "How come the price of gas is going up so much this winter?"

"I'm glad you asked that question. We buy our gas from producers, and now with deregulation they can charge us any price they want to, so we have to pass their costs on to the local gas companies we supply. We don't enjoy raising our prices because everyone thinks we're making a lot of money, which we're not."

"There seem to be an awful lot of Mercedes-Benzes out in the parking lot."

"They belong to the people in the gas pipeline end of the business. Perhaps you ought to talk to them."

"Where do I find them?"

"I believe they're somewhere on this floor. Wait a minute, I'll call my brother Fred. I think he's in charge of our pipeline division. Or perhaps my brother George is. In any case they both drive Mercedeses."

George was out buying a new Lear jet for his son's birthday so I got to talk to Fred.

"You can't blame the pipeline people for this winter's big increase," Fred told me. "All we do is ship the stuff for a modest fee which we base on the cost of gas. If the tariff goes up then the shipping costs have to go up, too. It takes a lot of energy to get gas from Texas to Virginia, and somebody has to foot the bill. If you want to know who is jacking up the price, go out and talk to the producers at the wells. They're the guys who know what is going on in the natural gas market."

I borrowed Fred's Mercedes and drove out to the Casa del Bunkum Oil and Gas Corral.

Bunkum invited me for a horseback ride. There were wells everywhere on his fifty-thousand-acre spread.

"You seem to have a lot of gas," I remarked.

"Too damn much gas," he said. "It makes the whole ranch stink."

"How come, if you have so much, the price is going up this winter? I would think you'd have to sell it cheaper."

"That's true if you want to sell old gas. But nobody's going to sell old gas when he can get a much better price for new gas. I've shut down all my old gas wells until the government will allow me to sell it for the same price as I can get for new gas. Someday Washington will phase out all gas regulations and I might sell my old gas. But for the moment, it's going to stay in the ground until I can make a fair profit with it."

"Then in your opinion it is not the gas producers, but government regulations that are driving up the price this winter?"

"Damn right. We barely can feed our families on what we're getting for the stuff now."

I flew back to Washington to talk to the people at the Department of Energy in hopes they could tell me why gas was going to cost the consumer so much more this year.

The man they turned me over to said, "You came to the wrong place. We don't concern ourselves with the price of gas. The faster the government gets out of the gas regulation business the better it will be for all of us."

"I'm sure of that, but aren't you concerned that a lot of people might freeze this winter when the price goes soaring?"

"That's not our department's job. If they have any complaints they should take them up with their local gas company."

The High Price of Politics

One of the richest men I know is Tarbaum. Therefore I was surprised to see him handing the clerk in the supermarket food stamps last Wednesday.

"What happened, Tarbaum?" I asked.

"I lost the election for the school board last week."

"I know that, but why are you on food stamps?"

"I spent six million dollars of my own money. I got wiped out."

"I don't believe it. Why would you spend six million dollars to be elected to the school board?"

"I didn't intend to. When I decided to run the most I was going to spend was four million dollars. But I didn't realize it would turn into such a dirty campaign. My opponent took the low road. He said I thought the Head Start program was a claiming race at the Laurel Race Track. I had no choice but to buy television time and say he believed remedial English was what Prince Andrew did on shore leave."

"I saw that commercial. It was quite effective."

"It should have been. It cost me a half a million bucks. When I started the race, the polls had me leading by fourteen points. I hired one of the best professional campaign directors in the country. He told me the only way to win a school board election was to promise to do away with the football team and put more money into textbooks. I bought time on all four TV stations to announce my plan, and the next day my opponent was leading me by twenty-six points."

"So you had to play catch-up," I said.

"It cost me two million dollars to deny I had said it."

"Did you ever think of bowing out of the race when it started costing you so much money?"

"Yes. But my wife wouldn't hear of it. She had invited all our friends and people who worked in my campaign to a victory party at our estate, and she said she'd be humiliated with the caterer if she had to cancel it. Besides, I found I loved campaigning and shaking hands with people, and handing out bumper stickers to strangers. Once politics gets in your blood you don't think about what it's going to cost you."

"So you just kept plowing ahead?"

"I fired my campaign manager and brought in two guys from New York who worked on Mayor Koch's campaign for governor. We redid all our television commercials and started with a fresh conservative slant. In the first TV spot, I promised if I was elected to the school board I would fire twenty percent of the teachers to balance the budget. The Teachers Political Action Committee sent in a half million dollars to defeat me. They plastered the town with billboards saying I was trying to buy the election."

"That must have hurt."

"Not as much as my second commercial when I reversed myself and said if I was elected I would hire twenty percent *more* teachers, and raise their salaries to the national level."

"So that took the teachers off your back?"

Yes, but it brought in the Political Action Committee Against Paying Teachers a Living Wage, and they decided to get me for caving in to the union."

"When was that?"

"I think it was about the time I had to sell my house to stay in the race."

"You sold your house?"

"And the boat and the car and my wife's diamond

engagement ring. You know I only lost by fifteen hundred votes."

"I saw the results election night. I'm sorry you didn't make it, Tarbaum. You certainly put your money where your mouth was. At least six million dollars of it."

"Oh, well, as we say in politics, easy come, easy go."

Love Boat USA

"This is your captain speaking. Welcome to *Love Boat USA*. We're going to have a wonderful trip because my crew has navigated a sure-fire course to get us out of these heavy seas."

"Permission to come on the bridge, sir."

"Permission granted, Stockman."

"Sir, we're in much deeper water than I predicted."

"Stay the course."

"When we set sail my calculations indicated that we would be short fifty billion gallons of fuel. But now because the ship is hardly moving, we could be short one hundred and eighty-five billion gallons."

"Let's give every passenger another fare cut. That should get the ship moving again."

"We have to find some way of getting more fuel. Giving everyone a fare cut now won't do it."

"Why don't we lay off more of the crew?"

"We've cut the crew to the bone. There won't be much savings there."

"Then cut down on benefits for the passengers."

"Yes, sir. All the passengers?"

"Of course not. Just those in tourist class. We don't

want to deprive the first-class passengers of anything they need. If the first-class passengers are happy, it will eventually trickle down to the tourist class."

"Chief Regan wants to speak to you, sir."

"What is it, Regan?"

"Bad news from the boiler room. We're running out of steam and the engines are only operating at half their capacity."

"Stay the course, Regan."

"Yes, sir, but if we can't produce steam we're going to have to use up even more fuel than we anticipated."

"Don't worry. When my fare cut goes into effect, we'll have all the steam we want."

"Captain, this is Officer Schweiker on C Deck. A lot of steerage passengers are seasick. Many of them are falling over the side."

"Put up some more safety nets."

"I don't have any safety nets. You ordered them thrown overboard to lighten the ship's load."

"Well, then, the passengers are going to have to stay in the water until we get things straightened out on the bridge."

"They're drowning, sir."

"My heart goes out to them, but stay the course."

"Captain, damage control says we're taking bilge in the cargo holds and the Gross National Product barometer is dropping fast."

"Tell them to reduce the prime interest rate valves."

"They have, sir, but the bilge won't stop. They want to know if you could turn the ship twenty degrees until they can pump out the water."

"I'm not interested in quick fixes to save a leaking boat. Stay the course."

"Chief Gunnery Officer Weinberger requests to speak to the captain."

"Of course, Caspar. What's up?"

"I'm going to have to put more sixteen-inch guns front and aft, sir, and I want laser-controlled depth charges and torpedoes on deck, and I must install MX missiles on the stern."

"I don't see any problem with that. Go ahead. Why are you sulking, Stockman?"

"Sir, if we put all that military hardware on deck in these heavy seas, we'll be short over two hundred and twenty billion gallons of fuel."

"As captain I have no intention of cutting back on the security of my ship. If Caspar says he needs all that stuff, then that's good enough for me."

"Captain, look at those waves! I think we're rolling into a depression."

"Keep your voice down, Dole, you'll scare the passengers. Stay the course."

Dooley Lives

The secret is out. Social Security is in a lot of trouble. The politicians will tell you that the system is going broke because: (a) the Cost of Living Indexing is too high, (b) the work force is not contributing enough money to pay for the retired, (c) the payout for people is three times what they and their companies put in, (d) all of the above.

But no one will dare mention the real reason. I found it out by talking to a man who said he was eighty-three years old.

"You don't look it," I told him.

"I am. And that's what is killing Social Security," he chuckled. "When Roosevelt started the thing in the thirties he expected me to die when I hit sixty-seven. That's what the whole damn program was based on. People were supposed to die a few years after they collected their money. Now we're all hanging around in our seventies and eighties and the government doesn't know what to do about us."

"I don't believe anyone wants you to die before your time," I said. "America reveres its old people."

"They do and they don't," he said. "They're not about to kill us, but at the same time, they're getting pretty darned mad they have to pay for us for being alive."

"Well, it is a burden on the working class," I admitted.

"Somebody should have thought of that when they started the system. The smart-alecks in the New Deal drew up these fancy graphs and said, 'If Dooley, that's my name, dies at sixty-seven and Mrs. Dooley dies at seventy, we should have enough in the pot to take care of them.' Well, Mrs. Dooley and I are doing quite well, thank you, and now the pot is empty."

"I guess they're going to have to come up with dire measures to replenish the pot."

"They haven't come up with any good ones yet. The thinking behind Social Security was they wanted us to all get out of the work force by sixty-five to open up the job market for the young folks. If they change it and say you can't collect Social Security until you're seventy, that means the younger folks are going to get furious because they can't have our jobs. If the politicians cut back on our benefits they've got a tiger by the tail because the senior citizens' vote is the most powerful in the country. And if they raise Social Security taxes for the people who are now working, nobody is going to be able to go out and buy the things that are supposed to get us out of the recession. You don't have to be an Alan Greenspan to figure that out."

"What's the solution?"

"There ain't one, son. That's what I keep telling you. The longer we live the worse it's going to be for everybody. Every time the medical profession finds a cure for a disease there is someone over in the Social Security Fund hitting his head against his computer."

"But we're a rich country. Surely we can take care of our old people in their September years."

"It isn't September, son, it's our December years. We're two months farther down the road than their actuarial tables. Look, don't think I'm cold-hearted about the problem. Mrs. Dooley and I were talking it over the other night and I said, 'Mama, do you want to die to save the Social Security system?' And she said, 'Not on your life! Do you?' And I said, 'Nope. I'm just hitting my prime.'"

"I think you both made the right decision," I said.

"We didn't have too many choices. But I'll tell you something, son. When that trust fund goes bust there are going to be a lot of people in this country who aren't going to look kindly on us for hanging around."

"As far as I'm concerned, you and Mrs. Dooley can live as long as you want to."

"That's mighty kind of you to say that, son. Well, I guess I better start my daily walk. My doctor says it adds years to your life."

"Where do you walk?"

"Past the White House, the Capitol, and the Social Security Building. Every time they see me strutting by it drives them up the wall."

On Her Majesty's Service

Well, they sent Geoffrey Arthur Prime to the cooler the other day for thirty years. Prime, if you don't keep up on British spies, was the chap who worked in the ultra-top-secret communications system in Cheltenham, and gave top secrets away to the Soviets for fourteen years. He blew the West's satellite operation, the one where we could listen in on every telephone call in the USSR.

The question arises, why are the British so slow to find out who their spies are?

I think I accidentally discovered the reason the other night when I watched the TV show *Smiley's People* starring Alec Guinness based on the book by John le Carré.

George Smiley is brought out of retirement to find out why the KGB's top man Karla has sent his daughter to a Swiss sanitarium. If they can prove Karla violated his KGB oath, by diddling with KGB funds, they can get Karla to come over to the West and make him tell every dirty little secret the KGB has. So much for the plot.

While watching it I suddenly got the clue as to why the British counterespionage people are so slow in getting their mole.

It appears that Her Majesty's Secret Service cannot deal with any problem without first offering the person they're talking to either a cup of tea or a drink.

"George, it's so good to see you again. How is Anne?"

"She's fine."

"Would you care for a cup of tea, George?"

"Thank you very much."

"Leggins, get George a cup of tea."

"I wanted to ask you a question. Why did Karla send Kirvosky to Paris?"

"Right, George. Do you take milk?"

"No milk, thank you."

"Of course not. You never did take it with milk. Let's see, Kirvosky. It seems he had a dustup many years ago with Kaminsky. One lump or two, George?"

"One lump will be fine, thank you."

"Only one lump of sugar for George, Leggins."

"Yessir. When I was a student at the Academy, Mr. Smiley always took one lump."

"Righto, Leggins. Most of the people in the Circus took two. But George always preferred to go it alone, and take one lump."

"About Kaminsky. You were saying?"

"Yes, Kaminsky and Kirvosky were once good friends. Is it too strong, George? Leggins tends to be very sparish with the hot water."

"It's quite good, as a matter of fact."

"There is nothing like a spot of tea when you're putting all the pieces of the puzzle together, is there, George?"

"I imagine not. You were saying Kaminsky and Kirvosky had a falling out. Do you know what it was about?"

"Something happened a long time ago between them. I don't want to get personal, George. But does Anne still make a good cup of tea?"

"I wouldn't know."

"Sorry to hear that, George. We all liked Anne."

"I was aware of that. Anne made tea for everybody but me. Can we get back to Kirvosky?"

"Of course. Kirvosky showed up in Paris some time ago as Karla's special boy. Kaminsky recognized him and told the head of the Free Estonian League. Another cup, George?"

"No, thank you. I think I'll be running along."

"Always happy to help. Let's have a drink next week. You're a Scotch man, aren't you, George?"

"Yes, no ice."

Well, that's how it went on the telly, and I can only assume that's how it went in real life when they were trying to find out who was blowing all the satellite secrets to the Soviets. It took the British fourteen years to catch up with Prime. And that, no matter how you add it up, takes in a lot of cups of tea.

Andropov's Honeymoon

"What do you plan to do about Yuri Andropov?" I asked a Soviet correspondent in Washington.

"We always give a new leader of the Soviet Union a honeymoon for six months before the press goes after him," he said. "The Soviet people don't want us to be too cruel at the beginning. After all, he won an overwhelming mandate and he should be given a chance," he said.

"We do the same thing in this country," I said.

"But if Andropov doesn't fulfill his campaign promises, then the power of the Soviet media will turn against him."

"I didn't know you could do that in your country."

"We certainly can and we will. Our readers expect us to keep our Soviet leaders honest. The function of our press and television is to tell the truth about our politicians no matter what position they hold in government."

"Do you think the fact that Andropov was head of the KGB might hurt his image with the people?"

"No. You people elected a former actor as your president, and it had no effect on Reagan's image."

"But an actor is not the same as a KGB director."

"It is in the Soviet Union. Our people revere the KGB. Anyone who rises to the top is in touch with *all* the people. He can identify with the workers, and the peasants, and the people trying to scratch out a living in the cold Siberian wastes. He knows about crime, and he has dealt with subversive elements in neighboring states. The KGB is much better training ground than Warner Brothers."

"Will the social life in Moscow pick up with Andropov in the Kremlin?"

"It always does when you get a new leader. Mrs. Andropov is now working with her decorator to change the living quarters, as she's very unhappy with what Mrs. Brezhnev did. She has ordered new china for state dinners. She believes the Kremlin belongs to all the Soviet people and she wants them to be proud of it. She's also ordered new clothes because she feels that the Russians pay close attention to what the first lady of the secretary of the Communist party wears."

"Style has always meant a lot to the Soviets," I said.

"It's good newspaper copy. But as far as we newspapermen are concerned it's what Andropov does that counts. He inherited a stagnant economy from Brezhnev and he was elected because he promised to lower the inflation rate, balance the budget, keep unemployment down, and restore confidence in the ruble. If he can do all this before he dies he could go down as one of the greatest Soviet leaders in history. But if his economic plan doesn't work we'll be as tough on him as we were on Brezhnev."

"Do you think he can do it?"

"He's a great communicator, thanks to his days in the KGB. And he has a lot of goodwill going for him. The people want change, but he's going to have to work closely with the leaders of the Presidium to get his programs through."

"I guess he'll have to throw a few bones to the right wing of the Communist party since they did so much work in his election," I said.

"He will. Andropov feels very strongly about prayers in school."

"Who would the schoolchildren pray to?"

"Marx and Lenin. Who else is there?"

"So we can't look for anything critical in the Soviet press about Andropov for at least six months."

"That's just about as long as the honeymoon will last. Then the Kremlin's correspondents will get bored and we'll start telling it as it is."

"At which point Andropov will say you people are distorting everything he is trying to do to save the country."

"We're used to that in the Soviet Union. When the honeymoon is over every Soviet leader thinks the press is giving him a raw deal. But all Andropov can do is send us to a Gulag for twenty years, and you know as well as I do, the Soviet public would never stand for that."

Telling the Truth

The Pentagon is seriously considering the use of lie detectors to test the veracity of its three million employees, as well as defense contractors and government workers in other departments. They say they want to use the polygraph tests for security reasons.

I have no objection to Defense resorting to lie detector tests provided that the top people take them, too, particularly when testifying on the Hill concerning the military budget.

It doesn't seem too much to ask Secretary Weinberger, his top assistants, and the high-level brass to put on electrodes when they face a House or Senate Armed Services

Committee. With the help of this equipment, all of us might be better informed as to what a weapons system will really cost.

"The congressional committee will come to order. General, are you comfortable? Let's just test the polygraph machine to see if it is working. What branch of the service are you in, sir?"

"Nothing can stop the United States Air Force."

"The lie detector checks out fine. We'll now proceed with the questioning. Could you give us some idea what the B-one bomber will cost?"

"Two hundred million dollars."

"Hmmm, the polygraph seems to indicate that is the wrong answer."

"I'm sorry, sir. I didn't understand the question. Do you mean with wings and wheels on it?"

"I'm afraid I wasn't specific. Yes, I do."

"To get it in the air it will cost $234,567,891.50."

"Good. Now this would only be the bare plane and not include such items as radar, communications, bomb racks, cruise missile launcher, and parking lights?"

"That's correct, sir. We might add on another forty million dollars for the equipment, give or take five million."

"The polygraph is acting up again, General. How much did you say?"

"Sixty-five million dollars."

"Very good, General. Now may I ask you about the tests the Air Force has made on the B-one? Are your people satisfied that the contractor will bring in the plane at that price without serious overruns?"

"We're certain of it, sir. They should deliver it on schedule without any bugs in it."

"The needle seems to be flying all over the place. Are you sure of this?"

"No, sir. We're not. But we need the plane."

"We're going to give you the plane, General. We just want to know what we're getting for our money."

"Every plane has bugs in it."

"Don't pout. We know that. Which brings us to the question of the C-five-A cargo plane. We understand a lot of cracks are showing up in the wings. How much will it cost to put on new wings?"

"Half a billion dollars."

"Would you like to try that again?"

"I meant to say a billion dollars. These electrodes are giving me a headache."

"We're sorry about that, General. But actually the idea for introducing the lie detector came out of the Defense Department. Since you people have been using it so successfully we decided to use it, too."

"We're only using it to find out who the whistle-blowers are in the department, and who is leaking detrimental stuff to the press. We would never use it on someone discussing the Defense Department budget."

"Why not, General?"

"Because when it comes to military spending testimony, we consider ourselves officers and gentlemen."

Cannibalism in Hi-Tech

Hi-tech industry, particularly computers, is recommended for people who are looking for a profession. For the moment, the computer industry is supposed to be recession-proof. Well, up to a point.

I heard this story about one of the largest computer companies in America:

"Dr. Frankenstein, I want to congratulate you on your new software program which makes it possible for a robot to do the work of one hundred human beings in one-half the time."

"It was nothing. The key was to get a computer to interface with the robot so they talk the same language. Once the robot was programmed to only respond to SAMPSON it learned to discriminate not only colors, but sizes, shapes, and verbal orders. One executive sitting in his home in Greenwich, Connecticut, with our 'Artichoke five-three-six' can now give orders to every SAMPSON-programmed robot in the Western World."

"We're aware of that and we're proud of your work. It has turned out to be better than anything we dreamed of."

"Have you sold the system already?"

"No, we've been using it in our own company first, to make sure there aren't any bugs in it."

"And?"

"You're fired, Frankenstein."

"I'm fired?"

"Yes, the system you perfected made it possible for us to lay off three thousand employees and still increase productivity by forty percent."

"But it was my idea. How can you fire the person who thought up the idea?"

"The SAMPSON robot has made it possible to eliminate your entire research and development department, which was a big financial drain on the company. We can now instruct the robot to do the same work you were doing at a hundredth of the cost.

"It has perfected a new merchandising program, which will eliminate ninety percent of our sales force, and it's already figured out how to cut our taxes and phone bills by seventy percent. Dr. Frankenstein, you created a work of art, and we plan to give you full credit in our next stockholders' report."

"That's great, but I still need a job."

"You should have thought of that when you started

developing the SAMPSON robot. Surely you knew that this labor-saving system would eliminate the need for people."

"I was thinking of other companies we could sell it to; not our own."

"We would be crazy not to use it ourselves. Our first responsibility is to cut labor costs as low as we possibly can. When you put a human being on the payroll, you not only have to add in his salary, but also his Social Security, medical benefits, pension, vacation, and coffee breaks. A robot can be depreciated over three years, and then it works for us for nothing."

"Well, if you feel that way about it, I'll go to another company and make a better SAMPSON than you have."

"I wouldn't do that if I were you. According to SAMPSON, which is now doing our law work, if you go to another firm and work on the same research you will be guilty of giving away trade secrets and our robot advises us to sue you."

"But you're taking my livelihood away from me."

"We're not taking it away from you. The robot you invented is doing that. If you were as smart as you think you are you wouldn't have programmed it to do research and development. Once you scientists take on a problem, you never think of the consequences of your successes."

"Well, if I can't work in R and D give me a job doing something else. I have only two more years before I get my pension. I'll work in the mail room."

"All right. I'll ask SAMPSON, on my computer."

"What did it respond?"

"He said he doesn't need some dopey person to get in the way. He can sort the mail alone."

Defensive Medicine

One of the reasons medical costs are soaring, according to a physician I know, is that doctors are now practicing "defensive medicine."

"The reason for 'defensive medicine' is that for every doctor practicing in this country, there are now two lawyers waiting to sue him for malpractice," said my friend, Dr. Ginseng.

"How do you practice defensive medicine?" I asked.

The M.D. said, "Suppose you come to see me with swollen tonsils. The first thing I would do is order an X ray of your stomach."

"Because?"

"In case I want to take your tonsils out I must make sure I'm not sued for giving you ulcers."

"That's only good medical practice."

"Then I have to order blood tests to protect myself in case you had malaria or yellow fever."

"Are swollen tonsils an indication of malaria or yellow fever?"

"It's highly unlikely, but your lawyers could always find a doctor who will say they are. After the blood tests I might order a brain scan."

"A brain scan?"

"Just a precaution in case you tried to claim that after I took out your tonsils you lost your memory. Of course, I would also have to give you an EKG and a stress test, so they couldn't get me for causing any heart damage."

"Swollen tonsils aren't what they used to be," I said.

"Neither are malpractice insurance rates. I now have to pay twenty-five thousand dollars a year to my insurance company before I can pick up a tongue depressor."

"So now after all the tests I'm ready to have my tonsils taken out?"

"I should say not. I still have to check out your liver, your thyroid gland, and I'd want pictures of your spine for my files."

"My spine?"

"That's what defensive medicine is all about. A doctor must be ready to prove that he checked out every part of your body before he dealt with the one that was giving you trouble. Suppose you had back trouble before I removed your tonsils. Six months later you could claim you got it on the operating table when I was working on your throat.

"If I can show the jury that you had back trouble *before* the operation, I'd have a better than fifty-fifty chance of not paying any damages."

"What else would you have to do to protect yourself?"

"After all the tests, I would make you sign a paper saying that you agreed to my decision to remove your tonsils. Of course, I would prefer you get a second opinion from another doctor, because that would bolster my defense that you had to have them out."

"Suppose I didn't want to pay for a second opinion."

"Then I would make you sign a second paper attesting to that fact, in case you denied it in court. It's only your word against mine."

"Okay, I've signed all the papers. Now will you take my tonsils out?"

"My insurance company would prefer I talk to another member of the immediate family. Many times the patient is willing to go along with the operation, but the rest of the family prefers to sue. After all, it isn't their tonsils that are swollen."

"I'm sure my wife isn't that type. If you say my tonsils have to go, she'll go along with your decision."

"I'd rather have it from her in writing."

"Let's say she gives you the green light. When can you take my tonsils out?"

"As soon as the anesthesiologist completes *his* tests."

"You mean he has to give me tests as well?"

"Certainly. My malpractice insurance just covers me. The anesthesiologist carries his own policy, and it's much more expensive than mine."

Certifying Human Rights

According to the law, the President of the United States has to certify to Congress that a country accused of violating human rights has made significant progress in ending abuses before the United States government can give it aid. This has presented some problems for Mr. Reagan, particularly where it concerns countries in Latin and Central America such as Chile, Argentina, El Salvador, and Guatemala, to name just a few.

One cannot be sure how Mr. Reagan knows if there has been progress made in the human rights area, because the President only has the word of the leaders of these countries that atrocities against the citizens are being kept to a minimum. My guess is that before White House certification is sent up to the Hill, this is what happens.

The State Department puts in a telephone call to the United States ambassador to the country to which Mr. Reagan has promised military aid.

The man in Washington says, "Mr. Ambassador, how's the human rights situation in your country?"

"Much improved. Last year the junta was holding one

hundred thousand political prisoners, but they've emptied out the prisons and as far as our intelligence people can find out, there are only ninety-five thousand hard-core criminals left."

"The President will be pleased to hear that. Do you see any signs of torture down there?"

"Wait a minute, I'll look out of my window.... No, it seems all quiet on the streets. No one is torturing anybody, at least not from my view. Do you want me to look on the other side of the embassy?"

"That won't be necessary. As long as you can't see anything from your window, that's good enough for me."

"Of course, they could be torturing at the local police stations, but I don't have the staff to go around checking every precinct in the country."

"The President wouldn't want you to. What does the opposition party say about the human rights situation in the country?"

"Come to think of it, I haven't seen any leaders of the opposition in three months. They all seem to have disappeared."

"Have you inquired as to their whereabouts?"

"I did ask one of the colonels the other night at a reception about them, and he said they were holding a party caucus on an island off the shark-infested seashore."

"So to your knowledge the opposition in the country is alive and well?"

"The colonel assured me they were in the best of health, and they all wanted to be remembered to the President."

"Good. What about the man in the street? Does he seem happier than he was a year ago?"

'I can't speak for everybody, but the ones guarding my embassy seem to be very happy. I spoke to one the other day and he said the army never had it so good."

"Could you give me a progress report on land reform?"

"It seems to be moving along. There was a photograph in the newspaper yesterday on the front page showing a peasant receiving a land grant from the president himself."

"Send us a copy of the paper. Now what about free speech? Can the people criticize the government without fear of being arrested?"

"Of course. We had a fellow in here the other day who ripped the regime to ribbons."

"What was he doing in the embassy?"

"He was asking for political asylum."

"All right. Let's move along. As you are aware, the President has to send Congress a certification that the human rights in your country have progressed to the point where he can resume military aid to the government in power. In your opinion can he truthfully do so?"

"Wait a minute, I'll take another look out the window."

The Battleships Are Back

President Reagan recommissioned the battleship *New Jersey* not long ago, and there wasn't a happier man in Washington than a ninety-one-year-old retired admiral I know.

"Didn't I tell you the battleship would come back, son?" he said at the Army-Navy Club.

"You told me every day," I replied.

The admiral was slapping his thighs and chortling. "Well, this is going to give them carrier fellows something to think about. They said we were finished, and they almost put us out of business. But you need a President like Ronald Reagan to know a dreadnought when he sees one. The flyboys and submariners can talk all they want about a 'modern Navy,' but it's the old values of a battlewagon that this country still longs for."

"I hope it will close the 'window of vulnerability' with the Russians. It cost us three hundred and sixty-five million dollars just to get it out of mothballs," I said.

"It's a bargain, son. You couldn't build a Navy tugboat for that now. By golly, when they de-mothball the *Iowa* next, we'll have the two greatest fighting ships in the world. When you put your feet on the deck of a battle-wagon, you know you're standing on a ship."

"You know more about it than I do, but it seems to me a battleship is outdated, compared to missiles and bombers and nuclear submarines."

"That's because you've never sailed on one. A battleship has something no carrier or submarine can provide—and that's firepower. You can sit twenty-six miles out at sea and lob in sixteen-inch shells on Soviet gun emplacements all day long, and the Russians can't do a damn thing about it. Take my word for it, the *New Jersey* is just the kind of ship to make the Commies yell 'Uncle.'"

"What worries me about a battleship is that it takes so many officers and sailors to crew one. The Navy is short of personnel now, and if you have to put fifteen hundred men on one ship, you're taking an awful lot of trained personnel away from other ships," I said.

"That's the kind of bilge the flyboys have been handing out for years. The reason they don't like battleships is that you can't sink one."

"I thought they sank quite a few of them in World War Two."

"Right, and we learned from that experience. Now we know where to put our heavy armor and how to protect our fuel tanks. It would take a nuclear torpedo to sink a ship like the *New Jersey* in the next war."

"So?"

"They're not going to fire nuclear weapons at a battleship because the *New Jersey* has nuclear weapons on board that can fire back."

"Are you trying to tell me they de-mothballed the *New Jersey* as *another* deterrent?"

"You're darned tootin'. That, and the fact that when we sail a battlewagon into a Third World power's harbor, they know we mean business. There's nothing that beats showing the flag on a battleship to scare the hell out of a small hostile country."

The admiral bought drinks for everyone at the bar. "Son, this is a great day for the Navy. When Reagan recommissioned the *New Jersey*, he not only sent a message to the Soviets, he also sent one to the naval Air Force that their days were numbered. I never thought I'd live to see the day that Pentagon chiefs would come to their senses."

"I'm happy for you, skipper," I said. "You battleship advocates have been fighting a losing war with Navy planners for years and now you have finally been vindicated."

"The reason is we never lost faith. We knew that as long as there was one battlewagon in mothballs, we had a chance of making a comeback. I think the President said it best when he called the *New Jersey* one of the most important cost-efficient additions to the United States fleet. And he's been in enough war movies to know what he's talking about."

The Worst TV Commercial

If there was a prize for the worst TV commercials, the Prudential Life Insurance Company would have to be a contender. In the past, Prudential simply asked you to "buy a piece of the Rock"—the rock being the "Rock of Gibraltar," which has been a symbol for as long as I can remember of a very solid institution.

But, lately, either because the Rock of Gibraltar isn't as strong as it used to be, or someone decided just owning a "piece of the Rock" wasn't selling enough life insurance policies, Prudential is using hard sell in its commercials by scaring the wits out of people.

They have two men dressed completely in white picking up people off the streets and taking them away on an escalator, presumably to heaven.

I probably wouldn't object if they took away people whose time had come, but the advertising people at Prudential have their two "agents" snatching people in the prime of their lives.

The other night I was watching one of the bowl games and during a time out, the two white-suited men picked a meter maid who was writing out a traffic ticket. She couldn't have been more than thirty, and seemed in the best of health.

One of the men, as I recall, had a clipboard and apparently the meter maid's name was on it. They gently escorted her away from the car, and in the next scene she was riding on the escalator above studio-made clouds, happy as a lark that her time had come.

The idea had obviously been stolen from the movie *Heaven Can Wait*. I believe that what I objected to most of all was that the meter maid did not protest when these two strangers came along and dragged her away. She seemed quite content riding on the escalator.

It was not only in bad taste, but smacked of false advertising. I have known many meter maids in my time, and I've yet to run into one who would be taken in by two wacky guys in white suits who told her to stop writing parking tickets and come with them. Meter maids have heard every story in the book.

The first thing the meter maid would say to the two guys is, "Is this your car?"

The men would deny it and then she would say, "Well then, don't bother me when I'm writing out a ticket."

"We're sorry, you have to come with us."

"In a pig's eye I'm coming with you. I have twelve more cars to ticket on this block."

"Your name is on the list and you have to go now."

"What list is that?"

"The Prudential Insurance list. It was made up by our advertising agency."

"You have to be joking. My policy is with Metropolitan Life. Now beat it before I give you both tickets for loitering around an expired parking meter."

"You have to come immediately. Our TV commercial goes on in a minute."

"I've heard some nutty stories in my time, but this one takes the cake. Now buzz off before I dump mud on your pretty white suits."

"But you're dead."

"The person who didn't put two quarters in this meter is dead. And if he doesn't come back in fifteen minutes, I'm going to call the tow truck."

"You'll never get to heaven if you don't come with us now."

"Where are you weirdos parked?"

"Our escalator is over there."

"I might have known it. You're right in front of a fire hydrant. That will cost you each twenty-five dollars."

Part Eight

GOODBYE, MA

GOODBYE, MA

Goodbye, Ma

One of the saddest things Americans will have to face in 1983 is the demise of "Ma" Bell, who, at the urging of the Justice Department, is going out of the telephone business and into "computers" and esoteric communications. From now on, each one of us will be at the mercy of his or her local telephone company.

I've always been very sentimentally attached to the old gal so I went over last week to say goodbye.

"We're going to miss you, Ma," I told her as she was packing some cable and silicon chips in her suitcase.

"I'm going to miss every last one of you," she said. "You were all my children and we shared many good times and bad times together."

"It doesn't seem right to break you up," I said bitterly. "You were the best telephone system in the whole wide world. I never told anyone this before, but you were the only monopoly I ever loved."

"I did the best I could," she said, wiping away a tear. "Some people did call me a monopoly, but I was a benevolent one. I had to make a profit for the widows and orphans who owned my stock. But I also made it possible for almost everyone in this country to own a telephone. I soaked the rich on long-distance calls, so I could subsidize the poor who wanted to make local ones."

"You were the last American monopoly who had a heart."

"My only desire in life," she said, "was to reach out and touch someone."

I handed her a Kleenex.

"When something went wrong with your phone," she sobbed, "I sent one of my people out there right away to fix it and I never charged you."

"And when we got lucky you always let us keep the change we found in the coin box at a pay phone."

"The girls I trained to be operators were the friendliest women in America. And I respected people's privacy. If you didn't want to be in the phone book, I always found you an unlisted number."

"You let our fingers do the walking in the Yellow Pages."

"I tried to make life a little easier for everybody."

"Tell me, Ma, of all the innovations you thought up during the years, which one were you the proudest of?"

"The collect telephone call. I made it possible for generations of children to keep in touch with their parents. I doubt without the collect call if some parents would have ever heard from their kids again."

"Only a mother would have thought of the collect telephone call," I said.

She put a Princess phone and a Touch-Tone dialer in her suitcase.

"The Justice Department never did like me. They've been out to get me for years. Well, at least I wired up the country before they won their case."

"If it hadn't been for you there wouldn't be telephone poles strung across this nation from sea to shining sea."

"Could you use an old switchboard?" she asked me.

"I'd like that. It would remind me of the wonderful times we had together."

"Well, I guess I'm all packed," she said. "It was nice of you to stop in and say goodbye. Most people forget."

"I'll never forget you. Every time the phone rings I'll say to myself, 'Ask not for whom the bell tolls. It tolls for Ma.'"

Tears began to well up in her eyes.

"I suppose now that I've been broken up, you'll never call me anymore."

"Of course I'll call you, Ma."

"When?"

"Friday."

"Mrs. Estrin's son Melvyn calls her every day."

Social Security Sweepstakes

There is one solution to the Social Security bankruptcy problem that has not been suggested yet, and that is that the government might hold a sweepstakes for eligible senior citizens. The Department of Human Resources could hire one of the professional sweepstakes companies to write and mail out brown envelopes to everyone on the Social Security rolls.

The letter would read:

Dear MRS. DALTON: Do not throw away this letter. You may have won one of 300 prizes adding up to $1,000,000 in the 1983 SOCIAL SECURITY SWEEPSTAKES. Yes, that's what I said, ONE MILLION DOLLARS in prizes offered to you absolutely free by the SOCIAL SECURITY CLEARING-HOUSE. All you have to do, MRS. DALTON, is return the enclosed coupon with your LUCKY number on it and you will be eligible for our MILLION-DOLLAR SWEEPSTAKES.

Just think, MRS. DALTON, if your number is picked on March fifteenth, you could win $250 A MONTH FOR THE REST OF YOUR LIFE. You may be holding the WINNING ticket in your hand right now. But if you don't send it back right away, you could be the sorriest senior citizen in America.

I know what you're saying. No one wins in a SWEEP-STAKES. But MR. CARLOS SEGURA, aged seventy, of Long Beach, California, won $50,000, MISS KITTY SOAMES of St. Louis, aged eighty-three, won $75,000, and MR. AND MRS. JASON MARKS of Sun City, Arizona, will receive Social Security checks for the next twenty years worth (are you ready for this?) over $100,000.

If they can win, MRS. DALTON, there is no reason why you can't join this illustrious list of people who took the time to send in their coupons.

Not only will you be eligible for the GRAND PRIZE of $250 A MONTH FOR THE REST OF YOUR LIFE, but you will also have a chance for other SUPER PRIZES in this once-in-a-lifetime SOCIAL SECURITY SUPER-SWEEPSTAKES DRAWING.

Listen to some of these other GRAND prizes.

A MONTH'S STAY in a PRIVATE room in the hospital of your choice, ALL MEDICAL EXPENSES PAID or $60,000 in CASH.

FOOD STAMPS FOR FIVE YEARS worth $20,000.

FREE HEATING FOR ONE YEAR worth $5,000.

A TWELVE-MONTH VACATION IN A NURSING HOME WITH YOUR OWN ROCKER WORTH $30,000.

PLUS HUNDREDS OF OTHER VALUABLE MERCHANDISE including EYEGLASSES at a fifty-percent DISCOUNT, PRE-SCRIPTION DRUGS AT COST, and a YEAR'S SUPPLY OF POL-IDENT.

Now you understand, MRS. DALTON, why we want you to send in your SOCIAL SECURITY LUCKY NUMBER right now.

You are probably asking how we can afford all these unbelievable prizes at NO COST TO YOU.

The answer is that the SOCIAL SECURITY ADMINISTRA-TION has a trust fund which was set up to take care of American senior citizens. The trust has decided the fairest way to distribute the money it has left in it is to hold a

SWEEPSTAKES, making it possible for people who otherwise would get nothing from the system to win a SUPER PRIZE.

This is how the SWEEPSTAKES will work. On March fifteenth all the Social Security numbers that people like yourself sent in will be placed in a large silver bowl in the Rose Garden of the White House, and Miss America of 1983, in the presence of the SECRETARY OF THE TREASURY, will draw the GRAND PRIZE WINNER—the person who will win $250 A MONTH FOR THE REST OF HIS OR HER LIFE. If you are the winner you will be flown by AIR FORCE ONE to WASHINGTON and PRESIDENT RONALD REAGAN will personally present you with your first SWEEPSTAKES SOCIAL SECURITY CHECK.

There is nothing to buy, and a Social Security employee will not call on you. Consider this SWEEPSTAKES the UNITED STATES GOVERNMENT'S way of taking care of its retired citizens who can now look forward to enjoying the September years of their lives, PROVIDING their LUCKY number is drawn.

No one has a better chance than you, MRS. DALTON, to win—so give your LUCK an opportunity to work for you. But you have to get your entry in NOW. The SOCIAL SECURITY CLEARINGHOUSE may never have as much money to distribute amongst its winners again.

A Lot of Bull

It seems that every time there is bad economic news on the evening television, the stock market goes up another ten points.

The only thing I've been able to figure out is that either Wall Streeters don't watch television or they're living in a world of their own.

I have a cousin who works for one of the large brokerage firms and I called him the other day to find out what was going on.

"I can't talk to you now," he said. "The new unemployment figures came out and I have to start buying stock."

"Why? Is unemployment going down?"

"No, but it only went up slightly compared to last month, so the bulls have gone into action again."

"Why are the bulls acting so bullish when all the indicators are bearish?"

"Because the bulls are betting the Fed is going to loosen up on tight money, and interest rates are going to come down."

"The feeling here in Washington is that, even if the Fed lowers the interest rates, the two-hundred-billion-dollar deficit will suck up any available investment money."

"The bulls aren't watching Washington."

"What are they watching?" I asked.

"They're watching each other. When one of the big bulls starts buying the others have to follow suit, or they'll be left back in the stampede. The word out on the street now is if you see a red flag, bid on it."

"Don't the bulls read the papers? They're closing manufacturing plants all over the country."

"That's why Wall Street feels it's the time to buy. If the plants stayed open, stocks would not be a bargain."

"But if the plants are closed, earnings will be down and there will be no dividends for the stockholders."

"The bulls are not looking for dividends. They're looking to make a profit on their stocks. The big boys can get in and out in a few days and make millions on their investments."

"It sounds like a crap game to me."

"It is a crap game. But as long as there are enough guys rolling dice, nobody is going to close down the table."

"I thought Wall Street was supposed to reflect the economy of the country."

"It used to. But now it's a game all unto itself. We're on a roll, and as long as everyone is making money, we're going to keep betting no matter what the rest of the country is doing. The only ones who have lost their shirts in the last year are the bears because they believed what they read in the newspapers."

"Does this mean the bulls on Wall Street don't care if the recession is on or over?"

"It's not their business. As long as they can buy low and sell high, they look like geniuses."

"But surely they must have some faith the economy is going to turn around or they wouldn't be investing their money in all the companies listed on the stock market."

"Of course they have faith in the economy. But they don't have time to wait for it to turn around. When you're sitting on five hundred million dollars of somebody else's money, you want results now."

"So the market is going up because the money managers have no choice but to buy stocks in the bull market which they made themselves, so everyone would look good?"

"It isn't that simple. When things were good, most company stocks were overpriced. Now that things are lousy, most of them are underpriced. So everyone wants to get in on the fire sale."

"Well, I guess if Wall Street isn't worried, I shouldn't be. After all, you guys seem to know what you're doing."

"Of course we know what we're doing. If we paid attention to everything that was going on in the country, we'd all be jumping out of windows."

Northrop
Has a Better Idea

The Northrop Corporation is now using newspapers and consumer magazines to advertise its new fighter plane, the "F-20 Tigershark."

From the ad, it looks like one heck of a plane, but I'm not certain if they want me to buy one or just admire it.

According to the advertising copy, the Tigershark is a new Mach 2-class tactical air defense fighter designed to deter or defeat the enemy. It can operate around the clock in all sorts of weather. It was financed by Northrop without government funding "in response to a United States government call for private development of a tactical fighter specially suited to fulfill United States mutual security policy objectives."

It so happens that I'm in the market for a new tactical

fighter and the looks of the Tigershark really appealed to me.

But my wife announced last Christmas that I couldn't buy a new plane until we paid for the children's orthodontic work.

I agreed with her, but I was so impressed with the ad that I showed it to her.

"It's a beautiful aircraft," she admitted, "but I think we should make do with the old F-five we have now until the economy improves."

"But the F-five can't do half the things the Tigershark can," I protested. "I'll be the laughingstock of the neighborhood if I'm tooling around in an F-five while everyone else is doing Mach two at sixty thousand feet."

"I don't understand why every time you see a new fighter plane in a magazine, you have to buy it."

"I don't want to buy every fighter plane I see in a magazine. But the Tigershark appeals to me. You can put an air-to-ground missile under each wing, flip it over on its back in a dogfight, and drive off anything twice its size in the sky. If people like myself don't buy one we'll never get the economy on its feet."

"Where do I and the children sit?" she wanted to know.

"It's not a family airplane. It's a one-seater, aimed at the type of person who reads *Playboy*."

"I thought as much. All you want is a new toy for yourself now that you're tired of playing with your Apple computer."

"That's not fair. I can defend our home, and the homes of everyone in the neighborhood, with the Tigershark. It says right here that it's the best deterrent money can buy."

"Even if you wanted an F-twenty now, how do you know that Northrop would let you buy it?"

"They're advertising it in *Newsweek*. They're not going to waste money on a four-color spread if they're not prepared to sell you one."

"Maybe they're aiming the advertisements at Third

World countries that can't afford a more expensive fighter plane."

"That's ridiculous. If they were doing that they would take space in Third World publications. This particular ad is directed at people like myself who can't afford a new Mercedes-Benz, but still want the speed and engineering that goes into one."

"How do you expect to pay for it?"

"I'm sure the Pentagon will finance it for me. After all, it's in their interest for me to buy an American fighter plane. The more they can sell, the cheaper Northrop can build them."

"Well, if you want to indulge yourself at the expense of the children's teeth, go ahead and buy one. What are you going to do with your F-five?"

"I'll give it to Joel. Then he won't be borrowing my Tigershark every time he wants to go on a mission."

Hello Out There

There is a communications revolution going on in the world right now. New technology has made it possible for people to communicate with each other by everything from satellites to car telephones. The only problem is that although scientists have made it possible to think up ways of keeping in touch with each other, no one seems to know if it's a good thing or a bad thing.

I came to this conclusion when I was riding with a friend in his car the other day. He had one of those new telephones attached under the dashboard.

"What do you need that for?" I asked him.

"I couldn't do without it. Look, all I have to do is hit this button and I can get my office." I heard the buzzing and a voice said:

"Thunderbird and Thunderbird."

"This is Mr. Thunderbird. Do you have any calls for me?"

"No I don't, Mr. Thunderbird."

"No calls at all?"

"No, Mr. Thunderbird. The phone hasn't rung since you left the office."

"Well, I'll be driving in my car for another twenty-five minutes. If anyone calls put them through to my car telephone."

"Business must be slow," I said. "When did your recession start?"

"Come to think of it, just about the time I put the phone in the car."

"That's tough. Just when it's possible for you to communicate by car phone with a client, there are no clients."

"You have to be ready for the turnaround in the economy," he said. "When it comes I'll be able to handle all my business from my car."

Just then the phone buzzed.

"There you are," said Thunderbird. "You see the importance of the phone? If I didn't have it, someone else might have gotten the business."

He picked up the receiver. "Thunderbird speaking."

"Is that you, darling?"

"Yes, dear."

"Where are you?"

"Massachusetts Avenue and Western."

"Would you stop at Wagshal's and bring home a pound of roast beef, some dill pickles, and a case of beer?"

"I've already passed Wagshal's. Why can't you send Tommy?"

"He's out driving somewhere, but he doesn't have a phone in his car."

Thunderbird muttered something and turned around.

"I guess there are pluses and minuses to having a phone," I said.

"I should have never given my wife my number."

The phone buzzed again. It was Thunderbird's secretary. "Mr. Thunderbird, Father Brooke of Holy Cross just called and said he needed the ten thousand dollars you pledged for the new science building."

"Did you tell him you couldn't find me?"

"Yes, but he said to call you in your car. *I* didn't tell him you had a phone in your car."

"I did," Thunderbird said. "I thought he'd be happy one of his alumni had made good."

We picked up the roast beef at Wagshal's and started back out to Bethesda. The phone rang again. It was Mrs. Thunderbird.

"Darling, be a dear and pick up Johanna at Holton-Arms. It seems she missed her car pool."

Thunderbird almost threw the phone out the window. It buzzed once more.

Thunderbird brightened up when he heard the voice.

"Hey, Eddie, where are you calling from?"

"My car. Where are you?"

"I'm in my car. I can hear you loud and clear. What's up?"

"Nothing. I just wanted to say hello."

"Well, hello, hello, and hidee ho!"

"Roger and out."

"Now you see the true value of a car telephone," Thunderbird said. "If I didn't have one in my front seat, I wouldn't have been able to talk to Eddie until I got home."

A Good News Story

WASHINGTON—Larry Speakes, as all presidential press secretaries seem to do when their boss is in trouble, took out after the press the other day. In a speech he complained about coverage of the bad economic news by the media, as opposed to the good news.

When inflation was at thirteen percent, he complained, the media reported it. Now that it is three percent (that's Larry's figure, not mine), the press has ignored the fact that the Reagan administration licked the country's number-one problem.

Speakes also questioned the public opinion polls that indicated the American people considered unemployment the present number-one problem.

"And why not?" he asked his audience. "Every night we have seen the unemployed line up and march across the television screen, and I certainly would not make light of the people who are unemployed. . . . But why is it that ten-point-eight percent is news, but eighty-nine-point-two percent of Americans who are employed and enjoy the highest standard of living is not?"

Larry posed a very good question. Why aren't the news programs covering the employed people instead of the unemployed? And how would they handle it, if they did?

"This is Tom Brokaw in New York. The big news tonight is that eighty-nine-point-two percent of all Americans who want jobs have them. Irving R. Levine reports on the plight of one of these men in Scarsdale, New York."

"This is Irving R. Levine and I'm standing here with

Frank Davis, a broker for E. F. Hutton, who is one of the millions of people now employed in the United States. To the Reagan administration, Davis is just another statistic. But in human terms, he and his family tell the real story of what is going on in America today.

"Frank, this is a lovely house you have."

"Yup. It's worth two hundred fifty thousand dollars. But since I'm working, I'm not about to sell it."

"How much do you make a year?"

"With bonuses about one hundred thousand dollars."

"Then you don't have to depend on food stamps or unemployment insurance, or use up your savings to keep going?"

"Certainly not. We eat very well, and we have enough money left over to own a boat, and send our kids to private schools, and go out to a good restaurant when it moves us. If the stock market keeps up the way it is, we might buy a second home in East Hampton."

"Does being employed make you feel any different than being unemployed?"

"Very much so. It makes me feel good. I like to work, and I enjoy being paid for it, and I'm not mad at anybody."

"How does your wife feel about you being employed?"

"She thinks it's just great. She's very supportive, as are the children, that I'm making it during the recession. I don't know what I'd do without them."

"But don't you get discouraged sometimes and say to yourself 'I'm sick and tired of working,' and I'm going to throw in the towel'?"

"I imagine the thought has occurred to me. But my wife and I like nice things, and if I threw in the towel, we couldn't afford them. We're going on a ski trip next week to Vail."

"Then you're not angry with President Reagan because you have a job?"

"Why should I be? Reagan's not to blame because I'm making a good living."

(Cut to Irving R. Levine standing beside the Davis swimming pool, alone.)

"Frank Davis is an example of one of the eighty-nine-point-two percent of the American working class blessed with all the things this country has to offer. Unlike the ten-point-nine percent who are unemployed, he believes in tax cuts, military aid to foreign governments, and an increase in defense spending. He may not represent all the employed people of this country, but his story is worth telling because it gives a true picture of what is really going on in the United States today.

"Tomorrow we'll talk to another employed person who is doing very well as a golf pro in Palm Springs, California. This is Irving R. Levine in Scarsdale, New York."

"Oh Boy"

This column is about sex. Parental discretion is advised.

The Reagan administration seems to be going ahead with a rule requiring that any organization receiving federal funds for dispensing contraceptives to a minor must notify the parents within ten days of the request.

The administration's heart is in the right place, but trying to put such a rule into effect presents problems. Many parents cannot talk with their teenagers about rock music, much less discuss with them the subject of sex.

Let's assume that the Wallingfords have just received a letter from Planned Parenthood, notifying them that their daughter Sue Anne has requested a prescription for the Pill.

Both are waiting for her when she comes home from school.

"Where have you been?" Wallingford demands.

"I was in school."

"And what were you doing in school?"

"I don't know. I just went to class, and stuff."

"What kind of stuff?" Wallingford yells.

"You know, just stuff. What are you guys all excited about?"

"Are you sure you didn't sneak off in a clothes closet and do it with some boy?"

"Do what? And with what boy?"

"Any boy," Mrs. Wallingford says. "We know everything," she yells, waving the letter from Planned Parenthood.

"So what do you have to say for yourself?"

"I knew if I asked you for permission to buy the Pill, you wouldn't give it to me."

"You're damn right we wouldn't give it to you. What kind of parents do you think we are?" Wallingford says.

"I know what kind of parents you are. That's why I went somewhere else to protect myself."

"Protect yourself from what?"

"From having a baby."

"What do you know about having babies?" Mrs. Wallingford asks.

"Well, when the male's sperm fertilizes the woman's ovum—"

"That's enough of that kind of dirty talk," Wallingford shouts.

"Relax, Daddy. I haven't done it. But if I ever decide to, I want to be protected. They told us at the clinic, it's the woman and not the man who has to take precautions. Men couldn't care less about the consequences."

"I don't believe I'm hearing this," Mrs. Wallingford says. "We've raised a nymphomaniac."

"You seem to know a lot about sex, young lady," Wallingford says to his daughter. "You certainly didn't learn any of this at home."

"I know. That's why I went to the clinic. Every time I brought up the subject you said it was none of my business."

"It isn't any of your business," Mrs. Wallingford says. "You're seventeen years old and nice girls don't discuss such things with their parents."

"Well, if it isn't any of my business, how come I can get pregnant?"

"You can't get pregnant unless you do it," Wallingford shouts again. "And your mother and I forbid you to do it."

"Anything you say. Now can I go?"

"Where are you going?"

"To the basketball game with Jack."

"So that's where you're going to do it," Wallingford cries.

"How am I going to do it at a basketball game?"

"In the parking lot," Wallingford says. "That's where I used to do it."

"I can't take any more of this. Goodbye."

After Sue Anne leaves, Mrs. Wallingford wipes the tears from her eyes. "You know, George, I think we both would be happier today if Planned Parenthood had never let us know."

Recessions Hurt Everyone

Recessions affect everyone, even people who are in love.

They also give some people who are in love reasons not to get married.

"I would marry you today, but where would we live?"

"What's wrong with here?"

"I wouldn't want my wife to live in this squalor."

"I've been living here for eight months."

"Yes, but it's one thing to live here because you're so in love you haven't noticed it. Once we get married the romance will go out of the squalor and you'll want to move to a place I can't afford."

"You're just using the recession as an excuse for not marrying me."

"How can you say such a thing? I told you when we met I was a romantic supply-sider. How did I know that interest rates would go through the ceiling, the economy would stagnate, and unemployment would be at an all-time high? How can a man contemplate wedlock when nothing is trickling down from the top?"

"Men are doing it every day."

"Yes, but what kind of men? The big spenders who don't care about a balanced budget, or the viability of the Social Security system, or the tight-money policies that have driven down inflation to five percent. Are you willing to go to the altar at a time when steel production is at its lowest since the Great Depression?"

"I'm starting to think that even if we were in a boom period you wouldn't want to get married."

"You're wrong. I would marry you tomorrow if the Gross National Product went up by only ten percent, unemployment was down to six percent, and automobile sales increased to their 1979 levels. Marriage is a very serious business and people shouldn't jump into it when they know we are going to have a one-point-six-trillion-dollar defense bill by 1986."

"I don't see what all this has to do with us. We love each other and if we don't get married soon, we never will."

"Of course we'll get married. President Reagan's advisers expect the economy to turn around in 1983 or '84 or '85. We could even have a mild recovery at the end of this year. The July tax cut might spur the consumer to go out and spend money again. With luck we could get married in any one of the next fiscal years."

"And if all these wonderful things don't happen?"

"Then marriage is out of the question until Reagan gets his house in order. Honey, why are you getting mad? Did I know when we started living together what the MX missile system would cost?"

"I don't care what the MX missile costs. I want a home and children and a husband who will take care of me. I'll continue my job if you're worried about the recession."

"Who said I was worried about the recession? I'm worried that I can't give you everything you deserve as a wife. I want the best for you and our children. When we live together no one cares about our lifestyle. Society accepts us now for what we are—two people living happily in sin. But once we take the marriage vows we'll be judged by much more materialistic standards. Do you think your parents would let you live like this if you were married?"

"I think you're full of it. If you don't want to marry me, I'm going to pack my things and move out."

"You can't do that. You have to stay the course.

Everyone has to suffer some pain if we ever hope to right the mistakes of the past forty years. Look, I'll tell you what I'll do. If Reagan can get the budget down by a lousy eighty billion dollars without endangering your national security, or increasing personal income taxes, I'll go down to City Hall and we'll take out a license the next day."

"You really play it safe, don't you?"

"What do you mean 'safe'? Jack Kemp, a leading supply-sider, is very optimistic."

Nice Guys Finish Last

I was walking down Pennsylvania Avenue with my wife when a nice fellow came out of this big White House and stuck a twenty-dollar bill in my hand.

"What's that for?" I asked.

"It's a tax cut," the man said, smiling, friendly as he could be. "I promised you one, and I always keep my promises."

"Take it," my wife said, "and don't ask any more questions."

This nice fellow said, "I'm going to give you one of those every week."

"What for?" I wanted to know.

My wife kept tugging on my arm.

"So you'll use it to do some good. I want you to go out and spend it or save it or use it to give someone a job. I want to spread the wealth."

"But if you keep giving away twenty-dollar bills, you won't have any for yourself."

The nice guy smiled. "That's what you think. The more

money I give away to people like you, the more I'll have coming back. It's a new economic theory and I can't miss."

My wife was getting angry. "It's his money and if he wants to give it to us, we should take it."

"There's a catch to it somewhere," I whispered to her so he couldn't hear. "No guy who lives in a big White House gives twenty-dollar bills away."

"Maybe he's an eccentric and wants to make other people feel good."

"Next year," the nice guy said, "I'm going to give you twice as much as I gave you this year."

"I think the guy has lost his marbles," I said to my wife. "Either that or it's some chain-letter scam."

The guy was handing out twenty-dollar bills to everyone walking by.

"I don't care what it is," my wife whispered. "Let's get out of here before the police come."

I stuck the twenty-dollar bill in my pocket and hurried down the street.

A few nights later my wife and I were taking a walk around the back of the big White House and a man came out of the shadows and said, "Your money or your life."

I looked around and much to my surprise it was the nice guy who had given me a twenty-dollar bill.

"What gives?" I said angrily. "A few days ago you were handing out money like there was no tomorrow and now you want to take it away from me?"

The guy smiled. "I made a mistake. I gave away more money than I thought I had. Now I have to get it back."

"Give it to him and don't ask questions," my wife said hysterically.

"You should be ashamed of yourself," I told him.

"I am, but I still want your money."

"All right," I said. "Here's your twenty dollars."

"I need more than that." He was going through my wallet. "I'm flat broke."

"You should have thought of that before you started giving everyone twenty-dollar bills."

"One thing has nothing to do with the other," he said. "What I do in front of the house is one thing. What I do in the back of it is another."

"Don't take my Social Security card, I may need it," I pleaded.

The nice guy just smiled. "I wouldn't be too sure of that."

The Sweet Smell of EPA

I walked past the Environmental Protection Agency in Washington some time ago with another newspaperman, and we were both nearly overcome by the stench coming from the building.

"What do you make of that smell?" I asked my friend.

"I don't know. It could be PCB or dioxin or some other industrial waste. It does have a familiar odor."

"I can't believe they'd be using the EPA building to store toxic waste," I said. "They may be incompetent, but they're not stupid."

"Let's go in," my friend said. "There could be a story here."

We went into the building and told the guard that we'd like to talk to someone about the EPA hazardous waste program. He handed me a pass and two gas masks.

When we went to the office he directed us to, we found a woman stuffing material into a paper shredder.

"What are you doing?" I asked her.

"I'm shredding material that the congressional committee has subpoenaed in regard to our superfund cleanup program."

"Isn't that dangerous?" my friend asked her.

"This stuff is poison and we have to get rid of it," she said.

"What's poisonous about it?" I wanted to know.

"It could compromise all the deals we've made with companies that are guilty of dumping toxic material. If these papers got into the wrong hands, many top people in the EPA could get sick."

"But isn't it against the law to shred paper that deals with toxic waste?" I asked.

"Absolutely not. These papers are being shredded under executive privilege."

"Aren't you afraid of being held in contempt of Congress?"

"I'm only doing my job. If you want to talk to anyone about the legal aspects, speak to Mr. Sniff in the next office."

Mr. Sniff was very nervous when we walked in. "I'm not allowed to talk to the press unless I have two witnesses with me." He called in two other lawyers, and turned on his tape recorder. "Now, what do you want to know?"

"Why are you shredding papers about your toxic waste program?"

"We don't want them to get into the wrong hands. We have several cases pending against companies that have been dumping chemicals, and we prefer their lawyers didn't see the evidence."

"But if you shred the papers, how can you use them in court?"

"We don't intend to go to court. We prefer to settle with them so they won't have to stand trial."

"If they violated the law, shouldn't they be brought to justice?"

"What would that accomplish? Our job is to get companies to clean up their acid pits. If we took a hard line, they'd only get mad at us and dump more waste."

My friend said, "What about the people who have been driven out of their homes by dioxin and PCB and those who are being poisoned by the water around the dumps?"

"We've done a study on that problem."

"Can we see it?"

"No, it's confidential. If we publish the results we might be revealing trade secrets of the companies who did the dumping."

A secretary came in and said, "Mr. Drum of Titanic Chemical is on the phone."

The lawyer picked up his phone. "Drum, we just got a report from the whistle-blower in our Pittsburgh office that your company is dumping uranium waste under the high-school football stadium. Are you aware that's a no-no?...Oh, you were? Well, be a good fellow and stop it. Thanks a lot. What Congress doesn't know won't hurt it." He hung up and turned to us.

"Now, if you'll excuse me, we've got a lot of work to do here."

I left with my newspaper pal. We handed in our passes and gas masks to the guard.

Suddenly, my friend said, "I know what this stench smells like."

"What?" I asked him.

"Watergate. It stinks like a Watergate."

I inhaled and said, "I think you're right."

Shouting at the President

My wife and I were watching the evening news on television the other night, when she said, "I feel sorry for President Reagan."

"How's that?" I asked.

"Every time he leaves the White House to go somewhere the reporters shout questions at him."

"Well, it's their job to ferret out news, and they hope he'll say something earth-shattering as he's leaving for Camp David."

"All he does is shout back one or two words to their questions. How much news can you ferret out of that?"

"It depends on how you phrase the questions. Suppose you shout, 'Mr. President, have you made up your mind about Dense Park?' and he shouts back, 'Yes,' that's also a news story. If he just smiles, shrugs his shoulders, and puts his arm around Nancy, it may not be a news story, but at least it's something to go with the film."

"Why can't he go to Camp David on the weekend without us having to watch it on the evening news?"

"Because the American people should know where their President is at all times. The White House doesn't mind the media covering his departure when he is going to Camp David because he's usually in a good mood. He's in an even better mood when he comes back. But you can't expect the press corps to just stand there like dummies when Reagan is getting on and off the helicopter. They owe it to the public to find out what is really on his mind. That's why they shout those questions at him."

"I think it's a very dangerous way to gather news. Half the time, with the helicopter motors whirring, he can't even hear the questions," she said.

"I don't think the President objects. Frankly, I think he prefers that type of questioning to a press conference. I know his staff does."

"But suppose someone yells a question and he says 'Yes' instead of 'No.' Isn't that scary?"

"Not really. Because if he gives the wrong answer, the press secretary can always say he didn't understand the question. What you have to realize is that Ronald Reagan, before he went into politics, attended an awful lot of movie premieres, so he's used to reporters shouting at him. He's an old pro when it comes to running a press gauntlet. Look at the way he waves his arm as he approaches the helicopter. He's a natural when he has to say goodbye."

"But the TV networks show the same scene every weekend. They could probably use stock footage from their files and save a lot of money."

"You don't understand how the White House communications people work. This is what is known as a 'photo opportunity.' It shows off the President at his best. He's usually wearing a cowboy outfit and boots and he doesn't look as if he has a care in the world. That's the image of Ronald Reagan they want to project. And frankly I believe that's the image the American people want to see. Would you feel any better if he came out of the White House to board the helicopter scowling and refusing to talk to anyone?"

"I guess not," she admitted. "But I don't know why the networks can't just say he went to Camp David and leave it at that."

"That's okay for the print people. But the electronic media can't just say it. They have to have the pictures to accompany the story. If they showed Sam Donaldson or Leslie Stahl or Chris Wallace standing in front of a darkened White House saying, 'The President is not here tonight,' you'd be worried sick."

"Maybe you're right. What are they yelling at him now?"

"They want to know if he's going to fire Ann Burford of the EPA."

"Does the press really expect him to answer that when he's leaving for Camp David?"

"Not really. But if you have to stand out in the cold for an hour, it's worth a try."

A Dirty Movie

We had just finished dinner when Winslow said, "I have a surprise for everyone. Come in the living room while I lock the doors and pull down the window shades."

We went into the living room. Winslow had set up a sixteen-millimeter projector and a movie screen.

"What are you going to show, Winslow?" someone asked. "*Deep Throat* or *Debbie Does Dallas*?"

"Something much worse. I managed to get an illegal print of a Canadian documentary on acid rain."

A murmur ran through the crowd. "Couldn't we get in trouble watching a dirty film from Canada?"

Winslow smiled. "You're damn right you could. The Justice Department has declared all Canadian films on acid rain to be pure propaganda, and they have to be clearly marked as such. They also told the Canadian Film Board it has to turn over to Justice the names of those who asked to see the films."

Martha Harrington said, "I've never seen a documentary on acid rain. This is going to be exciting."

"How in the devil did you get the film?" I asked Winslow.

"I smuggled it in from Toronto," he replied.

"You really took a risk. What if you had gotten caught?"

"I would have been fined and sent to jail. United States Customs has strict orders to look for Canadian Film Board movie prints. They're even training dogs now to sniff for them. The attorney general has given it top priority."

"Why are they uptight about films on acid rain?"

Winslow said, "They're afraid if Americans see them, without the films' being clearly marked as propaganda, we would believe that acid rain is an environmental problem."

"You would think the Justice Department would have more to do than worry about Canadian documentaries," Ed Harrington said.

"You don't know much about the Justice Department. They finally found a legal issue they understand. They've been so confused about civil rights, EPA, and antitrust cases that they jumped at the chance to sock it to Canada. The Canadians are going to think twice the next time they finance a film about pollution," Winslow told us.

"How long is it?" someone asked.

"It only runs thirty minutes. But it will blow your mind."

Bella Murphy said, "Suppose the FBI breaks in while we're watching it?"

"Don't worry about it, Bella," Winslow said. "My kids are outside on the lookout. If they ring the doorbell three times, I'll dump the print and substitute *The Devil in Miss Jones*. They can't touch us for watching a porno movie in our own home."

"Well, show it fast," Bella said. "I'm very nervous."

"Okay, lights out. Here we go."

We all sat in rapt attention as we watched fish and wildlife dying in the Canadian north. A few people got sick and had to go to the bathroom. At the end of the picture, Martha Harrington said, "What kind of degenerate mind could make a picture like that?"

"That's what the Justice Department would like to

know. If this film is shown throughout the United States, it could destroy the American way of life as we know it."

"How could Canada do it?"

"There are a lot of dangerous people in the environmental movement up there, and they have control of the film industry. If you think that one was bad, wait until you see the other one I smuggled in. It's about the horror of nuclear war."

"You can't show a Canadian picture against nuclear war in the United States," Bella screamed. "It's illegal."

"Of course it's illegal, that's what makes it so exciting," Winslow said. "Wouldn't you rather see a film forbidden by the United States authorities than watch *The Winds of War*?"

An American Hero

There are two kinds of people who don't pay any income taxes in America—the very poor and the very rich. One tends to look down on the poor when they don't pay taxes, because they're a burden on Society—but show me a rich man who doesn't pay any money to the government and I'll show you a real American hero.

My role model is Harvey Ripplemyer, a millionaire many times over, who has hardly paid a cent in income taxes to the federal government for the last ten years.

"How do you do it?" I asked Harvey the other day.

"I don't do it myself," he said modestly. "I pay people to do it for me. I believe it's an American's right, I might even add duty, to take advantage of every loophole our tax laws offer."

"I'm sure every taxpayer feels the same way. But not many of us can achieve the ultimate of not paying any taxes at all. What is your secret?"

"You need money not to pay money to the IRS. The more money you have, the less you have to give them. What you have to do is find paper tax losses to offset your real income. Then you prove that you've actually lost money in the fiscal year and therefore you owe the government a pittance."

"Okay, but how do you find a way to do that?"

"You hire the best tax lawyers that money can buy. They usually happen to be former IRS attorneys who know all the loopholes. They're experts on what will fly and what won't."

"What happens when the IRS closes a tax loophole for somebody like you?"

"Then my tax lawyers find another loophole. Fortunately our tax laws are such that when the IRS thinks they've got you trapped, you can always crawl through a hole they left open. It's really a poker game, but you have to have a big pot going in to play. What you need are large carryover losses, huge interest deductions, big depreciation write-offs, and solid tax shelters. Now, the average person doesn't have the stakes to acquire all these things, so he has to pay his taxes."

"What about your attorneys' fees? They must be very high."

"Not really. They're tax deductible."

"Do you ever have any guilt about paying hardly any taxes?"

"Does anyone have any guilt if they can beat the tax system? Go through your newspapers and magazines. Half the ads are from people who claim they can help you beat the IRS. The best seller lists always have a new book on ways you can keep your tax money. The only people who feel guilty in this country are those who have to pay their full share."

"It's lucky we have them or there wouldn't be any money in the Treasury."

"Now I don't want you to get the idea that just because I pay hardly any taxes I'm not a good American. I serve on the Committee for a Strong National Defense, I'm against large government deficits, and I don't believe in social programs that are bleeding this country to death."

"I never questioned your patriotism."

"Do you know why this is the greatest country on earth?"

"I think I do, but I'd like to hear it from you."

"Because if a man can beat the tax system he can keep everything he has. And it's possible to do it here without violating the law. You don't have to be born rich to avoid paying taxes. This country allows you to become rich and not give any of it away. That's why I love America."

"And that's why everyone loves you, Harvey. You're an inspiration to every taxpayer in America who aspires to be in your position right now."

"Anyone can do it," Harvey said. "With a little luck, a lot of money, and a good tax lawyer who really knows what he's doing, and has your interests at heart."

The U.S. Garage Sale

The United States government is continuing its garage sale. First, James Watt announced he was going to sell off a lot of federal land that we didn't need, and now the White House has announced President Reagan's plans to sell the United States Weather Service. The reason given, of course, is to save money and involve the private sector in activities that it might perform as well as or better than the federal government.

The irony of the decision is that while most Americans always complain about the weather, I've never heard anyone gripe about the United States Weather Service. It was one of the few services the government provided that worked well, whether you were on land, sea, or in the air.

I have no objection to Mr. Reagan selling off our weather satellites and ground stations to private enterprise, but the big question is how would a company make any money on the weather?

A weather analyst with Merrill Lynch told me he thought the profits were there, provided that enough people were willing to pay for a forecast.

"The company would have to set up a rate card for different types of weather," he told me. "For example, if you wanted to find out what the weather would be like tomorrow in your own town it might cost you a dollar. If you wanted to know what the weather was like in another area, it would be three dollars a prediction. And if you wanted the weather profile for the entire United States, it would be ten dollars."

"What about hurricanes and blizzards?"

"I believe hurricanes and blizzards would be worth twenty-five dollars. Tornado warnings would be fifty dollars, and there would be a surcharge for any predictions coming out of Canada."

"Why would someone pay for a weather forecast if they could get it free on television?"

"No company would buy the weather satellites unless it was assured that it would be the sole distributor of weather information. The TV stations would have to pay substantial fees for the service, if they're going to transmit this copyrighted information to their viewers for nothing."

"Who do you foresee as the large users of the private weather service?"

"The government will probably be the number-one

customer. They need weather information for planes, ships, and when the queen of England visits the West Coast. I predict the large government contracts for weather will pay for the system, and everything after that will be profit."

"If the government is going to pay millions of dollars for the service, why don't they just keep it, instead of selling it off?"

"The President wants the government out of as many things as possible. His philosophy is that the federal weather forecasters should get off the people's backs. He doesn't believe some Washington bureaucrat should be telling the farmers in Nebraska they're in for a hailstorm."

"What worries me," I said, "is that if a private company takes over the weather service it might tend to predict better weather than is actually coming, just to attract new subscribers."

"The company might at the beginning. But if they're wrong too many times, the customer will just cancel out on them, and tune in to the BBC for their weather reports."

"What do you think President Reagan will unload after the weather satellites?"

"The rumor on Wall Street is that he might sell the United States Coast Guard to the private sector. But no one has been able to confirm it. On the other hand, it makes a lot of economic sense. The Coast Guard is a big drain on the budget, and the federal government shouldn't be in the business of saving lives, particularly when they don't charge for it."

Retraining Horatio Alger

"Hi, Mr. Peters, remember me? Horatio Alger the Fourth. You laid me off from the company six months ago because I was unskilled labor. Well, I just completed a welding course, and I'm ready to go back to work."

"Sorry, Horatio, but since you've been gone, the company has decided to invest in robot welders. I don't believe your welding skills are necessary any longer. Now, if you knew something about robotics..."

"I don't, sir, but I'll retrain myself and become a robot serviceman. I'll see you in six months."

"That's a good idea, son. Come back when you know something about robots, Horatio, and there will be a job waiting for you."

"Hi, Mr. Peters. Well, sir, here's my certificate from the Consolidated Robot School. It says I can repair any kind of robot now on the market."

"This is very impressive. Let's see, according to your file, you were in this personnel office last July. Since you were here the company has invested in a state-of-the-art computer that can repair the robots that make our zits. We're no longer hiring service people to take care of the robots."

"But surely, sir, you must need someone to program the computers."

"As a matter of fact we do. Have you any experience in this field?"

"I don't at the moment, but I know I can be retrained

to become a computer expert. If I do well in school may I have a job with your company?"

"Of course you can. You show the spirit this corporation is always looking for."

"Hello, Mr. Peters. Long time no see."

"As I live and breathe, it's Horatio Alger the Fourth. What have you been up to for the past two years?"

"I've been going to advanced computer programming school, sir. I am now fluent in BASIC, PASCAL, and FORTRAN, and can work with any software on the market. I assume the company is still looking for programmers."

"We were for a while, Horatio. But then we subcontracted all our programming work to a software company which specializes in improving robot production for zits. We no longer have a computer division of our own, except for a small section that devotes itself to collating data on the zit market and then making economic predictions on how the company should expand."

"Don't worry, Mr. Peters, I will retrain myself to become an economist with an emphasis on long-range zit planning."

"You'll need a doctorate before I can hire you."

"Do not fear, sir. I will drive a taxi during the daytime and go to school at night. If becoming an economist is the only way I can get a job, so be it—I will become one."

"You show gumption, boy. Bring me that sheepskin and you'll be on the payroll."

(Three years later.)

"Do my eyes deceive me? Is this the little Horatio Alger the Fourth who used to drop in here to see me about a job?"

"The very same, and I have something to show you. Here, sir, from the Harvard Business School, is my doctorate in Hi-Tech Economics. And here is my doctoral thesis on the future of the zit market in the twenty-first century, as broken down by continents and countries throughout the non-Communist world. Now that I am retrained, may I have a position with the company?"

"Horatio, please sit down. Since you went off to get your economics degree, we've moved the entire company's operations to South Korea. We don't do anything here except distribute zits to our dealers."

"I understand, sir, and I certainly don't blame you for going where you can make a better product for much less cost."

"What are you going to do now, Horatio?"

"The same thing any ambitious American boy would do. I'm going to retrain myself to be a South Korean."

Why Jason Can't Read

Newsweek's cover story last week dealt with parents who are pushing their kids earlier and earlier into schools. The post-Spock generation of parents believe the sooner their babies get an education the better chance they will have of being successful when they grow up.

I thought *Newsweek* was exaggerating about mothers and fathers wanting their toddlers to become early achievers until I went over to dinner at the Markses' the other night.

There was tension in the house.

"What's going on?" I wanted to know.

"We're waiting on word whether Jason will be accepted in Culpeper's pre-pre-nursery school."

"I shouldn't think you'll have any trouble," I said. "After all, Jason seems like a very bright two-year-old to me."

"He is bright," Mr. Marks said. "But they won't take him unless he's potty trained. We only have until September, and so far he won't cooperate."

"I see the problem," I said. "But you would think if Jason really wanted to go to school he'd get his act together."

"That seems to be the trouble. He doesn't seem to care if he gets into the school or not," Mrs. Marks told me. "Every time we mention pre-pre-nursery school, he tries to crawl into a shopping bag."

"Maybe he wants to take a year off to find himself," I suggested.

"This isn't a joking matter," said Mr. Marks. "I laid out sixteen ninety-five for a toilet trainer last week. You sit the baby on it and it plays music every time he does something. But Jason still won't use it."

"Maybe they're not playing his song."

"We never had this kind of trouble with his brother Ben," Mrs. Marks said. "He's a brilliant student."

"How old is Ben?"

"Almost five, and he's been accepted by three of the best nursery schools in the area."

"Perhaps the pressure of living up to his brother Ben is too much for Jason to handle right now," I suggested.

"We're not just going to let him sit at home for a year and twiddle his thumbs," Mr. Marks said. "He has to learn there is no such thing in life as a free lunch."

"You can't imagine the humiliation parents have to go through to get their kids in pre-pre-nursery school," Mrs. Marks said. "Our friends Ed and Anne Weinberg went for an interview with their son, and swore to the admissions director the child was potty trained, and right in the middle of the interview the kid told his mother he had to be changed. The Weinbergs never heard from the school again."

"Well, you've got until September. Jason could shape up by then. Maybe if you don't make a big deal of having to go to school, he might just use the potty trainer without being forced to."

"That's easy for you to say," said Mr. Marks. "You don't have to live with the anxiety of it all. If Jason doesn't get into pre-pre-nursery school, he'll never get into nursery school."

"It can't be that big a deal," I said.

"Oh, yeah?" Marks said. "How would you like to raise a kid who, by the time he reaches four, can't even pin a tail on a donkey?"

"Is Paris Burning?"

"Is Paris Burning?" You bet your sweet croissant it is.

President François Mitterrand, in order to get his financial house in order, has just issued the most controversial edict since he took office. He has told the French if they want to leave the country on vacation they may only take the equivalent of $427 with them, and they can't use their credit cards outside of France's borders.

This is the equivalent of pulling an Iron Curtain down on French tourists, who, contrary to myth, are far more passionate about their vacations than their love affairs.

I just received a letter from a Parisian friend.

Cher Ami,

You have probably read by now that our crazy French president has made it impossible for us to leave the country for *vacance*.

Until his proclamation, our main concern was the placement of American missiles on the Continent. Now our only worry is how we can get out of France in the summertime.

Everyone knows the one thing that makes the Frenchman happy is to travel abroad to see how primitive other cultures are. Once we taste their food, and drink their wine, we come home reinforced in our belief that France is still the only civilized nation in the world.

Besides, a trip outside the country is the only opportunity we have to get away from foreign tourists who make our lives so miserable by telling us how happy they are that the French franc is so weak and that Paris is once again the tourist bargain it used to be.

I am not saying the French are not to blame for this sad state of affairs. We all voted for Mitterrand because we were bored with watching Giscard d'Estaing on television. Mitterrand said he was going to do a lot of stupid things, such as nationalizing all the banks and the industries, which sounded like good fun at the time. But he never said anything about only letting us take the equivalent of $427 out of the country for our vacations.

Had he mentioned this just once in his campaign, he wouldn't have even won the votes of his own family.

When I told Giselle that we couldn't go to England for our holidays she was grief-stricken. Giselle hates the English and was looking forward to spending four weeks there, so she could show the children how miserably the British live, how awful the weather is, and how fortunate they are to be French.

My brother Gérard already had made his reservations for Portugal this summer, just to let the family see how bad European plumbing really can be.

Uncle Jacques was prepared to go to Switzerland, which he despises, but considers the perfect vacation spot because it is the dullest place in Europe. When he returns to the madness of Paris, he feels like a new man.

Now our entire family must cancel their plans and find a place in France for our holidays, which is impossible, because nobody expected the French to stay home this summer.

The reason I am writing to you at this time is that if you had any plans to come to Paris this year, please let me know. Do not bring any money with you. I will be happy to supply you with all the French francs you need at a very good rate.

If you spend enough money here I could come to the United States and you could repay me in dollars without that idiot Mitterrand being any wiser.

I must be honest with you. America was not my first choice, particularly since Giselle is afraid the children will have a good time and spoil the vacation for all of us. But we will have to take this chance just so we can get out of the country for a few weeks.

If you weren't planning on coming here I urge you to do so. If Mitterrand does not rescind his order by August first, you could be a witness to the second French Revolution.

Last week ten thousand people marched to the Ministry of Finance gates shouting, *"Vacances, liberté,"* and do you know what Mitterrand said when he heard the noise? He said, "Let them eat credit cards."

No Conflict of Interest

I worry about doctors. Not all doctors. But just the ones who have investments in private hospitals. The reason I worry about them is that when you're a stockholder in a hospital you might have a conflict of interest between doing what is right for the patient and what is good for the corporation.

Dr. Wesley Heights, who owns a piece of the Kidney Stone Memorial Hospital, told me he saw no ethical problem in a doctor investing his money in a private hospital.

"Doctors should own hospitals," he said. "Then they can personally see that their patients get the best treatment money can buy."

"But some people argue," I said, "that if a doctor has a financial interest in a medical facility he may subconsciously hospitalize people, just to keep the occupancy rate up."

"That's ridiculous," Dr. Heights said. "I've never put a patient in Kidney Stone Memorial unless he absolutely needed to be there. The board of directors does not pressure me to send them patients. As a matter of fact I don't even put all my sick people in Kidney Stone. I send many of them to the Sisters of Mercy, which is a nonprofit hospital."

"How do you decide?"

"It's strictly a medical decision. If they have a good health insurance plan I put them in Kidney Stone. If they don't, I find them a bed at Sisters of Mercy."

"Sisters of Mercy must be thrilled to get all your indigent patients."

"They probably would like more who can pay their way, but Kidney Stone Memorial's computers are not set up to handle noninsured patients, while Sisters of Mercy has been doing it for years. So I know when I send a destitute patient to Sisters he'll get much better treatment than he would at Kidney Stone."

"Will Kidney Stone take a noninsured person?"

"Of course we will if it's a life or death situation. But as a profit-making hospital we owe it to our stockholders to make sure our loss-per-bed is held to a minimum. Some people have accused us of trying to put the nonprofit hospitals out of business. This is not true. We need them as much as they need us."

"Why do they need you?"

"Because we take the burden off them, by providing services for people who can afford them. If we didn't take these patients, they wouldn't be able to accommodate the nonpaying patients who also need hospital care."

"I guess what troubles me is not the idea of private hospitals, but the thought that doctors own stock in them. That doesn't bother you?"

"On the contrary. Medical people should own a piece of the hospital they put their patients in. Who knows better how to keep costs down, and make sure the institution is being run at a profit? Private hospital employees are on their toes because they know we're watching them as carefully as we're watching our patients. What makes Kidney Stone a great hospital is that our doctors worry about the bottom line."

"I guess that's the only thing you have to worry about," I said.

"What the heck does that mean?"

"If you worry about the bottom line *and* your patient, you could have a conflict in medical judgment."

"The patient always comes first," Dr. Heights said angrily. "I don't know one doctor at Kidney Stone who has ever kept a client there longer than was absolutely necessary, unless it was a nice weekend and no one was waiting for the bed."

"You don't have to get sore."

"When I graduated from medical school I took an oath that I would treat all patients alike whether they had Blue Cross, Group Health, or Medicare. I've never violated that oath. As a matter of fact, since I became an owner in Kidney Stone Memorial, I've been able to look at medical care not only from the patient's viewpoint but also from the stockholder's. This has made me a better doctor, and richer for the experience."

Play Ball

The income of baseball players seems to be getting more attention from the media than how they play the game. Pretty soon we can expect to hear the sports announcers on television describing a contest like this:

"Coming up to bat is Paul London, the million-dollar wonderboy right fielder. London, who became a free agent last year, is the highest-priced left-hander in baseball. His deal is, every time he gets to first base he receives a thousand-dollar bonus and a new automobile.

"On the mound is Too-Tall Dawkins, who was given the Empire State Building as a bonus when he signed up with the New York Yankees. Dawkins, who owns two hundred and ten Kentucky Fried Chicken franchises, made an unsuccessful bid to buy Sears Roebuck last week with the trust fund set up for him by George Steinbrenner. Strike one.

"The infield is expecting a bunt. Third baseman Pedro Cappello, who earns one million dollars a year doing commercials for the Wallin Savings and Loan Company, is playing in close. Don Kirby, the shortstop who made seven hundred fifty thousand dollars last year and held out this season during spring practice because they wouldn't renegotiate his contract, is covering second base. Dawkins winds up—here comes the ball, London swings—it's a line drive over Pablo Hernandez's glove into right field, and London is safe on first. Hernandez and London have the same business manager and they seem to be having a heated discussion on a tax shelter they're both in.

"The next hittter is Ron Dirksen, who gets a big ovation from the crowd. Ron has a golden-parachute deal with the Red Sox. If he is ever traded or hurt he still gets five hundred thousand dollars a year for ten years, plus ten percent interest on his money.

"Hernandez has gone over to speak to Dawkins. Apparently London just gave Hernandez a tip on a hi-tech stock, and he wants to talk it over with Dawkins, so they can call their brokers after the inning is over.

"The umpire has joined the group and he is writing down the name of the stock. Dirksen is at the plate and play is resuming. Dawkins throws a fast one over the corner and it's called a ball. Catcher Sam Francisco, who does light beer commercials for the Sudsy Brewing Company, is protesting the call. The umpire tells him to put his mask back on.

"Here comes the pitch—a grounder to second baseman Bip Doctorow, who tried to corner the copper market last week—he tags London and then throws to first for a double play.

"Two out, and Fernando Gravas comes to bat. Fernando was not expected to play today, when his private Gulfstream Three had engine trouble in Tampa. But fortunately he hitched a ride in center fielder Max Newman's Lear jet and suited up in time.

"... The count is three and two. Dawkins shakes his head to the catcher. This could either mean he doesn't like the pitch called for, or Dawkins doesn't want to go into a condominium deal catcher Francisco is developing in Fort Lauderdale. Dawkins throws, and Gravas swings and misses for a strikeout. The side is retired and Dawkins has earned the Empire State Building from George Steinbrenner today.

"Here comes Red Sox pitcher Arnie Ballow, whose record in pork belly futures this year is twenty and one...."

IRS Squealers

I know it is going to come as a surprise to some people, but the Internal Revenue Service has a "squeal" rule. If someone is cheating on his or her taxes, and you tell the IRS where to look, and they manage to collect the hidden money, you can get a reward of up to fifty thousand dollars.

You would think that the tipster money is what attracts income tax whistle blowers to the IRS, but this is not always the case.

"I would like to see the man in charge of tax cheaters."

"I am that person. May I help you?"

"I want to tell you about a man who bilked you out of two million dollars over five years."

"Before you do, may I ask you why you are telling me this?"

"Because I'm a patriotic American, and I feel everyone should pay his fair share of taxes, so we can protect our way of life."

"That's good to hear."

"The person also happens to be my third husband, and you'll never meet a more devious rat in your life."

"Then you have a personal motive in turning him in?"

"There's nothing personal about it. I'd turn him in if he were a stranger. Anyone who runs off with his secretary when he's married to a wonderful woman who gave him the best years of her life deserves to feel the full weight of the IRS on him."

"You say he's been cheating on his taxes for five years. Why did you come to us now?"

"I found these love letters in his closet last week. Smell them. Have you ever sniffed such cheap perfume? Now most women would have immediately gone to a lawyer like Marvin Mitchelson. But I'm not the vengeful type. I decided to come here instead. I said to myself, 'Rose, it isn't what he did to you that matters, it's what he did to his country. The money he has cheated the United States of could be the difference between war and peace, freedom and slavery, and prosperity and recession.'"

"Did you say anything else to yourself?"

"Come to think of it, I did. I said, 'Rose, I'd like to see that blonde floozy's face when she sees Milton behind bars.' But that was just a second thought, and it's not why I'm here today."

"I understand that. You say Milton cheated us out of two million dollars. Do you know where the money is?"

"He spent a lot of it. We had a boat, he bought me fur coats, jewelry, and a new BMW. Believe me, if I knew it was Uncle Sam's money I wouldn't have accepted any of it."

"How did you find out he was not declaring his full income?"

"I discovered he was also paying for a penthouse apartment on Park Avenue for his tootsie, and it suddenly dawned on me it must be coming out of the IRS's pocket. So I immediately came down here to let you know. I can't live with a man who lies on his income tax return."

"Are you aware that the IRS pays rewards to people for turning in tax cheaters?"

"I'm not here for the money. I just want to help my country and President Reagan and our fine boys in the armed forces, and the senior citizens and the poor and homeless, and everybody else who depends on our tax dollars for support. If Milton has to suffer horribly for his cheating ways, I can live with that too."

"Well, Rose, I'll turn you over to our criminal investigators, and you can provide them with the leads for a full investigation. We can't tell you how much we appreciate your visit."

"I was only doing my duty as a citizen."

"We know that, and as a small token of our appreciation we'd like to present you with this American flag. If it weren't for selfless patriots like yourself, our job would be so much harder."

About the Author

When Art Buchwald isn't watching Ronald Reagan, he writes a syndicated column, which appears in 550 newspapers throughout the world. Each article is processed at 400 words per minute on his computer. He is 58 years old, married, has three children, and owns a Honda. For relaxation he prefers marathon running and mountain climbing.